Rock of Ages?

Rock of Ages?

The Changing Faces of the Christian God

John Butler

Ⓛ

The Lutterworth Press

The Lutterworth Press
P.O. Box 60
Cambridge
CB1 2NT
United Kingdom

www.lutterworth.com
publishing@lutterworth.com

ISBN: 978 0 7188 9296 8

British Library Cataloguing in Publication Data
A record is available from the British Library

First Published, 2013

For Gillian, my wife and soulmate of fifty years

Contents

Timeline

Prehistory Portable gods in nomadic societies

BC

c. 12,000 Static gods in farming communities
c. 5000 Established gods in urban communities
c. 1800 Yahweh appears to Abraham
c. 1750 Isaac and Jacob
c. 1400 Moses and the Exodus from Egypt
c. 1400 Yahweh gives Moses the law on Sinai
c. 1000 Composition of many of the Psalms
c. 538 Return of the Jews from exile in Babylon
c. 570 Xenophanes born
427-347 Plato

AD

c. 33 Death of Jesus of Nazareth
c. 37-100 Flavius Josephus
c. 50-60 Letters of St Paul written
c. 56-117 Tacitus
c. 60 Mark's gospel probably written
c. 69-122 Suetonius
c. 70-80 Luke's gospel probably written
c. 80-90 Matthew's gospel probably written
c. 90-100 John's gospel probably written
c. 103-165 Justin Martyr
c. 110 Ignatius of Antioch died
c. 120-202 Irenaeus of Lyons
c. 133-190 Athenagoras of Athens
c. 150-216 Clement of Alexandria
c. 160-225 Tertullian of Carthage
185-232 Origen of Alexandria

c. 210	Praxeas of Carthage active
c. 210	Sabellius of Libya active
c. 250-336	Arius of Alexandria
296-373	Athanasius of Alexandria
313	Christianity is accepted in the Roman Empire
325	First Council of Nicaea
326	Alexander of Alexandria died
c. 329-379	Basil of Caesarea
337	Constantius becomes Emperor
341	Eusebius of Nicomedia died
347-407	St John Chrysostom
354-430	St Augustine of Hippo
c. 360-435	John Cassian
c. 374	Marcellus of Ancyra died
381	Council of Constantinople
c. 390-418	Pelagius active in Rome
451	Formulary of Chalcedon
529	Council of Orange
540-604	Pope Gregory the Great
589	Council of Toledo
809	Synod of Aachen
1033-1109	St Anselm of Canterbury
1054	Split between Western and Eastern Churches
1079-1142	Peter Abelard
1225-1274	St Thomas Aquinas
1265-1321	Dante Alighieri
1267-1337	Giotto
1326	William of Ockham condemned as a heretic
1369-1415	Jan Hus
1466-1536	Desiderius Erasmus
1473-1543	Nicolaus Copernicus
1475-1564	Michelangelo Buonarroti
1483-1546	Martin Luther
1485-1531	Huldrych Zwingli
1489-1565	Guillaume Farel
1504-1575	Heinrich Bullinger
1505-1572	John Knox
1509-1564	John Calvin
1509-1553	Michael Servetus
1519-1605	Theodore Beza
1522-1590	Dirk Koornhert
1539-1604	Fausto Sizzini

1542-1621	Cardinal Robert Bellarmine
1545-1563	Council of Trent
1548-1600	Giordano Bruno
1560-1609	Jacob Arminius
1563-1641	Frances Gomarus
1564-1642	Galileo Galilei
1596-1650	René Descartes
1598-1680	Gianlorenzo Bernini
1618-1619	Synod of Dort
1623-1662	Blaise Pascal
1632-1704	John Locke
1635-1705	Philipp Spener
1642-1727	Isaac Newton
1657-1733	Matthew Tindal
1664-1729	Jean Meslier
1670-1722	John Toland
1694-1778	François-Marie Voltaire
1694-1768	Hermann Reimarus
1700-1760	Nicholas Ludwig, Count Zinzendorf
1703-1768	Jonathon Edwards
1703-1791	John Wesley
1707-1788	Charles Wesley
1711-1776	David Hume
1712-1778	Jean-Jacques Rousseau
1713-1784	Denis Diderot
1714-1770	George Whitefield
1714-1773	Howell Harris
1723-1789	Paul Heinrich, Baron of Holbach
1724-1804	Immanuel Kant
1743-1805	William Paley
1749-1827	Pierre-Simon Laplace
1768-1834	Friedrich Schleiermacher
1770-1831	Georg Hegel
1792-1822	Percy Bysshe Shelley
1797-1878	Charles Hodge
1804-1872	Ludwig Feuerbach
1808-1874	David Strauss
1809-1882	Charles Darwin
1813-1855	Søren Kierkegaard
1822-1889	Albrecht Ritschl
1837-1920	Abraham Kuyper
1837-1899	Dwight L Moody

1840-1908	Ira D Sankey
1841-1919	Arthur Ainger
1851-1930	Adolf von Harnack
1851-1921	Benjamin Warfield
1854-1928	Amzi C Dixon
1854-1941	James Frazer
1856-1928	Reuben A Torrey
1858-1917	Emile Durkheim
1860-1925	William Jennings Bryan
1861-1947	William B Riley
1863-1914	Johannes Weiss
1869-1937	Rudolf Otto
1875-1965	Albert Schweitzer
1878-1969	Harry E Fosdick
1881-1936	J Gresham Machin
1884-1976	Rudolf Bultmann
1886-1968	Karl Barth
1886-1965	Paul Tillich
1893-1971	Reinhold Niebuhr
1894-1962	Richard Niebuhr
1900-1970	John T Scopes
1906-1945	Dietrich Bonhoeffer
1918	Billy Graham born
1919-1983	John Robinson
1928	Hans Küng born
1928	Elie Wiesel born

Acknowledgements

I am deeply grateful to the many friends and colleagues over the years with whom I have discussed and debated the nature of God, and without whose help and encouragement this book might never have been written. They are too numerous, and their contributions too varied, for me to name them individually, but they have clearly left their marks upon my thinking. I would, however, like to express my particular gratitude to a smaller number of friends who kindly read all or parts of the manuscript and whose comments have been invaluable in keeping my ideas on track: Barbara Bishop, Ted Bishop, John Bown, Gillian Butler, Jill Butler, Derek Crabtree, Warren Hickson, Richard Llewellin, Clare Nicholson, Doreen Rosman and Lewis Ryder. They bear no responsibility for the errors and imperfections that the book undoubtedly harbours.

I would also like to record my thanks to Philip Law for his invaluable advice about getting the book published, and to Fiorella Day-Dell'Olio at The Lutterworth Press for masterminding the copy-editing with great tact and efficiency.

John Butler
Canterbury
May 2013

Introduction
The Author and the Book

This book is a personal exploration of the God of the Christian faith. I have written it in the hope that others may find interest and benefit in the illuminating and sometimes surprising journey that I have undertaken for myself. There must have been many occasions in my life when I have been asked, or asked myself, whether I believed in God; and I can now only image the answers I may have given at different ages. Until well into my teens I would probably have given a straightforward 'yes', for I was brought up in a quietly Christian family and I absorbed the non-conformist faith of my parents along with many other dispositions. As childhood gave way to adolescence and I began to think about religion for myself, doubts crept into my hitherto unquestioned beliefs, and by my late teens my answer would, I think, have changed: 'I don't know whether I believe in God, but probably not'. This agnostic phase did not, however, last for long, and by the time I entered the world of work, my answer to the question of whether I believed in God would have reverted to the affirmative 'yes' of my childhood.

It was to remain the answer for much of my adult life, though for many years I gave little systematic thought to what I meant by 'believing in God'. I was far too busy doing other things. God was simply there, the Rock of Ages, the eternal and immutable presence that I unthinkingly assumed him to be. I had no pressing reason to interrogate the images that I had of him, for to question the nature of God was never considered necessary in the circles in which I mostly moved. If asked, I would certainly have ruled out a bearded old man in flowing white robes who lived in the sky, but otherwise I would have fallen back on the images I had garnered from a very selective reading of the Bible and from the hymns and prayers of the non-conformist tradition in which I had grown up. By the time I was into adulthood, these familiar images had lost whatever power they may once have had to challenge or intrigue. As long as I didn't have to articulate my beliefs about God in any great detail, he could remain as a safe and unexamined backdrop to my life.

As middle age loomed, however, I found myself thinking far more seriously about the origins of these taken-for-granted images of God. I began to study the Bible more systematically and I started enquiring into the foundations of the Christian faith. I read up on the history of the Christian Church and I dipped a hesitant toe into the chaotic whirlpool of Christian theology. As I went on, I realised that the historical God of the Christian faith was far more complicated than the carefully selected and sanitised God whom I had come to know through decades of non-conformist church-going. In spite of the hundreds of sermons I must have heard, there was suddenly a great deal about him that I was picking up for the first time. I was, for example, very familiar with the stories in the early books of the Old Testament about the God (Yahweh) who had led the Hebrews out of captivity in Egypt, sheltered them on their forty-year trek through the deserts of the Sinai peninsula, and delivered them to their new home in Canaan. I had never encountered, however, the violent and temperamental God who had wreaked unconscionable havoc against the king of Egypt and his people, who had gratuitously slaughtered the Egyptian army at the Sea of Reeds, who had almost abandoned the Israelites in the desert lest he should be tempted to kill even more of them than the thousands he had already obliterated, and who had passed death sentences on Moses and Aaron because of their faithlessness to him at the waters of Meribah. This didn't seem at all like the loving God in whom I had been enjoined to place my faith.

Or again, I was very familiar with the God who had given Moses the Ten Commandments on Mount Sinai; but it was a surprise to find that I knew almost nothing about the hundreds of other laws that Yahweh had given to Moses at the same time and that carried the same weight of divine authority as the Ten. I did not know, for example, that Yahweh had approved of soldiers taking comely women who had been captured in battle as trophy wives for as long as it pleased them and then discarding them when they no longer satisfied. I was intrigued to find that it was an abomination to Yahweh for steps to be placed in front of altars lest the people should chance to see the private parts of the priests ascending them. I felt a little betrayed to discover that nobody had warned me, upon reaching adolescence, that Yahweh had sanctioned the stoning of unruly teenagers at the entrance to a town or city. I was startled to read that women who grabbed the genitals of men with whom their husbands were fighting should have their hands cut off. The puzzling question then arose of why some of God's laws were still very much in vogue while many others had slipped quietly away. Why, to take an obvious example, were the prohibitions on homosexuality still treated by many in the

Church as the unquestioned will of God while the punishments mandated for those found guilty of marital infidelity were never mentioned? What did it say about the authority of God that many of his commandments, enshrined in the scriptures of the Christian faith and available to be read in acts of Christian worship, had long since disappeared from view?

Questions continued to intrude when my inquisitiveness moved on to the New Testament and I found myself struggling to understand the relationship between the God of the Old Testament and the God of the New. How could the blood-thirsty Yahweh of the Pentateuch possibly be the same God whom Jesus had called his father? The conventional answer – that Jesus was revealing a truer and more complete face of God than people had been allowed to see in earlier times – raised even more questions. If Yahweh was *not* in fact the tyrant he is often portrayed as being in the early books of the Old Testament, why did he reveal himself in such a misleading way? Why did Jesus unreservedly commend the God of Abraham, Isaac and Jacob if the scriptural portrayal of him was so inaccurate? And why were these apparently false revelations included in the Christian Bible? These difficulties were compounded by the fact that for Christians, Jesus was not just the one who revealed a more acceptable face of God but God himself. Jesus *was* God. Yet it stretched my imagination almost to breaking point to believe that the micro-managing God of Mount Sinai, who had issued hundreds of laws to Moses about everything from the proper disposal of human excrement to safety in the building of houses, was the same God who had become incarnate in Jesus of Nazareth. Where did this astonishing idea come from?

The creeds that I had been dutifully reciting for many years raised yet more questions as my voyage of discovery progressed. The Nicene Creed, for example, went out of its way to emphasise that Jesus had been 'begotten and not made'. In saying the Creed I was declaring my belief that this was true, but I had never given so much as a passing thought to either the meaning or the origins of such a puzzling assertion. What was the difference between Jesus being 'begotten' and being 'made', and why was it of such overwhelming importance that it had become a creedal tenet of the Christian faith? As far as I could see, the New Testament was silent on the matter, and I could not recall ever having heard a sermon in which the distinction had been explained. I had, therefore, to face the challenging question of whether I was being entirely honest with myself in believing something that I had never taken the trouble to understand.

The doctrine of the Holy Trinity was another central plank of the

Christian faith that seemed to raise searching questions in the light of my new discoveries about God. I was familiar with the Church's orthodox teaching that God was a single and indivisible being made up of three entirely separate persons. I understood, too, that there were occasions when it was necessary to emphasise the one-ness of God (to defend Christianity from the charge of polytheism) and other occasions when it was equally necessary to emphasise the separateness of the three persons (to avoid the possibility that the Father and the Holy Spirit had died with Jesus on the cross). Yet the origins of this Trinitarian doctrine were entirely unknown to me. It is true that the New Testament speaks of a Father, a Son, a Word, and a Holy Spirit, but I could find no biblical authority for the full-blooded doctrine of the Trinity enshrined in the Nicene Creed. If not from the Bible, for example, where did the idea come from that Jesus had been 'begotten' and not 'made'? And why did the Word (which, according to the prologue to John's gospel, had been with God from the beginning of time and which dominated many of the theological debates of the early Christian Church) find no place in the Creed? When was the Word ejected from the formula, and why?

The crucifixion and resurrection of Jesus was yet another cornerstone of Christian belief that needed to be rethought. I had been familiar from an early age with the words from the famous Good Friday hymn: 'There was no other good enough to pay the price of sin; he only could unlock the gates of heaven and let us in'; but I had never thought to ask who had locked the gates in the first place and why God had needed the human sacrifice of Jesus before he was able to open them again. I could, moreover, find little in the New Testament to explain how the death of one man at a particular time and place in history had 'paid the price of sin' for all eternity. The synoptic gospels of Matthew, Mark and Luke are almost entirely silent on the matter. John's gospel hints at an answer that invokes the Jewish ritual of the sacrificial lamb; and St Paul's letters introduce the novel but difficult idea that people's sins are forgiven and their place in heaven assured as they die symbolically with Jesus and rise with him again. By the end of the first thousand years of the Christian faith, further explanations had appeared on the scene that seemed to have no biblical authority at all. A number of theologians had, for example, explained the death of Jesus as a ransom paid for the return of sinful man to the forgiving arms of God; but they differed as to who had paid the ransom and to whom it had been paid. Some argued that the ransom had been paid by God to the devil, others that it had been paid by Jesus to God. Yet others rejected the idea of a ransom entirely, preferring instead to see the cross as a symbol of God's unconditional love and an encouragement to righteous living. So how did the meaning of Jesus' crucifixion come to be understood in such conflicting ways? If not from the Bible, where did these explanations come from? Did they not reflect fundamentally different faces of the Christian God?

A final example of the questions arising from my new-found discovery of the multi-faceted God of the Christian tradition lay in the notion of salvation. Much of the evolution of Christian doctrine, I discovered, was best understood in the context of mankind's continuing search for salvation. Always there is the eternal question: What must I do to be saved? St Paul's answer, when the question was put to him by his jailer in Philippi, was: 'Put your trust in the Lord Jesus'. Other – rather different – answers have, however, illuminated the history of Christian theology. At one extreme are those who have argued that there is nothing we can do to aid our own salvation. It is God alone who decides whether human souls are saved or damned, and if people were able by their freewill actions to influence his decision, even to the tiniest degree, then he would not be the omnipotent God that he is. At the other extreme are those who have argued that there is quite a lot that people can do to help themselves. In particular, they can respond to the love of God by trying to lead good and morally responsible lives. God won't force himself upon us, but if we make the effort to follow his teachings, we will meet him coming towards us. There are assorted intermediate positions too. Such contradictory answers to the question 'what must I do to be saved?' seem to betoken entirely different faces of God. A God who chooses to save only *some* souls can hardly be the same deity as a God who invites the salvation of *all* souls. How did such a contradiction come about, and does it matter?

It is clear from these introductory illustrations that many different faces of the God of the Christian tradition have been unveiled in the stories and narratives that have come down to us across the years. Far from being the immutable Rock of Ages that I had imagined him to be, the historical God emerges as a complex and changing deity whose images have formed and reformed like the pieces of a kaleidoscope. If I am now asked whether I believe in God, I reply that it all depends on the kind of God the questioner has in mind – for it is meaningless to ask whether people believe in God unless some definitions are first agreed.

Does God unilaterally choose some souls for hell and others for heaven, or doesn't he? Does God manipulate the laws of the natural world in response to people's prayers, or doesn't he? Did God create the world and all its inhabitants in six days, or didn't he? Is the God of the Old and New Testaments the same God who is worshipped by Jews and Muslims, or isn't he? Did God require a once-and-for-all human sacrifice before he was able to forgive human sin, or didn't he? And so on. God comes in many different shapes and sizes; so tell me the shape and the size of the God you have in mind, and I will tell you whether it is a God in whom I can believe.

Lying behind these awkward questions is an even greater one that unites them all: why is it that people across the ages have claimed to have experienced so many different and sometimes contradictory faces of the Christian God? If there is one true God, and if he is known to those who believe in him through the revelation of himself in history, why hasn't a consistent understanding of him emerged from the witness and testimony of those who have experienced his presence and told their stories? There are various possible answers. One is that God has deliberately revealed himself in different guises over time – an answer implicit in the common Christian assertion that the true nature of God was revealed much more fully in the life of Jesus than in his dealings with the early Israelites. Somewhere along the line between Abraham and Jesus, the argument goes, God started showing himself in a different and truer light. Somewhere in the course of those two thousand years, his revelation of himself as the warrior God of Sabbaoth or the micro-managing God of Sinai metamorphosed into his later revelation in Jesus as a God of universal grace. Perhaps, but why would an omnipotent God behave in such a misleading way? Why would he deliberately want to confuse people by giving out incomplete (or even false) messages about himself to earlier generations, only to correct them in later generations? It seems a very unlikely thing for God to have done.

A more convincing answer, perhaps, is that God has actually been changing over time, and the revelations that people claim to have experienced are the manifestations of a deity who is continually evolving new and different faces. Perhaps the angry and vengeful Yahweh of the early Old Testament learnt from his mistakes and became incarnate in Jesus as a more compassionate kind of God. The stories in the Old Testament that link him with such foundational figures as Abraham and Moses portray him as someone who was perfectly capable of changing his mind. It could be argued that he has continued to do so in the millennia that have followed. From this point of view, God appears to be a kaleidoscopic God because he *is* a kaleidoscopic God. It is not, however, an argument that has very much to commend it. A God who feels the need to change within a time span that, in cosmological terms, is less than the blink of an eye can hardly be a God who created the cosmos in the first place.

Much stronger is the likelihood that many of the faces of God that people have claimed in good faith to have seen over the ages have simply been wrong. Believers may sincerely have thought that they were receiving true revelations from God, but in fact (for all sorts of good and human reasons) they were mistaken. Revelation is always mediated through human perception; and human perception can often act as a distorting prism. Since there are, as far as we know, no neural pathways within the human brain that are dedicated exclusively to the reception of divine messages, one man's revelation of truth can be another man's fanciful imagination; and there are no objective criteria for deciding which is right. There are numerous examples in this book. Plausible though such an explanation of the multi-faceted God of Christian history may be, it raises searching questions about certainty and doubt. Can we *ever* be sure that what we are experiencing, through whatever means we may experience it, is genuinely from God? Is it ever possible to see the 'true' face of God, or must we necessarily make do with the disparate and distorted images that have come down to us through the witness and testimony of the ages? Those who yearn for certainty will believe that, through the teachings of their Church and the authority of the Bible, they are indeed seeing the true face of God. Those who are content to live with uncertainty will reach their own conclusions from the array of images on offer.

There is, of course, a fourth possible answer to the question of why people have experienced so many different and contradictory faces of the Christian God – that he simply doesn't exist outside the human imagination. God could be an entirely human invention. In many ways, this is the easiest answer of all. Human inventiveness is endlessly creative, and if God is among its finest creations, then there is every reason to expect a rich diversity in the way he has been portrayed. From this perspective, the historical portrait gallery of God is stocked with nothing more (but also with nothing less) than the sum of human hopes and fears, and while they may tell us a great deal about the human condition, they can tell us nothing about God because he is not 'really' there. This is, though, rather too glib an answer. Whatever people may or may not personally believe about God, the human awareness of something beyond the ordinary world of everyday experience has been among the most potent drivers of human history. This awareness cannot be explained *simply* as the product of a collectively deluded mind. It would not be true to the historical record to dismiss the human experience of God *simply* as the triumph of hope over experience, or romanticism over rationality, any more than it would be true to the record to portray him as the eternally immutable Rock of Ages. The truth is likely to be far more ragged and complex than either of these absolutes imply.

Against this autobiographical background, my aim in this book has been to lay out the fruits of my search for a less selective and sanitised image of God than the one I grew up with. The book is set within an historical framework, beginning with the gods of Canaan from whom the Yahweh of the Old Testament probably emerged and ending with the non-theistic faces of God that were gaining traction by the end of the twentieth century. It is, quite deliberately, a brief history, for as any writer knows, the quickest way to bore one's readers is to tell them everything. I have necessarily been highly selective in the examples I have included in the story, and I have surely omitted much that others would consider far more relevant. I plead guilty as charged. It is not my aim to offer an exhaustive account of the history of God – others have done that far more ably than I could possibly do – but to present what seem to me to be some of the major milestones in the human understanding of God within the main stream of Christian faith.

I offer no answers to the question (which runs as a consistent thread throughout the text) of why people across the ages have experienced so many different and sometimes contradictory faces of the Christian God. I have merely tried to supply the evidence upon which readers can decide for themselves. I hope that some will allow me to escort them on a journey that I have already undertaken for myself and that has led me to some surprising but ultimately sustaining conclusions; but if any decide not to, I will entirely understand, for the journey is not without its hazards, especially for those in search of certainty.

Chapter 1
The Origins of the Gods

In about 1800 BC a man called Abram (or Abraham, as he was later to be named) set out from his hometown of Ur, in Chaldea, bound for Canaan. He was accompanied by his father Terah, his childless wife Sarai (or Sarah, as she was later to be named) and his nephew Lot. The story is told in the Old Testament book of Genesis. The family reached Harran, where Abraham decided to settle and where Terah later died at the ripe old age of 205. Then, without any apparent warning, a God appeared to Abraham and promised to make him the father of a great nation. The God told him to complete his journey to Canaan; and although he was now 75 years of age, Abraham obeyed and set off with Sarah, Lot and all their possessions. At Schechem, a city on an important trade route north of Jerusalem, the God promised Abraham that he would give the whole of the country to his descendants. Abraham built an altar there before moving on to settle in the land between Bethel and Ai.

Who was this God who commanded Abraham's obedience? Judaism has accepted him as the God who eventually united the various ethnic groups that made up the people of Israel, and Christianity has proclaimed him as the God who became incarnate in Jesus Christ. The early biblical stories about him are, however, far from consistent, for they originated in different places and were written many centuries after the events to which they bear witness. The first five books of the Old Testament (the Pentateuch) did not exist in their present form before about 900 BC and they were not brought together until several centuries after that. Generations of oral tradition must have separated the life of Abraham from the only record of it that now exists – and stories can change quite dramatically as they are told and retold across the ages. It is by no means certain that Abraham even existed.

A further difficulty in identifying the God who appeared to Abraham is the variety of names that he bears in the early books of the Old Testament, a legacy in part of the different sources from which the Pentateuch was compiled. Following the death of King Solomon in 922 BC the single kingdom of Israel split into two separate kingdoms, each adopting a different name for Abraham's God. Documents from the southern kingdom of Judah favoured the name of YHWH, while those from the northern kingdom of Israel preferred the name Elohim. They had to be treated with care, for the naming of gods in the ancient world was a risky thing to do, but it would have proved impossible to write the religious history of a nation without referring to the central character in the drama. Although the proper name of Abraham's God could never be spoken, it was written in a number of different ways. The most common form in the Old Testament, occurring more than six thousand times, is YHWH, the name that was typically used in the southern kingdom of Judah. It is usually pronounced in Western speech as either Yahweh (the form used in this book) or Yehovah, and it is conventionally written in English translations of the Bible as 'the LORD'.

The slightly later writers in the northern kingdom of Israel favoured the name of Elohim, a plural or composite form of El. Among the ancient mythologies of the Middle East, El was the high god of Canaan and the consort of the goddess Ashera. Other gods in the Canaanite pantheon included Mot, the god of sterility and death, and El's son Baal, the god of fertility and new life whose worship went back at least to the time of the ancient Semites living in Bronze Age Canaan. Baal and his consort Astarte, the goddess of sexual love, were prominent deities in the eastern Mediterranean, ensuring the continuation each year of the great cycle of germination and fruitfulness. The fertility rituals performed by the priests of Baal and Astarte included temple prostitution and other symbolic enactments of conception and birth. Elsewhere in Canaan, first-born children were sacrificed to the Ammonite god Milcom, the young victims being slowly burned to death in the outstretched arms of the idol. King Solomon, the exemplar of Jewish wisdom, was a worshipper of both Astarte and Milcom, even erecting a shrine to Milcom on the Mount of Olives to please his foreign wives. The story, narrated in the first book of Kings, was taken up by John Milton in *Paradise Lost* where he depicted Milcom as 'the horrid King besmear'd with blood of human sacrifice and parents tears'.

It was this polytheistic culture, presided over by the high god El, that Abraham would have encountered when he travelled to Canaan in about 1800 BC. The Genesis stories about him and his descendants give various names to the God who came suddenly into their lives. The God first introduced himself to Abraham as Yahweh (the LORD); but when Abraham was blessed by the priestly King of Salem, Melchizedeck, the blessing was in the name of El Elyon (usually translated into English as

God Most High). When the God appeared to Abraham in his hundredth year he introduced himself as El Shaddai (God Almighty). Other names that appear in the Genesis narratives include El Roi (the God who sees), El Olam (the everlasting God) and El Bethel (the God of Bethel).

It is natural to wonder about the relationship between these appellations. Were there several gods, each with its own name, or was there just one God introducing himself under different titles? Moreover, was there any connection, other than the obvious linguistic one, between the God who appears in the Genesis stories as El and the ancient Canaanite god of the same name? The confusions multiply when the narrative moves on a few hundred years to the time of Moses, for although Yahweh had by now been worshipped by the Hebrew people for generations, Moses did not recognise him when he appeared in the burning bush on Mount Horeb. Speaking through the flames, Yahweh identified himself as 'the God of Abraham, Isaac and Jacob'; yet in spite of coming face to face with his tribal deity, Moses had to ask what name he should use when he returned to Egypt and told the people about the encounter. Later, Yahweh explained the reason for the confusion: in his earlier appearances to the patriarchs he had always called himself El Shaddai, not Yahweh. Moses' mistake was, perhaps, understandable after all.

Whether there were one, two or several gods at this very early stage in Jewish history is a question that does not lend itself to normal historical enquiry. By the time the early books of the Bible came together in their present edited form in about the third century BC, Judaism had been a monotheistic faith for several centuries, and it is all too easy to assume that the early patriarchs had been committed to a single God. Yet there is no necessary reason why Abraham, Isaac and Jacob, moving among the polytheistic communities of the Middle East, were ever devoted to a single God. When Jacob's wife Rachel moved out of her father's home in Mesopotamia, for example, she took with her the portable gods that had been in the family for a long time. Although, therefore, the Hebrew tribes had been familiar with Yahweh from a very early time, other gods were not only well known to them but also (according to the record in the Old Testament) were worshipped by them. As well as Yahweh, the name of the Canaanite high god El still survives in such familiar Old Testament names as Bethel, Penuel, Ishmael and of course Israel.

Although the origins of the deity who entered the lives of Abraham and Sarah must remain forever obscure, we do know something of the ways in which people first became conscious of the spirit world around them and of the gods who populated it. For this, we have to thank the work of cultural anthropologists, especially in the late nineteenth and early twentieth centuries. Sir James Frazer's (1854-1941) compendious text *The Golden Bough*, published in stages between 1890 and 1915, made a particularly significant contribution to our understanding of the origins of religious belief. His findings caused a stir among late Victorian and Edwardian clerics who saw them as a calculated challenge to the religious certainties they were preaching, and *The Golden Bough* was widely condemned as a book that was neither safe nor proper for Christians to read. Frazer's work, however, proved too popular to be dismissed out of hand; and once he had drawn aside the veil concealing the primitive origins of many religious practices, Christians could never again be wholly innocent about the complex antecedents of their familiar beliefs and rituals.

In the early stages of human religious awareness, gods took many forms: stones, trees, animals, figurines, totem poles, statuettes, seas and rivers, sun and moon, and so on. Since they were typically the gods of nomadic people, they had to be either portable or universally available. The divine objects were believed to be animated by spirits that could transmit their life-force to those who worshipped them, protecting them from disasters and endowing them with valuable advantages in the remorseless struggle for life. By the early Mesolithic period in Europe (from roughly 12,000 BC), nomadic lifestyles were giving way to more settled farming communities, and gods could become larger and more static beings, sometimes with their own dwelling places. Temples were appearing in Mesopotamia (modern day Iraq) by about 5000 BC as gods became embedded in the history and culture of local settlements, commanding the allegiance of successive generations of worshippers. Some of the earliest deities were feminine, their pendulous breasts and prominent genitalia betraying the supreme importance of fertility in the life of agricultural communities. As towns and cities expanded and urban cultures developed, female deities gradually gave way to male. By about 2000 BC elaborate rituals, mainly involving the worship of male gods, were already well established in India, China, Mexico and parts of North America.

As the gods became increasingly important in their local communities, elaborate cults grew up around them involving priests, rituals, and holy objects. The ruling elite in a community typically appointed themselves as the chosen servants or priests of the local god, attending to his needs, managing his affairs and interpreting his wishes. The lower strata of society, the labourers and agricultural workers, provided the sacrifices needed to appease and satisfy him. The biblical story of the Babylonian god Bel is a vivid account of a local middle-eastern cult in about the second century BC. Superintended by temple priests who ensured that he received the food he needed, Bel 'miraculously' got through twelve bushels of flour, forty sheep and fifty gallons of wine a day – though in reality, of course, these vast provisions were being siphoned off by the priests for themselves and their families. As well as their physical presence in their temples on earth, gods sometimes led other, transcendental lives in the cosmic sphere above. They had their abodes among the pantheons of heaven as well as their dwelling places on earth. Seated on their thrones above the celestial firmament, they were spiritual sovereigns exercising their power remotely over their temporal subjects on earth: lords of lords and kings of kings.

At some point in the evolution of religious beliefs, people began to think of gods as inhabiting, or even becoming, human beings. Throughout the history of religious belief, outstanding men (and very occasionally women) have been thought to be possessed by a deity, or at least to have such a high degree of supernatural power as to be a virtual god. With the status of divinity came also the sacrificial homage of the people. In many cases these human gods had regal as well as divine authority, turning their kingdoms into theocracies. There are numerous examples throughout recorded history. Egyptian pharaohs, Chinese emperors, Mesopotamian and Babylonian kings, American Indian tribal leaders, Inca emperors, Nepalese kings and Japanese emperors were all worshipped in their lifetimes as human gods, the last two until well into the twentieth century. European monarchs were rarely deified (though some were canonised), but many claimed a God-given right to the exercise of absolute power. To be touched by a king was to be favoured as if by a direct blessing from heaven. The 'king's touch', as it came to be known, could also mediate the healing power of God. As late as the seventeenth century, scrofula (tuberculosis of the lymph nodes) was thought in England to be curable through contact with the monarch. Charles I (1600-1649) 'cured' a hundred patients at a time in his chapel at Holyrood Palace in Edinburgh, and Charles II (1630-1685) is said to have touched around a hundred thousand scrofulous subjects in the course of his reign. The king's touch, however, could not survive the progress of science: William III (1650-1702) contemptuously refused to engage in such magical antics, declaring on the only recorded occasion on which he touched a subject: 'God give you better health and more sense'.

The religions of ancient Greece and Rome, which were flourishing in the pluralistic hothouse of the Mediterranean world at the time of Jesus, provide some of the clearest examples of the fusion between the human and the divine. Gods still embodied the pure essence of divinity, of course, but human beings could be raised to divine status through the gifts they possessed or the powers they displayed. An inscription on the acropolis on Mount Mycale in modern-day Turkey describes the first of the Roman emperors, Caesar Augustus (63 BC – AD 14), not only as Emperor but also as the Son of God. He was worshipped in his own lifetime as Lord, Redeemer, and Saviour of the World – all titles that were later used by Christians to emphasise their emerging belief in the divinity of Jesus Christ. Plainly, some careful analysis is needed to distinguish between the divinity of Augustus and that of Christ.

A quantum leap in the evolution of religious belief took place in the Hebrew faith when the gods became God. Among the descendants of Abraham the conviction gradually emerged, probably over a long period of time, that there was, in fact, only one true God. When and how the transition occurred cannot be mapped in any great detail, but there are clues. When Yahweh gave Moses the tablets of commandment on Mount Sinai in about 1250 BC, he was making no claims to uniqueness. In his first commandment to Moses he acknowledged that he was not the *only* God, merely the one who demanded the undivided loyalty of his people: 'You shall have no other gods before me.' Yahweh was not alone among the deities on offer in those polytheistic times: in theory, and often in practice too, the people had a choice. When some four hundred years later Elijah challenged the prophets of Baal to call down fire on a sacrificial bullock, the prophet's argument was not that Baal did not exist, merely that he was a less potent god than Yahweh. By the time the long-suffering Job appeared on the scene in about 700 BC, however, the Jewish scriptures were beginning to depict their God as the sole surviving resident in the formerly populous pantheon of the Canaanite gods. He was also someone with whom an interactive relationship was possible.

It was a step change. Gods (including Yahweh, if the Pentateuch is anything to go by) had often been seen as remote and fearsome beings who appeared wreathed in smoke on the tops of mountains and who spoke through thunder and lightning. Their divine anger at the wickedness of their people could only be appeased by sacrifice and worship. People had good reason to tremble and bow before their gods, for if their fate depended upon the will of a powerful deity, it was prudent to respect his holiness and acknowledge his majesty. Yet here was Job audaciously complaining to the God of Israel, arguing with him, and even calling him to account for his actions. The dramatic story of Job's dialogue with Yahweh, which has few parallels in the Hebrew Scriptures, is a striking example of human autonomy flexing its muscles in protest against the actions of a seemingly capricious God. Job had the self-confidence to rail not only against the slings and arrows of outrageous fortune that came his way but also against the deity who was hurling them. His daring and risky interrogation of Yahweh, who had shown himself more than capable of obliterating those who crossed his path, is a dramatic milestone in mankind's long and continuing search for the meaning of life. Why was God condemning him to an existence of unbridled misery? What had he done to deserve such divine disfavour? God's hand, Job complained, was heavy upon him in his trouble; and he refused to be fobbed off by those who thought he was playing with fire in calling God to account. Job demanded an explanation – and it had better be a good one. It was, by any standards, a breath-taking display of bold self-righteousness.

The introduction of the moral language of sin and expiation allowed another momentous step to be taken in the development of religious consciousness when the 'scapegoat' emerged as a practical way of dealing with the mountain of human sinfulness and guilt. The problem was, in essence, quite straightforward. Gods laid down the rules of human behaviour; people sinned by breaking them; and if the resultant anger of the gods was to be appeased, ways had to be found of atoning for sin and repairing the fractured relationship. The scapegoat became a highly effective mechanism for doing so. In *The Golden Bough*, James Frazer defined a scapegoat as an animal or a person onto whom the sinful burdens of individuals and communities were symbolically laid. By then disposing of the animal, often in a ritual sacrifice overseen by priests, the sins would die with the scapegoat and the favour of the gods would be restored. A new start could be made, unencumbered by the weight of the personal and corporate guilt of the people and the wrath of the gods.

The Jewish faith, from which the later Christian ideas of sin and atonement developed, attached a great deal of importance to the ritual sacrifice of scapegoats in the temple in Jerusalem. Various animals, cloven and otherwise, were symbolically saddled with the sins of the people and then slaughtered in a particular way before being burnt at the altar by a priest. Sins would be blotted out in the sight of Yahweh as the scapegoat shrivelled and burnt. Detailed rules were set out about the form and conduct of these sacrificial ceremonies, each part of which had to be followed to the letter if Yahweh was to be satisfied. Different kinds of sacrifices were offered in atonement for different kinds of sins, but most of the rituals had a common template. Typically, the scapegoat had to be a young and flawless animal, its blood had to be poured out at the base of the altar, and its fat had to be removed and burnt separately as a soothing balm for Yahweh's pleasure.

At various times in Jewish history the prophets spoke out against the whole cultic system of scapegoat and sacrifice, demanding instead a more humane and contrite response to God's calls for repentance. Micah, writing in about 700 BC, declared that sacrifices were anathema to Yahweh: it was far more important that people should act justly and walk humbly with him. Amos, too, was saying much the same thing at about the same time. For a long time, however, the sacrificial offering of animal scapegoats was central to the Jewish understanding of Yahweh and his relationship with the people. There are also examples in the Old Testament of the cultic use of a living scapegoat. According to the book of Leviticus, Yahweh commanded Aaron, the first high priest of the cult, to take a live goat, place his hands upon its head and confess all the sins of the Hebrews. Aaron was then to send the animal into the wilderness where it would carry the iniquities of the people into the oblivion of the desert, there to be lost forever.

People as well as animals could sometimes be coerced into duty as scapegoats for the misdemeanours of their fellows. In *The Golden Bough*, James Frazer reported several interesting examples from around the world of human scapegoats cancelling out the sins of others by undergoing some form of substitutionary punishment in their stead. In parts of India, the sins of a rajah would be ritually transferred to a convicted criminal who earned his pardon by vicariously suffering in place of the ruler. In other places a local Brahman was paid to pick up the rajah's sins and then to die on his behalf. In some countries of Africa, the services of sickly men and women were purchased each year by public subscription. Those who had committed a serious offence such as theft or adultery were expected to atone for their misdeeds by paying for the cost of these human scapegoats, and a man from a neighbouring town was hired to kill them. In all of these examples the slate of moral accountability was wiped clean by the vicarious suffering of the scapegoat: the gods were appeased and life was able to begin afresh, free from the fear of divine retribution.

Even a human god could, on occasion, become a scapegoat. Frazer thought that where this happened, two separate traditions were brought together in a single act of deicide. One was the use of human scapegoats; the other was the killing of living gods before they had time to be ravaged by the decrepitude of old age. If human gods were to be killed in any case before they became too infirm to be of any further use, they might as well be killed as scapegoats. A divine scapegoat is likely to be a far more effective atonement for sin than a merely human one. It would then make sense to heap the sins of a community onto the human god and kill him in a sacrificial manner to ensure that the evil deeds would die with him. The atoning power of a divine sacrifice has been a consistent leitmotif in the human imagination. The Christian story of the death of Jesus, in which a divine man was killed to atone for the sins of all mankind, is not unique among the stories that have come down from the ancient world.

So Yahweh, the LORD, the God whom Christians later came to believe was incarnate in Jesus Christ, appeared on the scene some four thousand years ago, revealing himself to Abraham through a series of extravagant promises. As Abraham and his descendants were soon to discover, he did much more than scatter promises.

Chapter 2
The God of Israel

The God who appeared to Abraham at Harran in about 1800 BC was a God who commanded and promised. According to the narrative in Genesis, he commanded Abraham to travel to a country that would be shown to him, and he promised to make him the father of a great nation. He was also a partisan God of capricious power. When Abraham and Sarah journeyed to Egypt to escape a famine in Canaan, Abraham, fearing that the pharaoh would kill him and take Sarah as his wife, begged her to say that he was her brother, not her husband. The deceit worked and Abraham's life was spared; but God was firmly on his side, and instead of chiding him for his duplicity he turned on the luckless pharaoh, infesting his palace with awful diseases. At this very early stage in Jewish history, Yahweh was still a local God who protected his own people and would have no truck with foreigners. As if to emphasise the point, he later promised Abraham that he would punish not only the Egyptians but any other nation that was rash enough to enslave his people. The promise was bound up in a covenant with Abraham where God pledged himself to Abraham's family if he and all his male descendants yielded up their foreskins as a symbol of their commitment. Abraham agreed and he, together with his illegitimate son Ishmael and all the other men in his household, were circumcised.

As well as promising Abraham an extravagant future and demanding in return a distinctive ritual of allegiance, God also had a more homely side to him. One day, as Abraham was sitting outside his tent by the ancient Canaanite shrine of El at Mamre, near Jericho, Yahweh came to him in the guise of a man accompanied by two angels also dressed as men. They caused Abraham's post-menopausal wife Sarah to chuckle as they promised her that she would have a son. 'At my time in life I am past bearing children', she said to herself, 'and in any case my husband is old'. God also told Abraham of his intention to destroy the city of Sodom, on the Jordan plain in the south of Canaan, because of the sexual depravity of its citizens. Realising that innocent people in the city might perish along with the guilty, Abraham daringly reminded Yahweh that if he really was a God of righteousness, he was obliged to act justly. 'Far be it for you', he said, 'to kill innocent people along with the wicked'. For a brief and dramatic moment, Abraham stood on a higher moral plane than God; but rather than smite him for his temerity, God accepted Abraham's argument and entered into a kind of Dutch auction with him over the number of innocent people there had to be in Sodom for the city to be spared. Will you spare Sodom if there are fifty innocent people?, asked Abraham. Yes, if that is the number of innocent people, the city will be spared. Forty-five? Yes. Forty? Yes. And so it went on. Eventually Yahweh agreed to spare Sodom if only ten innocent people were found in the city; but either he was unable to find ten innocents or he reneged on his promise, for the next day he caused burning sulphur to rain down on both Sodom and the neighbouring city of Gomorrah, destroying them and all their inhabitants. Yahweh stood revealed to Abraham as a God of terrible and vengeful power.

Another of God's promises was, however, made good in the fullness of time when Sarah gave birth to a son, Isaac. Sarah laughed in celebration as she recalled the earlier visit of the man with the two angels. Then God tested Abraham by ordering him to kill the boy and burn his body as a sacrifice. It was an extraordinary command: not only was Abraham to kill the only son of his marriage to Sarah, thereby destroying the life of the very one through whom God's dynastic promises were to be fulfilled, he was to do so by offering a child as a human sacrifice. The ghastly ritual, mimicking the sacrificial offering of children to the Canaanite god Milcom, was only halted at the very last minute when God provided the alternative sacrifice of a ram caught in a nearby bush. Abraham's preparedness to kill and burn his son in obedience to God has marked him in both Jewish and Christian eyes as a man of great faith; but from a modern viewpoint, such a repugnant test of fidelity could only have been set by a God of grotesque moral sensibilities. Far from being lauded for his faith, a father in the twenty-first century who came within a whisker of killing and burning his child in response to what he believed to be a direct command from God would rightly be detained in state custody for a long time. As with any biblical story, however, the historical and cultural context in which the sacrifice of Isaac occurred is central to the way it should be read. Times change profoundly, and the acceptable faces of God change with them.

The Genesis story moves on. Having narrowly survived this childhood ordeal, Isaac married his cousin Rebecca. It was while he was living with her at Gerar, between Gaza and Beersheba, that he repeated the deceit of his father by trying to pass Rebecca off as his sister in order to save his own life and prevent Rebecca from becoming a concubine of the Philistine king, Abimelech. On this occasion, however, Yahweh did not repeat the vengeful act that, in the previous generation, he had carried out against the Egyptian pharaoh. Instead, he chose to make Isaac a very rich man. In one year with God's help Isaac harvested a hundred times as much as he had sown – a staggering rate of return on his investment. The family's duplicitous tendencies surfaced again in the next generation when Isaac and Rebecca's younger son, Jacob, tricked his older brother Esau out of his inheritance before leaving the family home in Beersheba to work for his uncle Laban in Mesopotamia. During the journey, Jacob had a dream in which he saw a staircase running from earth to heaven, with angels travelling up and down. Suddenly, Jacob was aware of God standing beside him, and having repeated the promise he had given to his father and grandfather that his descendants would be as numerous as all the specks of dust on earth, God vowed to protect Jacob wherever he went.

Far from being comforted by these words of extravagant promise, Jacob woke from his dream in a state of terror, declaring that he must be in the very house of God. He named the place Bethel – the place of El. Jacob, however, showed himself a man of some resilience, for despite his terror at meeting Yahweh, he somehow mustered the confidence to set conditions to their relationship. *If* Yahweh would protect him on his journey, and *if* he returned safely to his father's home, *then* Jacob would accept him as his God. Jacob's response to his night-time terror was reassuringly human as well as daringly audacious: he wanted evidence that God would be as good as his word before throwing in his lot with him. Jacob's next encounter with God was equally dramatic. After many years spent working for Laban under terms that he regarded as unfair, Jacob finally fled his uncle's household and set off for home in Beersheba. He took with him his two wives, Rachel and Leah, together with all his possessions. As he was nearing home, Jacob became understandably anxious about the reception he would receive from his brother Esau. Fearing the worst, he reminded God of the bargain they had struck at Bethel. That night Jacob found himself wrestling with an unknown stranger who refused to reveal his name but whom Jacob later recognised as Yahweh. As at Bethel, Jacob by no means disgraced himself in the encounter. The stranger told him that he had struggled with God and won, and as a result his name was changed from Jacob to Israel. Later, God told Jacob to return to Bethel, and there he repeated the promise he had already given to Abraham and Isaac that he would be the ancestor of kings and the fount of nations.

Some four to five hundred years after Jacob's death in Egypt, Yahweh appeared to Moses while he was tending his father-in-law's sheep near Mount Horeb, in Sinai. The story begins in the third chapter of Exodus.

Speaking from the midst of a burning bush, God introduced himself to Moses as the God of Abraham, Isaac and Jacob, and he established his credentials with two miracles that would convince the Hebrew people of his authenticity when Moses returned to them in Egypt. In the first, a rod was turned into a snake and back again, and in the second, one of Moses' hands was first made leprous and then restored to health. By stressing his historic connections with Abraham, Isaac and Jacob, the God of the patriarchs was merging imperceptibly with the God of Moses to become the tribal God of Israel. His involvement in the dramatic events of the exodus from Egypt to the Promised Land of Canaan was greatly to enhance his status among the Israelites, earning for himself the majestic title of the God of Sabbaoth – the God of hosts, the warrior God of armies and battles.

This new face of Yahweh, of which there are but few harbingers in the very early stories of the Old Testament, began to be revealed when he commanded Moses to seek the release of the Hebrews from their bondage in Egypt. A god of Yahweh's power could presumably have brought about the liberation of his people with a minimum of collateral damage by simply persuading the pharaoh to let them go; but that is not how it happened. Far from allowing the Hebrews to leave Egypt and worship God in their own way, the pharaoh's mind was deliberately set by Yahweh against any such act of clemency. 'I shall make him stubborn', Yahweh said to Moses, 'and he will not listen to you'. Having ensured the pharaoh's intransigence, God then had a reason to unleash a dreadful catalogue of divine retribution against the Egyptian people. Plagues of frogs, flies, boils and locusts descended on Egypt; the Nile was turned into blood; a terrible hailstorm blew up; and the land was covered in darkness. After each appalling catastrophe had subsided, the pharaoh behaved exactly as Yahweh had said he would, ignoring the pleadings of Moses and refusing to release the Hebrew captives. Finally, in the most terrible act of all, God arranged for the first-born children in every house in Egypt, from the grandest to the humblest, to be slaughtered in their beds at night. First-born cattle were also decimated. It was the last straw for the pharaoh, and, summoning Moses and Aaron in the middle of the night, he commanded the Hebrews to leave the country at once together with their sheep and cattle and all their possessions. Yahweh had eventually triumphed by revealing himself as a God of unconscionable death and destruction.

Following Yahweh's vindictive rampage through Egypt, the Israelites finally left the country of their enslavement and set off on the journey to the land that God had promised to give them. According to the numbers given in the book of Exodus, there could have been as many as two and a half million men, women and children, together with vast herds of sheep and cattle. They would have formed an enormous and unwieldy caravan, taxing Moses' powers of leadership to the full. During their travels, which took forty years, God continued to wreak his revenge on the Egyptians. His campaign moved from Egypt to the Sea of Reeds (possibly the modern Lake Timsah) where, pursued by the Egyptian army, the Israelites found themselves on the shores of the lake with no way over to the other side. Behind them, the Egyptians were closing fast but Moses waved his staff for the waters to part and the people – two million or more of them – crossed to safety. The soldiers, following them into the passage between the watery walls, were drowned as their chariots became bogged down in the mud and the waters closed over their heads. It was, according to the narrative in Exodus, a gratuitous act of mass murder. Although Yahweh could presumably have closed the waters as soon as the Hebrews were safely across, he waited until the Egyptian army was trapped in the middle before drowning them all. The hapless soldiers and their horses were no match for a God who first impeded their retreat and then condemned them to their watery graves. The Israelites were deeply impressed, singing ecstatic songs of praise to their great defender. 'We shall sing to the LORD, for he has risen up in triumph.' Yahweh had once again proved himself an awesome and powerful deity, the greatest of all the gods, the God of hosts, the God of Sabbaoth.

So Moses and his brother Aaron led the people of Israel to the dramatic climax of their wilderness years. Sustained by the food and water that God had miraculously provided for them in the desert, and guided by a pillar of cloud by day and a pillar of fire by night, they came to Mount Sinai, a terrifying mountain of noise, fire and smoke. Trembling with fear and foreboding, the people were led by Moses from their campsite to the foot of the mountain, which convulsed in a volcanic shudder as smoke rose from its cone like fumes emerging from a kiln. Then, amidst a rising crescendo of trumpeted sound, Yahweh appeared on the summit – a God of awesome and holy terror. Only Moses and Aaron were permitted to make the journey up the mountainside and into his presence. The priests and people prudently kept their distance lest the voice of God became the pronouncement of a sentence of death.

There, on Mount Sinai, Yahweh entered into a covenant with Moses, sealed with the blood of some bulls that had been slaughtered on an altar hastily erected at the foot of the mountain. For their part, the people were to worship no other deities and to do everything that God required of them. For his part, God promised to harass the enemies of the Israelites, cure their illnesses, endow them with long life, and prevent miscarriages among the womenfolk. He also vowed to create a cordon of terror around the Israelites as they moved on through the desert, panicking those whom they encountered and driving out the tribes already colonising the Promised Land of Canaan. In contemporary language, God pledged to carry out an act of ethnic cleansing against the Amorites, Hivites, Canaanites, Philistines, Perizzites, Jebusites and Hittites who were already living there. Provided the Israelites made no alliances with the indigenous people and shunned their gods, they would become the sole possessors of all the land from the Red Sea to the Euphrates. The people agreed and the new covenant was signed and sealed with the blood of the sacrificed oxen. As Moses splashed them with the sacred blood of the bulls, the Israelites shouted: 'We shall obey and we shall do all that the LORD has said'.

Yet such was the attraction of other gods in the polytheistic culture of the times that even before the blood was dry on their clothes, the people had forgotten their promise. Under the direction of Aaron the Israelites fashioned a bull (a traditional effigy of the indigenous Canaanite god, El) from golden trinkets they had melted down and hailed it as the deity who had led them out of Egypt. When Yahweh saw what was happening, he told Moses to leave the people in no doubt as to his displeasure at their rejection of him. Indeed, so angry was God that he decided to break his everlasting covenant with Abraham, wipe the Israelites from the face of the earth, and begin again with the descendants of Moses. It took the cool head of Moses to prevent another killing field. As Abraham, centuries earlier, had tried to talk God out of the destruction of Sodom, so Moses begged him not to go back on his promises to Abraham, Isaac and Jacob. For a brief moment Moses, like Abraham before him, held the moral high ground and, like Abraham, he prevailed. Yahweh recognised the evil he was planning to do and called off his threatened genocide of the Israelites.

That was not the end of the matter, however. Acting on God's instructions, Moses called the people of the tribe of Levi to him, armed them all with swords, and told them to go through the camp slaughtering their brothers, sons, friends and neighbours. The Levites obeyed, killing some three thousand of their fellow Israelites. Yahweh was pleased with the carnage and installed the Levites as his priests, declaring that by killing their sons and brothers they had brought blessings upon themselves; but then came an unexpected shaft of mercy in an otherwise relentless rampage of violence. Having been appeased by the killing spree of the Levites, God promised to blot out the transgressions of the people and obliterate their sins from the book of reckoning. It was, though, no more than a temporary reprieve, for Yahweh went ahead regardless with the punishment of those who had taken part in the ritual of the golden bull. More than that, he declined to accompany the people any further on their journey towards the Promised Land lest in his anger he should be tempted to destroy them. Having commanded the people not to kill, God evidently did not trust himself to refrain from slaughtering those with whom he had entered into an eternal covenant of salvation.

As soon as the Israelites were on the move again after their epoch-making encampment at Sinai, the familiar pattern of complaint and retribution continued. The story is now taken up in the book of Numbers. The people grumbled to Moses about their dreadful conditions and Yahweh (who had evidently decided to remain with his people) responded by setting fire to their camp. Greatly distressed, Moses asked God why he was so displeased with him: if he was doing such a bad job as leader, then God might as well put an end to him. For a while God relented; but it was not long before he was calling Moses' bluff. Irked yet again by the people's endless complaints, he threatened to take Moses at his word and kill him and everyone else over the age of twenty, scattering their corpses across the wilderness. Eventually Yahweh relented and on this occasion confined his killing to ten of the twelve scouts whom Moses had sent ahead to spy out the land ahead. Joshua and Caleb alone were spared.

As the Israelites continued to wend their way towards the Promised Land, the cycle of populist whinge and divine retribution repeated itself. On the road to the Gulf of Aqaba the people registered their disgust at the food they were given to eat, and God sent poisonous snakes to kill them. In the Valley of Acacia, where the Israelite men had sex with the local women and worshipped the indigenous god of Peor, Yahweh instructed Moses to punish them by executing all the tribal leaders in broad daylight. Another potential massacre was avoided only when one of Aaron's grandsons, Phinehas, took a spear into a tent where an Israelite man, Zimri, and a Moabite woman, Cozbi, were having sex and skewered them to death. Suitably impressed, God changed his mind about killing the leaders in broad daylight and he rewarded Phinehas by promising eternal priesthood to him and his descendants.

Finally, as the book of Deuteronomy takes up the story of the wilderness years, the tribes of Israel arrived on the plains of Moab, across the River Jordan from Jericho. As he looked over to the Promised Land, Moses assured the Israelites that Yahweh would protect them by terrorising all who bullied or threatened them. He would deliver kings to the Israelites for slaughter and drive the native people out of Canaan. He would give the Israelites a fertile land of wheat and barley, vines and fig trees, olive oil and honey, copper and pomegranates. He would bless their harvests, rid them of their diseases, and cure their impotence and infertility. It was an irresistible menu of promises, and the people rejoiced. Their God had come up with the goods. For them, he was a God above all others, a God to be feared, loved and served with every fibre of their being. He was, in spite of his apparent track record to the contrary, a merciful God who would never fail or destroy his own people whatever destruction he might inflict upon their enemies. He was a God who gave justice to the widowed and the fatherless and showed charity towards the stranger.

All of this was, however, to come at a price, for the God of Deuteronomy, like the God of Exodus and Numbers, was still a fiery and jealous God who would brook no opposition and stomach no rivals. He was, after all, by no means the only god in the religious marketplace: other local deities, offering attractive terms and conditions, were also available for worship. Any act of disloyalty by the Israelites, or any repetition of the treacherous incident at Mount Sinai when they bowed their heads before a golden calf, would be met with dire retribution. God would destroy them as surely as he planned to liquidate Israel's opponents. The curses that Moses pronounced on the children of Israel in the name of Yahweh were violent and blood-curdling in the extreme, including affliction by incurable boils, tumours, scabs and itches; blindness and stupefaction; hunger to the point where people would devour their own children and women would secretly eat their afterbirths; the loss of crops and animals; and much else besides. The full litany of curses is set out in the twenty-eighth chapter of Deuteronomy.

The story of the exodus from Egypt closes with the death of Moses in the manner ordained by God. On the summit of Mount Nebo, overlooking the plains of Moab and in sight of the Promised Land of Canaan, Moses was condemned to die by Yahweh for losing faith in him at the waters of Meribah earlier in the journey. It was the same fate that his brother Aaron had earlier suffered on Mount Hor. Yet just before he died, Moses pronounced some final blessings on the tribes of Israel, culminating in an explosion of triumphant praise to Yahweh: 'Happy are you, Israel, peerless, set free! The LORD is the shield that guards you, the Blessed One is your glorious sword'. Why did Moses bless God? Because he would enable his people to trample their enemies into the ground. Right up to the boundaries of the Promised Land, Yahweh seems to have rejoiced in his status as the God of Sabbaoth, the God of hosts, the God of armies and of the vengeance and death that comes with warfare.

Chapter 3
The God of Laws and Psalms

The centrepiece of the Israelites' wilderness journey from Egypt to Canaan was their encounter with Yahweh at Mount Sinai where Moses received a stone portfolio of divine laws, including the Ten Commandments, that were to govern not only the religious life of the Israelite people but many aspects of their social and private lives as well. These laws, which offer some extraordinarily detailed glimpses of the face of God in a critical period of Jewish history, are presented in the early books of the Old Testament as three main collections.

The first collection of laws, in the book of Exodus, deals with such matters as the construction of altars for the worship of God, the buying and selling of slaves, violence towards other people, the responsibilities of those who keep animals, the repayment of debts, the proper treatment of widows and orphans, the administration of justice, the celebration of holy festivals, and much else besides. They embody an enduring social ethic very similar to those of other legal codes from the distant past, touching as they do upon such fundamental issues as the primacy of justice and the rule of law, the boundaries to permissible sexual behaviour, obligations to the poor, and the honouring of private property. The Babylonian code of Hammurabi, for example, which dates back to an even earlier time than Moses, reflects a remarkably similar understanding of the legal framework needed to sustain a just and ordered society. Though attributed to the God of Israel, the laws in Exodus can be seen in a wider context as the accumulated wisdom of tribes and nations about the proper governance of human societies if they are to flourish and prosper. Few of these laws, other than those that specifically concern the worship of Yahweh, can be said to apply *uniquely* to the people of Israel.

The second great collection of laws, in the Old Testament books of Leviticus and Numbers, deals mainly with religious rules about sacrifice, cleanliness, holiness and the worship of Yahweh. In Leviticus the laws fall roughly into four main groups. Firstly, there is an elaborate set of sacrificial rites and rituals, some of which are to be carried out by priests of the Jewish cult and others by lay people seeking forgiveness for their sins. Secondly, Leviticus prescribes the way in which the priests are to be ordained and installed. Most of these prescriptions are directed at Aaron, the first high priest, and his sons. Thirdly, there is a lengthy set of laws about the maintenance of ritual purity and cleanliness, including the avoidance of forbidden foods, the proper treatment of leprosy, and the institution of a scapegoat to carry the sins of the people into the wilderness. Finally, Leviticus contains a detailed code of conduct about the ways in which priests and people must behave if they are to retain the favour of God.

The laws of Leviticus are continued in the book of Numbers, the first ten chapters of which more or less carry on where Leviticus ends. These opening chapters concentrate on the rights and obligations of the various tribes of Israel, with the Levites coming in for special treatment because of the priestly duties and responsibilities that Yahweh had laid upon them. In addition to these tribal concerns, the book of Numbers also contains further laws and requirements about purity, holiness and sexual behaviour that build on those in Leviticus. Some of them seem, to modern eyes, primitive and sexist. When, for example, a woman is suspected by her husband of committing adultery, she is to be brought before a priest and made to drink a bowl of holy water mixed with sweepings from the floor of the tent of God's presence. If she is innocent, she will emerge from her ordeal unscathed, but if guilty her stomach will swell up and her genitals will shrink. No parallel ritual is mandated for husbands suspected of infidelity by their wives.

At face value, the great collections of laws in Exodus, Leviticus and Numbers date from the time of Moses when the Israelites were camped at Mount Sinai, and there can be little doubt that they have a long and complex history. Yet they are so obviously out of place in the midst of the wilderness stories that they must surely have been written in their present form at a much later date. Merely to read them is to realise their very limited relevance to a vast caravan of homeless people, wandering in barren territory, with no means of growing their own food and with no idea of their ultimate destination. Far from applying to the life of nomadic tribes, they are the laws of a well-established and cohesive society with highly developed systems of justice, commerce, religion, marriage, agriculture, slavery, immigration and banking.

Little is certain in the dating of ancient manuscripts but the contents of Exodus, and even more so of Leviticus and Numbers, are now thought to be based very largely on texts that date from the much later deportation of the Jews to Babylon following the fall of Jerusalem in 597 BC. They seem to reflect the dawning realisation among Jewish religious leaders of the time that the earlier prophets might, after all, have been right in what they had to say about the nation's neglect of God. The catastrophic sacking of Jerusalem by Nebuchadnezzar and the subsequent exile into Babylon had badly shaken the Jewish people. Whether in their worship or in their social and personal morality, something must have gone dreadfully wrong for God to have allowed Jerusalem to be plundered by a foreign power and Solomon's great temple on Mount Moriah to be desecrated. It may have been for reasons such as these that the laws in Leviticus and Numbers were devised, detailing the ways in which the Jewish people were henceforth to regulate their personal, social and religious lives if they were to please God on their return from exile. They seem much more like the laws of a mature and settled society with a long experience of God than of a loose confederation of millions of people and animals on the move through desert lands.

The third great collection of laws in the Pentateuch comes in the book of Deuteronomy. These laws, numbering hundreds, also purport to date back to the time of Moses, ostensibly forming part of the farewell discourses that he delivered to the people of Israel on the eve of their entry into Canaan. The text of Deuteronomy, however, is now thought to be no more contemporary with Moses than those of Exodus, Leviticus or Numbers. The things that Moses says in the book were seemingly put into his mouth by an unknown author several centuries later. What we now know as the book of Deuteronomy was probably written in the time of either King Hezekiah (who reigned as King of Judah from about 727 to 698 BC) or his son, King Manasseh. Whatever its exact date, the book cannot safely be read as an eyewitness account of what was said and done at the end of the Israelites' trek through the wilderness. The laws of Deuteronomy, ostensibly written by God on tablets of stone and given to Moses on Mount Sinai, are more realistically seen as the product of an established nation trying to rediscover the social and spiritual values that it had allowed to fall into disregard.

There is a good deal of overlap between the three collections of laws; but the added variety and complexity of the Deuteronomic laws mark them out as the sign of a remarkably mature and generous society. Deuteronomy signals the high watermark of Jewish legalism – an essential and practical handbook of commands and punishments for those destined by birth to live in the light of God's righteousness. The laws begin with the reiteration of a familiar theme: the God of Israel is a jealous God who will tolerate no rivals. Accordingly, the Israelites must not only turn away from all other gods, they must actively destroy all the trappings of the other cults they would be encountering in the course of their occupation of Canaan, including altars, pillars and idols. Those found worshipping local gods must be put to the sword or stoned to death and their buildings destroyed. The killings must be carried out by the town gate, the first stones being thrown by those who had witnessed the act of religious treachery. In effect, the God of laws was imposing a zero tolerance of religious freedom within the Promised Land. The modern concept of the human right of people to worship freely in ways of their own choosing was alien to Yahweh.

Most of the laws in Deuteronomy are not, however, explicitly religious in their content: they extend also to numerous secular areas of both private and public life. They are the closest that the Bible comes to the legal basis of a theocratic state and, to modern eyes, they are a bewildering amalgam of justice and oppression, liberty and discrimination, humanity and brutality. The God who is supposed to have promulgated them was a God of striking contrasts, at one moment compassionately exempting a frightened soldier from battle, at the next declaring that a comely woman who is captured in battle may be taken as a trophy wife for as long as it pleases the captor and then discarded when she no longer satisfies. Some of the laws, particularly those relating to diet, are dizzyingly complex. The prohibition against the eating of pork is well known, but kites, falcons, crows, pelicans, ospreys, storks, cormorants, bats, three kinds of vultures and eight kinds of owls were also banished from the Hebrew meal table. Yet this obsessively detailed menu of forbidden dishes is followed immediately by some feisty rules about parties and some compassionate ones about people in debt. Every two years, people were to set aside a tenth of all their crops to provide for an alcohol-laden party to celebrate the presence of God among them, and at the end of every seventh year all outstanding debts were to be written off. The Israelites were always to treat their fellow-citizens with compassion and their slaves with dignity, remembering that they themselves had once been slaves in Egypt. The deep sense of moral obligation contained in many of these laws, especially an obligation towards the poor and the oppressed, mark them out as one of the high points in the history of civilisation. Many of them are deeply humane laws made sacred by the divine imprimatur of a God who, in this mood, stands as the epitome of enlightened compassion.

The later chapters of Deuteronomy contain a miscellany of laws about many different aspects of daily life. These too are a very mixed bunch. All lost property, including livestock, must be returned to the rightful owners.

Nobody may dress in the clothes of the opposite sex. When a new house is built, a parapet must always be placed around the roof. If a man commits adultery with a married woman, both must be put to death. If a man rapes a virgin who is not yet engaged, he must take her as his wife and pay her father fifty pieces of silver. If a man falsely accuses his wife of not being a virgin when he married her, he must pay a hundred pieces of silver; but if the accusation is true, then the woman has behaved like a prostitute and must be stoned to death. Camp latrines must be signposted and those who use them must carry a trowel to dig a hole in which to relieve themselves. Newly married men are to be exempt from public service in order to stay at home and make their wives happy. Workers must be paid promptly and the remnants of a harvested field or vineyard must be left for the fatherless and the widowed to glean. A woman must have her hand cut off if, while trying to drag her husband away from a fight with another man, she grasps that man's genitals. All weights and measures must be accurate, and interest may not be charged on loans to fellow-Israelites. Oxen must not be muzzled while treading grain and only one kind of seed may be sown in the rows between vines. The earnings of prostitutes cannot be given as gifts in the house of God, and men whose testicles have been crushed cannot enter the tent of God's presence.

Many of these are self-evidently sensible laws that would be accepted even in modern secular societies. That the Israelites believed them to have been handed down to Moses by Yahweh makes them neither more nor less acceptable. Few reasonable people would question them and no God is needed to justify them. Of course lost property should be returned to the lawful owners, human excrement disposed of hygienically, workers paid their wages promptly, houses built in ways that minimise the likelihood of accidents, weights and measures accurately calibrated, the widowed and fatherless cared for, and so on. It is not necessary to be religious to recognise such laws as part of the tapestry of a civilised society. By contrast, some of the other laws in Deuteronomy are, to modern eyes, quite simply wrong. They are the products of a particular time and culture, made sacred through a human belief in their divine origins. It would now be seen as barbaric – at least in most Western societies – to cut off the hands of women who grab the genitals of their husbands' assailants, or to kill a married woman who has sex with a man who is not her husband. It would be stupid to try to ban women from wearing trousers or men from wearing kilts and cassocks. It would be illegal for disabled people to be denied access to religious premises. Such laws are simply unacceptable in most of the modern world whether or not they represent the word of God. Yet not only does Deuteronomy declare them to be the everlasting and unchanging will of God, it regards all infringements of them as equally reprehensible. There is little sense in

Deuteronomy (other, perhaps, than through the tariff of punishments attached to them) of any gradations among the offences. All appear to be equally sinful in the eyes of God and all deserve the punishments set out for them. The God of laws is not only a God of mercy and compassion, he is also a God of strict accountability and punishment.

The most complex and multi-faceted images of the God of Israel are found in the Old Testament book of Psalms. It is a book of immense significance to both Jews and Christians, containing as it does some of the most profound reflections about the nature and character of the God of Israel that are to be found anywhere in the Bible. In the Psalms, Hebrew poets have taken the insights and experiences of generations of Jews and woven them into one of the greatest collections of sacred poetry in the world – poetry that encompasses songs of joy, sorrow, thanksgiving, anger, lamentation, desolation and praise. The God of Psalms may be full of contradictions and inconsistencies but he is, unquestionably, a God who can be known, loved, praised, feared, berated, respected and even challenged.

The Psalms were almost certainly written by many different people over a long period of time and their authorship cannot be assigned with any great certainty. Seventy-three of them carry the name of King David and others are associated with Asaph, Solomon, Heman, Ethan, Moses and Korah (whose family came to a nasty end when God opened up the ground beneath their feet and buried them alive). David's authorship of many of the Psalms has been questioned on the ground that they reveal a very different character from the often belligerent and insensitive man of Jewish history. Can the David whose name is associated with the exquisitely solicitous twenty-third Psalm really be the same David who slaughtered two hundred Philistines and presented their foreskins to Saul as a marriage dowry for his daughter Michal? Many scholars think that the large number of Psalms ascribed to David (almost half of the total) may merely indicate that they were favoured by him or were used in special acts of royal celebration in his court but, since there are references in the Old Testament to David as a musician and poet, some could indeed be his own compositions.

Questions about the authorship and, therefore, the dating of the book of Psalms are important in understanding the different faces of God that they reveal. The God of Psalms is astonishingly diverse in his nature – at one moment the ancient, vengeful God of Sabbaoth, lashing out at the enemies of his chosen people, at the next the kindest of shepherds, leading his children into paths of peace and walking with them in the valley of the shadow of death. God is angry but he also protects. He punishes but he also forgives. He judges but he also blesses. He destroys the enemies of Israel but he is also Lord of the entire earth. If the Psalms had all been composed as the Jews were re-establishing themselves in Jerusalem and rebuilding the temple after their return from exile in Babylon in 538 BC (as might be implied by the traditional description of the Psalms as the 'hymnbook of the second temple'), then Jewish impressions of God at that time were very mixed. In fact, the Psalms almost certainly cover a much wider time span, reflecting the changing images of the God of Israel across many centuries of Jewish tradition. Many of them do indeed refer explicitly to the return from exile in Babylon, although similar hymns of praise also date from much earlier periods of Jewish history, as far back even as the exodus from Egypt. The book of Psalms is perhaps best seen as a collection of traditional Jewish songs of praise to God that had been sung from at least the exodus to at least the period of the second temple.

A dominant theme in the Psalms is the all-pervasive action of God in the history of Israel. These are, above all else, Jewish songs of praise to a God who saves his people when they most need him. They are emotional outpourings of gratitude to a God of salvation, and their impact is lessened if they are divorced from their historical context. Some of the Psalms recount the history of Israel in great detail, stressing at every turn and twist in the story not only the power of God in saving the Israelites from their enemies but also his anger in the face of their own rebellion and disobedience. God is praised as a partisan God who defends his own people while bringing chaos and destruction to everyone else. He is a shield to his people against the fury of their enemies. He gives military victory to the Israelites but he destroys their opponents, scattering them like thistledown before the wind and consigning them to the fiery furnace. He strengthens the anointed kings of Israel but rains down fire and brimstone on the wicked. In the Psalms we see the face of an involved and committed God, defending his chosen people and visiting chaos upon their enemies.

There are, then, unmistakeable echoes in the Psalms of the vengeful, bloodthirsty God of Sabbaoth who angrily and furiously stalks the pages of the Pentateuch. Yet words also tumble out of the Psalms that tell of a very different kind of God – a God who has dominion over all the nations of earth, not just the people of Israel. God is the Lord above all nations to whom all kings pay homage. He judges the people with equity and guides all the nations on earth. Everyone on earth stands in awe of him. These are confident assertions about a God whose kingdom is far flung and whose rule is universal. The children of Israel may have been the apples of his eye, at least in the early stages of Jewish history, but now there are other fruits in his basket as well. He is the universal Lord of all who created the world and who sustains it in all its parts. He causes the stars to shine, the tides to turn and the seasons to come and go. His voice thunders over the mighty waters of the sea, he separates the summer from the winter, he spreads out the heavens like a tent, and he satisfies every living creature with his favour. His kingdom is an everlasting kingdom and his dominion will endure throughout all generations. This is no mere local God of clans and tribes in the Middle East. This is a majestic God of boundless creation who veils the sky in clouds, clothes the hills with grass, and moves the seasons through their cycles.

With God's creative and sustaining power comes also his justice, which is like a deep ocean, and his righteousness, which is like a lofty mountain. If some of the Psalms revere him as the military leader who delivers victory to his own people, others proclaim him as a God whose justice and righteousness is available to all, Gentile as well as Jew. He is the source of all laws and statues, he administers justice and passes sentence on the guilty. The law of the Lord, the Psalms proclaim, is the heart of wisdom, and wisdom is the beginning of joy. The law is perfect: it revives the soul and it makes the simple wise. God's precepts are right and give joy to the heart. His commandments are pure and give light to the eyes. He judges the world with fairness and brings justice to those who have been wronged. Surely, a Psalmist writes, goodness and mercy will follow me all the days of my life.

The Psalms, however, are not merely about a deity who administers justice and exercises mercy. The God of Psalms is a God of holiness who is worthy of the kind of honour and praise that in any other context would be mere idolatry. Many of the Psalmists worship him with all their hearts and they bless his holy name. They sing his praises in song, music and dance. They see his holiness in the wonders of the natural world and they trust him to protect them. They abound in their confidence in him, knowing that he is a God who heals, liberates, rescues, protects and saves. He is a refuge and strength to those who fear him, their rock and their salvation.

The book of Psalms also has something to say about the way in which God should be worshipped, especially in the matter of sacrifices. Does he or does he not require the sacrificial offering of animals? The answer is ambiguous. A Psalm traditionally attributed to David declares it fitting to praise God with sacrifices as well as with songs; and in a Psalm attributed to Asaph, God welcomes the sacrifices offered to him at the temple in Jerusalem. Yet elsewhere God is unimpressed with the Jewish cult of animal sacrifice. If any sacrifice is to be offered, it should be the obedience of a penitent heart, not the life of an innocent animal. A Psalm of repentance that may have been written for King David following his reprehensible treatment of Uriah and Bathsheba (when he engineered the death of Uriah in order to marry Bathsheba) proclaims that God has no delight in any sacrifice other than a broken spirit. Such ambiguities over the place of sacrifice in the worship of God may merely reflect the gradual shift that occurred in Jewish attitudes at the time of the exile in Babylon. The sacrifice of burnt offerings in the temple at Jerusalem had been an important part of Jewish worship since the time of King Solomon; but by about 700 BC, when Micah was prophesying in the northern kingdom of Israel, a different message was abroad. All that God wanted of his people was for them to be just, merciful and trusting. Animal sacrifice did not come into it.

A final feature of the God of Psalms may be noted that has surfaced in every generation, Christian as well as Jewish: he seems often to be a hidden or even an absent God. Some of the Psalmists interrogate and even complain to God about his absence. Why are you so distant, they ask, why so hidden in times of trouble? For how long will you hide your face and forget your people? God's absence may be most noticed when he is most needed. Tears are my food day and night, laments a Psalmist, while all day long people ask me, where is your God? Why do you hide your face, heedless of our misery and our sufferings, demands another. Even Jesus' lament of despair from the cross was an anguished cry of desolation from the Psalms: 'My God, my God, why have you forsaken me?'

The God of Psalms seems often to be a God on the cusp of change. Some of the images of him look back to the early days of the Jewish faith, when he vented his anger on the enemies of Israel and behaved towards his chosen people in a violently partisan way. Yet there is another face of God to be seen in this hymnbook of the second temple, a face barely glimpsed in the earlier books of the Old Testament that was recognised by the people of Israel only after the traumatic events of their exile in Babylon and their later return to Jerusalem. It is the face of a God who not only delivers his people from danger while bludgeoning the enemies of Israel into submission: it is also the face of a God whose kingdom is universal, a God of international mercy and justice who abjures the rituals of ancient religious rites in favour of honesty, justice, love and decency. It is a harbinger of the face of the Christian God that was to be revealed in it fullest manifestation in Jesus of Nazareth.

Chapter 4
The God of Messianic Expectation

Christians of almost all traditions and denominations believe that the God of Israel was uniquely revealed in the human person of Jesus of Nazareth. As St Paul put it in his correspondence to the church at Corinth, 'God was in Christ, reconciling the world to himself'. For Christians, then, it is in Jesus that the most authentic faces of the Christian God are to be seen. Yet this God did not emerge unheralded from a cultural and religious vacuum. The New Testament leaves no room for doubt that the God whom Jesus called 'Father' was the God of Abraham, the God of Moses, the God of Sabbaoth, the God of laws, the God of Psalms. He was, in short, Yahweh. And, as we have seen, the evolutionary trail must surely go back farther even than Abraham, for the religious mists from which Yahweh emerged in about 1800 BC were themselves the result of thousands of years of human reflection about the unseen world of spirits, forces and powers. Without this ancient heritage of numinous experience there might have been no Yahweh; without Yahweh there might have been no Jesus; and without Jesus there would certainly have been no Christianity. As we shall see, after several hundred years of intense and often acrimonious debate in the early Church about the relationship between Jesus and God, the belief finally became embedded in the Christian creeds that Jesus Christ was not merely a *witness* to the God of Israel, he was the very *incarnation* of that God – Yahweh made flesh. He was, in the words of the fourth-century Nicene Creed, 'light from light, true God from true God, of one being with the Father'.

Although almost everything that is known about the life of Jesus is contained within the New Testament, there are passing references to him in non-biblical texts. He is mentioned in early Roman manuscripts by Tacitus (*c.* 56-117) and Suetonius (*c.* 69-122); but these do little more than confirm his existence as an historical person. Of slightly greater value is the fleeting reference to Jesus in *The Antiquities of the Jews*, a monumental work completed in about 92 by the Jewish historian Flavius Josephus (*c.*

37-100). In the third chapter of the eighteenth volume of his great work, Josephus described Jesus as 'a wise man . . . who accomplished surprising feats and was a teacher of such people as are eager for novelties. . . . He was the Messiah. When Pilate . . . condemned him to the cross, those who had loved him from the very first did not cease to be attached to him. On the third day he appeared to them restored to life.' New Testament scholars have long suspected that this famous passage, which seems at face value to bear independent witness to Jesus' messianic status and his physical resurrection, was altered at some point from the original text, for there is no reason why the Jewish Josephus should have gone out of his way to cast a patina of Christian interpretation over his account of Jesus' life. His depiction of Jesus as the Messiah who was restored to life is widely thought to have been a later insertion into the text by a Christian hand.

Other non-biblical texts also report the words that Jesus said and the things that he did. The most important of these texts were discovered in 1945 near the Egyptian town of Nag Hammadi. Written mostly in Coptic and dating to about the end of the second century, they may have been part of the library of one of the many groups of Gnostics (a sect that, as we shall see, persistently challenged the emerging orthodoxy of the Church) that were proliferating in the Middle East in the early Christian period. One of the texts, known as the *Apocryphal Gospel of Thomas*, has been dated to within about a hundred years of Jesus' death. Opening with the words: 'These are the hidden sayings which the living Jesus spoke, and which Judas Thomas the Twin wrote down', the gospel comprises a hundred and fourteen sayings of Jesus. Many of them correspond to words attributed to him in the biblical gospels; others have no direct parallels in the gospels, though they sound very like the kinds of things he might have said. Some New Testament scholars are prepared to accept the sayings in the *Apocryphal Gospel of Thomas* as of equal authenticity with those in the biblical gospels while others are more cautious.

Other apocryphal gospels that have come to light since the New Testament was compiled in its present form in about 400 include the *Gospel of Mary*, the *Gospel of Philip*, the *Protevangelium of James* and the *Infancy Gospel of Thomas*. The latter contains stories about the miracles that Jesus is said to have performed as a child, including one where he made twelve clay models of birds on the Sabbath. When this transgression against the Jewish law was reported to his father Joseph, Jesus clapped his hands and bade the birds remember him as they flew away. On another occasion, Jesus restored a child to life who had died after falling from a roof. Also of some interest is the *Gospel of Peter*, fragments of which were discovered at Oxyrhyncus in Upper Egypt in 1886. It contains an account of Jesus' death and resurrection that agrees in broad outline with the New Testament narratives but differs in many details, including a rather bizarre reference to a walking and talking cross at the scene of the resurrection.

By far the most important sources of information about the life of Jesus are the synoptic gospels of Matthew, Mark and Luke. Although they were not written until several decades after Jesus' death, the stories they contain must have been circulating by word of mouth for many years and are therefore likely to contain a strong basis of historical truth. Mark's gospel is now widely (but not quite universally) seen as the first to have been written, perhaps as early as 60, followed by Luke's in the late 70s and Matthew's in the late 80s, though some scholars are prepared to give them earlier dates.

The stories of Jesus in the synoptic gospels are pitched at two obviously different levels, one human and one divine. At the human level, Jesus is presented as a Jewish rabbi of authority who taught, preached, healed and performed miracles. In this, he was not unique: others were doing much the same. Honi the Circle Drawer, who was proficient at conjuring up rain, was operating as a teacher and miracle worker in Galilee in the 1st century BC; Hanina Ben Dosa, who had miraculous powers of healing, was doing the same in the 1st century AD. The human Jesus comes across from the pages of the synoptic gospels as a man of striking contrasts. He was an austere person who cared little for his own welfare but was known to the public as a glutton and a drinker. He was tender and protective towards children but dismissive of his own family. He was capable of deep anger, to the point of causing offence among those at whom it was directed, yet he also displayed great compassion to those in need. He was a man of ordinary human frailties but he showed an almost superhuman courage in the face of an arguably unjust trial and a cruel death at the hands of the Romans. He trusted God for each and every need in his life yet he contemplated his end with great foreboding. The humanity of Jesus, including the contradictions as well as the virtues of his character, is central to the image of him in the synoptic gospels.

As a teacher and moralist, Jesus has been respected even by those who have not accepted the Christian belief in him as the divine son of God. Merely to read the synoptic gospels is to understand the reasons. He attracted large crowds and his teaching was seen by his audiences as authoritative: those who heard him were repeatedly amazed at what he said and wondered where it had come from. They were spellbound by his words and full of admiration for his message. Much of Jesus' teaching in these gospels was focused on the kingdom of God as both a present reality and a future expectation. The social and moral values of the kingdom are timeless in their prescriptions for a good society: love, justice, mercy, humility, compassion, faith, charity. In sharp contrast to much contemporary Jewish religiosity, Jesus taught that God's kingdom was a place of moral righteousness where people were judged by the contents of their hearts, not the external formalities of their religious observances. He is reported as saying in Matthew's gospel that: 'Wicked thoughts, murder, adultery, fornication, theft, perjury, slander – these all proceed from the heart; and these are the things that defile a person; but to eat without first washing his hands, that cannot defile him'. What counted for Jesus was a righteous heart, not a punctilious religiosity. It was very different from the meticulously articulated laws that Yahweh had handed down to Moses on Mount Sinai.

Yet the Jesus of the synoptic gospels is not *just* a Jewish rabbi who taught, healed and performed miracles; he also stands in a complex relationship to God that can only be understood in the religious context of first-century Palestine. Jesus was a Jew living in a Jewish country; his God was the God of Israel; and his scriptures were what is now known as the Old Testament. He was, therefore, a product of the Judaism of his time; and although there were many different strands in the web of Jewish belief, there was a shared narrative, rooted in Jewish history, that defined the special relationship between the Jews and their God. There was, the narrative asserted, one true God who had created the world, who had revealed himself to Abraham, and who had marked Abraham's descendants as his chosen people. A series of covenants had been forged in which the Jewish people committed themselves to God in obedience and he to them through his saving power. Since God had shown his people how they were to behave by giving them the law, any transgressions against the law were also sins against him; and repentance and sacrifice were central to the process of reconciliation between sinners and God. There was also a common expectation that God would, at a time of his own choosing, enter human history to bring all nations to him, including non-Jewish nations. Meanwhile, as they patiently waited for that time to come, the faithful were to worship God in their traditional ways, to observe the laws of Moses, and to seek forgiveness for their sins.

The Jewish scriptures were blurred about the time of God's involvement in human history; but in the fullness of time a saviour, or Messiah, would be sent to rescue the Jewish people from their oppression and usher in God's rule on earth. It is here that Jewish expectation intersects with the life of Jesus, for his followers believed that he was the long-awaited Messiah. For the gospel writers, Jesus was the culmination of the long centuries of expectancy and promise. In him, their hopes were finally to be fulfilled. He had been chosen by God, anointed by the Holy Spirit at his baptism, and now was destined to become the king in God's new age. It was good news for the gospel writers, and they were breathless to convey it to what they evidently believed would be an expectant world. To do so convincingly, however, they had to show that Jesus stood centrally within the framework of Jewish salvation history, reflecting all that had been prophesied in the past and pointing to all that was expected in the future. A Messiah who stood apart from the weight of Jewish history and the burden of Jewish expectation would be no Messiah at all. Jesus' messianic credentials could not be taken for granted: they had to be established. It was to do this that the synoptic gospels were written.

Though their emphases were different, the authors of Matthew, Mark and Luke addressed the issue of Jesus' messianic status through the use of two inter-connected devices. Firstly, they linked him firmly into the past by interpreting the key events in his life as the culmination of centuries of Jewish prophecy. Things happened to Jesus that had been foreseen by the prophets of old. In Matthew's gospel, in particular, the actions of Jesus are explicitly interpreted as the fulfilment of many time-hallowed prophecies: he was born in Bethlehem, he journeyed out of Egypt, innocent children were massacred on his account, he went into Galilee, he healed the sick, he spoke in parables, he rode into Jerusalem on an ass, he was betrayed for money, he was silent in the face of his persecutors, he was mocked and spat upon, and he suffered and died for his people. According to Matthew, all these things had happened to Jesus precisely because they had been foreseen in the Jewish scriptures. Luke too was anxious that his readers should not miss the point: when Jesus met two of the disciples on the road to Emmaus on the evening of his resurrection, he 'started from Moses and all the prophets, and explained to them in the whole of scripture the things that referred to himself'. The Jesus of the synoptic gospels did not emerge from nowhere to take everyone by surprise. To those who believed in him, his coming had long been foreshadowed – and any account of his life had therefore to be rooted in the portents of which the prophets had written.

The second way in which the authors of Matthew, Mark and Luke sought to convince their readers of Jesus' messianic credentials was by giving him the authentic hallmarks of the Messiah. He had to be shown to be saying and doing the kinds of things that a messianic leader was expected to say and do. It was, though, a far from straightforward matter, for Jewish expectations about the Messiah had developed over many centuries and, in Jesus' day, they were made up of several different strands. There was no commonly agreed template of what the Messiah would be like or how he would behave. His life had to be a fulfilment of Jewish prophecy, of course, but beyond this were a number of different traditions about the kind of person the Messiah would be.

Firstly, there was a royal strand: when he came, the Messiah would be a mighty king, a descendant of David who would conquer the powers of evil and establish God's reign of justice and peace. As Isaiah had predicted, the kingdom over which he ruled would be filled with the glory of God, just as the waters filled the seas. Secondly, there was a priestly strand in the messianic weave. The Dead Sea scrolls, discovered at Qmran in 1947, hint at two Messiahs: one a kingly descendant of David and the other a priestly descendant of Aaron, the first high priest of the Jewish cult. The Messiah would have a religious as well as a secular authority. Thirdly, there was a link to the prophets of old: the Messiah would do for Israel what the great prophets of the past had done – men like Moses, Elijah and Elisha. He would reaffirm Israel's special identity as the chosen people of God, living under God's rule and worshipping him in the ways that he had appointed. Finally there was an element of expectation stemming from Isaiah's moving vision of the suffering servant. Isaiah had spoken of one who would come in servile form to bring good news to the poor, bind up the broken-hearted, and proclaim liberty to captives. The Messiah would be a servant as well as a prophet, priest and king.

The synoptic gospels incorporate most of these messianic hallmarks in their portrayal of Jesus, some more explicitly than others. Most obviously, they go to considerable lengths to establish him as a descendant of King David. Both Matthew and Luke's gospels contain a genealogical tree for Jesus, and although the two trees have few names in common, they both include David. The birth narratives of Matthew and Luke reinforce the royal lineage, locating Jesus' birth in Bethlehem, the city of David. Matthew goes further than this, reminding his readers that the circumstances surrounding the birth of Jesus were the fulfilment of several Old Testament prophecies. Isaiah had prophesied that a young woman would conceive and bear a son,

Hosea that God would call his son out of Egypt, and Jeremiah that the voice of Rachel would be heard weeping for her children. For Matthew, these prophecies had been fulfilled in the virginity of Mary, the flight of the holy family into Egypt, and the massacre of the baby boys of Bethlehem on the orders of Herod the Great. There is a royal story behind the gospels' acclamation of Jesus as the Messiah. He was a scion of the house of David.

The prophetic strand is also evident in the three synoptic gospels, for each presents Jesus not only as a royal king but also as the last and greatest of the prophets of Israel. Matthew tells how Jesus lamented that a prophet had no honour in his own town, and Luke reports him as saying, shortly before his death, that it would be unthinkable for a Jewish prophet to die anywhere other than in Jerusalem. Many of those who heard Jesus also recognised his credentials as a prophet: 'He is a prophet like one of the prophets of old', they said. Others, however, were sceptical, and even those who saw Jesus as the reincarnation of an Old Testament prophet were not sure which it was. Jesus was variously seen as the embodiment of John the Baptist, Elijah, Jeremiah or 'one of the other prophets'. His transfiguration on the unnamed mountain in Galilee, reported in all the synoptic gospels, is the clearest example of the way he is linked into the prophetic tradition of Judaism. Like Moses centuries earlier on Mount Sinai, Jesus' face shone like the sun and his clothes became as white as light. Then Moses and Elijah appeared, talking to Jesus about the law. The gospel writers were clearly presenting Jesus as the successor to Moses and on speaking terms with Elijah. It was a pedigree every bit as impressive as his descent from King David, confirming him as the one who had been sent by God to minister (as Matthew puts it) to 'the lost sheep of the house of Israel, *and to them alone*'(emphasis added).

This was not, however, all that the synoptic evangelists had to say about the special status of Jesus. Having sought to establish his credentials as the Jewish Messiah, and having stressed his God-given mission to 'the lost sheep of the house of Israel', they then pushed their claims about him beyond the traditional boundaries of Jewish expectation into territory that was hinted at but not elaborated in the Hebrew scriptures – the idea that God was the God not only of Israel but also of the Gentile nations. For the gospel writers, Jesus was not *just* the Jewish Messiah of ancient prophecy and fervent expectation; he was also the one who would come on clouds of glory to establish God's kingdom in all the earth and rule it in justice and peace. He was not *just*

a prophet in the tradition of Moses or a king in the lineage of David or a servant in the mould of Isaiah; he was also the saviour of the whole world. Jesus is proclaimed as Messiah not only because of his demonstrable links with Jewish history and Jewish expectation but also because of his unique role in God's purpose for all mankind. If Jesus himself had doubts about his mission beyond the religious confines of the Jewish world, the evangelists had seemingly set them aside by the time they came to write their gospels. When Jesus sent the disciples out on their mission, he explicitly instructed them not to 'take the road to gentile lands'; but the evangelists recognised no such limitations. They believed that Jesus had commissioned them to make disciples of all nations and to baptise *everyone* in his name. What may have started as the narrow aim of establishing Jesus as the Jewish Messiah became the gospel of salvation for the whole world.

Yet although the synoptic gospels portray Jesus of Nazareth as God's Messiah and saviour for the whole world, they are reticent in explaining what salvation meant or how it was to be accomplished. For Matthew and Luke, the death and resurrection of Jesus plainly had something to do with it, but neither anticipated what the early Church came to see as the atoning properties of the Easter events. They report the empty tomb and the post-resurrection appearances of Jesus but they have little to say about their meaning. Mark's gospel, which was probably the first to be written, has even less to say about it. The earliest versions of this gospel end abruptly at the point where the women who had discovered the empty tomb ran away in fear and amazement. Either the author of Mark's gospel was unfamiliar with the resurrection stories or he counted them of minor significance. It was left to St Paul (who was writing before the authors of Matthew, Mark and Luke) and the author of the fourth gospel, John, (who was writing after them) to try to explain the theological significance of the cross; and it is to them that we must now turn. For Paul, especially, the death and resurrection of Jesus lay at the very heart of his message.

Chapter 5
The God of the Damascus Road

It would be difficult to over-estimate the influence of St Paul on the course of Christianity, both in its earliest phases and in the long-term development of its theology. From being a self-confessed and zealous persecutor of the fledging faith, Paul became its most creative and inspirational apologist, elevating the crucified and risen Jesus to a position of saving power far exceeding anything found in the synoptic gospels. It began in a dramatic fashion. On a road close to Damascus, Saul (as he was then called) was thrown to the ground by a brilliant light and heard a voice which, on being questioned, identified itself as that of Jesus. It was a mystical and life changing experience for him. Writing to the church at Corinth several years later he said that he had been caught up as far as the third heaven, as far as paradise, where he heard words so secret that human lips could not repeat them. It was upon this dream-like foundation that Paul constructed his idiosyncratic interpretation of Jesus' crucifixion and resurrection. The gospel he preached was, he declared, no human invention: it had been given to him not by any man but through a direct revelation from Jesus. Paul was so confident of his mission that he began to preach about Jesus without consulting anyone, least of all the disciples who were still in Jerusalem and whom he could easily have contacted. He even threatened expulsion from his newly established churches in Asia Minor if anyone dared to challenge him.

It has often been remarked that the person whom Paul encountered on the Damascus Road was less the human Jesus than the resurrected Christ. In this sense, Paul's experiences were very different from those of the disciples. He had never known the living Jesus; they had known him intimately, and the gospel writers leave no doubt that the Jesus who appeared to the disciples after his resurrection was physically recognisable as the man whose company they had kept for the previous three years. He could be touched, fed and conversed with. Paul, on the other hand, saw only a bright light and heard only a voice that was inaudible to his travelling companions; and it was only because the voice identified itself as that of Jesus that Paul knew who was speaking to him. Paul's overwhelming conversion experience, in other words, did not depend upon the same kind of post-resurrection appearances of Jesus that had so galvanised the disciples in Jerusalem and Galilee. Thereafter, it was the disembodied spirit rather than the human man that became the burning centre of Paul's life and work. Indeed, he almost went out of his way to avoid meeting those who had known Jesus, and even though he did eventually go to Jerusalem, there is no indication that he visited the place of the crucifixion or the site of the tomb. For one who was so obsessed with the death and resurrection of Jesus, it is an intriguing omission.

In the light of Paul's experience on the Damascus Road, it is hardly surprising that his theology of salvation owes relatively little to the human Jesus whom he almost certainly never met. If his letters were the only source of information we had about Jesus' life and ministry, we would know very little about the man whom the Christian church was later to recognise as a fully human being. It is as though Paul saw little of any great significance in Jesus' earthly life. As he wrote to the church at Corinth: 'Even if [worldly standards] once counted in our understanding of Christ, they do so now no longer'. He could scarcely have expressed himself more clearly. It was through the crucifixion and the resurrection that the earth-bound Jesus became the heavenly Christ of eternal glory; and once the transformation had been wrought, the human man was of little residual significance.

Paul's clearest account of the distinction between the earthly Jesus and the risen Christ comes at the beginning of his letter to the Romans, where he writes of Jesus at 'two levels'. At the human level, Jesus was a descendant of David, born to an unnamed Jewish woman at a particular time in history. He had a human ancestry and a human life. At the spiritual level, he became the Son of God 'by an act of power that raised him from the dead'. Jesus' humanity was real enough, but it was not this that made him the saviour of the world. Of infinitely greater worth, in Paul's view, was his status as the Son of God – a status acquired not though the circumstances of his birth but through those of his death and resurrection. For Paul, it was the resurrection rather than the incarnation that created the possibility of human salvation. The idea that God emptied himself of his divinity and became a dependent human baby has softened the hearts of countless Christian believers through the ages. Paul, one feels, was made of sterner stuff. Not for him Luke's sentimental scene in the stable at Bethlehem, with ox and ass, shepherds and kings, star and angels.

Who was this resurrected Christ, and how did he save? It is here that we begin to approach the mysterious heart of Paul's understanding of the relationship between Jesus and God. Unlike the writers of the synoptic gospels, Paul had little obvious need to establish Jesus' credentials as the Jewish Messiah. He was writing predominantly for Gentile converts to the new Christian faith who would not have shared the messianic hope of Judaism and who would hardly have been impressed by the acclamation in the synoptic gospels of Jesus as the anointed successor to King David. Nor did Paul regard Jesus as standing in the great line of Jewish prophets. Whoever he was, the risen Christ was far above that. Paul even avoided the title of 'the Son of Man', so favoured by the writers of the synoptic gospels. To do so might have been to dwell for longer than he would have wished on the humanity of Jesus. Instead, he made extensive use of the title of 'Lord' as his favoured expression for the risen Christ.

Whether Paul went so far as to see Jesus as the incarnation of God is a matter of some contention. There are texts that suggest he did and others that suggest he didn't, but either way it does not appear to have been a question that greatly troubled him. He was writing long before the earnest theological debates began in the early Church about the precise nature of the relationship between the Father, the Son, the Holy Spirit and the Word. There was little in his understanding of the risen Christ that required him to face what was later to become the intractable theological problem of the Holy Trinity. In any case, he must have been so immersed in the Jewish tradition of monotheism as to regard anything that hinted at two Gods, one in heaven and one on earth, with deep revulsion. There is certainly nothing in Paul's letters that anticipates the Church's later dogmatic assertion in the Nicene Creed that Jesus was 'true God from true God . . . of one being with the Father'.

Paul can hardly be blamed for any lack of clarity in his letters about the precise relationship between Christ and God. For one who had very little contact with the circle of those who knew Jesus, and who was blazing a pioneering theological trail in commending the Jewish God to Gentile congregations in the Greek-speaking world, his views about the risen Christ were imaginative and sophisticated. That he failed to answer all the problems that were later to cause the Christian Church innumerable headaches does not detract from the heart of his message that God was at work in Christ, reconciling the world to himself. It was in turning to the saving power of Jesus Christ that Paul's innovative theology came most abundantly into its own.

At the heart of Paul's great, mystical drama of salvation was the vast and ugly domain of sin and death. Sin was for him the great and powerful enemy, dominating people's lives and alienating them from God. Human sinfulness began with Adam, whose singular act of disobedience in the Garden of Eden became the template of all human sinfulness. 'It was through one man that sin entered the world', Paul wrote in his letter to the Romans, 'and through sin death, and thus death pervaded the whole human race'. Adam's particular sin had been to sample the forbidden fruit of the tree of the knowledge of good and evil. Paul argued, however, that it was not until God gave Moses the vast and detailed body of the Jewish law that sin could really begin to flourish. It was only when the Jewish people knew exactly how God wanted them to behave that the full possibilities of sinful behaviour were laid out before them; and since the law concerned itself with so many detailed aspects of daily life, each and every action was fraught with the possibility of sin. For Paul, Jewish legalism was a constant obstacle race in which the more barriers that were erected, in the shape of the laws of Moses, the greater the chances of stumbling over them and sinning against God. Before Moses, the barriers were few and far between; after him, they were all over the place.

The argument is not without its pitfalls, and Paul was well aware of them. If the floodgates of human sinfulness were finally opened through God's gift of the law on Mount Sinai, what had been happening during the millennia between Adam and Moses when there had been no law? How could a loving and gracious God have provided his people with such a golden opportunity to sin by giving them the law? Why, if the law had been God's great gift to the Jews, was Paul no longer requiring them to accept it as a condition of salvation, substituting instead the seemingly simpler requirement of faith in the risen Christ? These were troubling questions for Paul and he devoted a large part of his letter to the Romans to searching for the answers. So sure was he of his position, however, that he pressed on remorselessly, stacking up the negatives and positives on each side of the great divide of human sinfulness. On one side were the corruptions of the flesh, opposition to God, and death. On the other side were the antitheses: the fruits of the spirit, the forgiveness of God, and everlasting life. These were intimately connected: when people died and rose with Christ, they were saved from their sins, their fractured relationship with God was restored, and their bodies after death were transformed from earthly to spiritual forms. How did this happen? How did Christ's death and resurrection make possible the forgiveness of sins and the promise of eternal life?

The synoptic gospels of Matthew, Mark and Luke had very little to say about the meaning of the death and resurrection of Jesus, but Paul had plenty. In fact, it is possible to discern in his letters two different accounts. Firstly, there are occasional but unmistakeable references to what was later to become a central plank in the Church's explanation of the cross – that Jesus took upon himself the sins of the world and died on behalf of sinful men and women to make things right again with God. Jesus' death, in other words, was a sacrificial atonement for human sin. The idea was taken directly from the Jewish cult of sacrifice in which animals were slaughtered at the temple in Jerusalem and offered to God as an act of expiation. Paul would have been totally familiar with such rituals, and it was these that he seemed to have had in mind when he wrote in his first letter to the Church at Corinth that: 'Christ died for our sins to be the means of expiating sin by his death'. Drawing even more explicitly from the Jewish tradition of sacrifice and atonement, Paul went so far as to link the human sacrifice of Christ to the saving power of the Passover lamb: 'Christ our Passover lamb has been sacrificed', he told the Corinthians.

This was not, however, the most important element in Paul's analysis of the saving power of Christ's death and resurrection. Instead, his theologically fertile mind came up with something that had no such precedent in Jewish thought or experience and that later generations were to find baffling, uplifting, impenetrable and inspirational. It had its genesis in Paul's deeply pessimistic view of sin. For him, sin was not *just* a transgression of the Jewish law, nor was it *just* a lapse in moral behaviour that could be cancelled through a routine sacrificial offering in the temple. It was much more than that. Sin, Paul believed, was woven into the very fabric of humanity, permeating every sinew of the body. It was a power that could dominate and enslave people, causing them to do things that they didn't want to, and to fail to do things that they did. Indeed, sin was so powerful that it could only be conquered by a total transformation, and the only route to such an absolute transformation was death. It was only by dying in the flesh and rising again in the spirit that the old could be transformed into the new. The defeat of sin, which came into the world with Adam's transgression in the Garden of Eden, could only be accomplished through the death of the mortal body and the assumption of a new spiritual body. It was through his own death and resurrection that Jesus, the second Adam, had made it all possible. What Adam had sullied, Christ had redeemed.

Herein, for Paul, lay the real power of Christ's crucifixion, not as a sacrificial offering but as a template of the death that we ourselves must undergo if we are to be freed from the vice-like grip of sin. As Christ died to sin, so must we. There is no other way of defeating the dreadful hold that sin has over us. As Christ was raised from death in the glory of his spiritual body, we too can be raised with him as spotless people on the way to eternal life. Paul wrote in his letter to the Romans: 'If we have become identified with him in his death, we shall also be identified with him in his resurrection. We know that our old humanity has been crucified with Christ but we believe that we shall also live with him, knowing as we do that Christ, once raised from the dead, is never to die again.' By joining ourselves mystically in the death of Christ we become mystically joined with him in his resurrection also. Sin is finally overcome and God's glory is revealed throughout creation.

Fine words; but do they mean anything in the lives of ordinary people? Are we to read Paul's cosmic drama of death and resurrection literally or symbolically? Is resurrection into our spiritual bodies something that will 'really' happen to us after death or is it to be thought of only as the best that words can do to inspire a search for spiritual truths in our earthly lives? The answer seems to be a bit of both. At one level, Paul clearly did believe that people really would, like Christ, rise from death in a new kind of body. As he wrote to the Church in Corinth: 'We shall all be changed in a flash, in the twinkling of an eye, at the last trumpet call. For the trumpet will sound, and the dead will rise imperishable, and we shall be changed.' Paul also believed that the general resurrection would happen very soon – so soon, in fact, that many of those to whom he was writing would live to see it. Indeed, so clear was Paul about the reality of this future triumph of life over death that he was able to describe the final scene in wondrous detail: 'When the command is given, when the archangel's voice is heard, when God's trumpet sounds, then the Lord himself will descend from heaven; first the Christian dead will rise, then we who are left alive shall join them, caught up in the clouds to meet the Lord in the air.'

There are clearly problems with such a huge and imaginative canvas – not least that it simply has not happened as Paul predicted it would. To the constant dismay of those who claim to know the exact date when all things shall end, the trumpet has never sounded and Christ has never returned from heaven in the way that Paul envisioned. The living and the dead have yet to be wafted up into the air to meet the risen Christ in the clouds. This, for the modern reader, must change the entire thrust of Paul's elaborate theology of dying and rising with Christ. If the sound of the trumpet and the meeting with the Lord in the air are discounted as a factual description of something that will happen in real time and space, then the ethereal poetry of Paul's mystical visions becomes a symbol – an inspirational aid to holy living for those who have the imaginative capacity to respond to it. For those who can find themselves truly caught up in Paul's empyrean drama of death and resurrection, trumpets, clouds and all, the result may well be a profound sense of forgiveness and renewal. For them, its impact is spiritual and psychological, not temporal and physical.

St Paul was thoroughly Jewish. An Israelite and a Pharisee, of the stock of Abraham and the tribe of Benjamin, he had been a zealous practitioner of the Jewish way of life before his dramatic conversion near Damascus. Yet Paul claimed for himself the mission of taking the gospel of Christ to non-Jewish, Greek-speaking places. The division of labour that he eventually hammered out with the disciples in Jerusalem was clear: Peter was to go to the circumcised, the Jews, Paul to the uncircumcised, the Gentiles. In making the God of the Jews accessible to non-Jews, he succeeded beyond anything that he might have imagined. He did it, moreover, through his own imaginative theology of the risen Christ. For the Jews, the mark of their faith was the physical circumcision of the penis: for Paul, true faith was manifest in the metaphorical circumcision of the heart, brought about by dying with Christ and rising again with him. Paul had no particular need to rehearse the history of the Jewish people or to trumpet the merits and achievements of Yahweh. Those things were in the past. In Christ, Paul said, God was making all things new, and what had gone before was merely the prelude to the great transformation that he was about to make in the world.

Above all, then, St Paul set out a vision of the Christian future. The God of the Damascus Road is a God of grace as much as command, who deals with people not according to their obedience to the ancient laws of Moses but to their faith in Jesus Christ. People are justified, or saved, by the grace of God through their faith in the resurrected Christ *and nothing else*. Obedience to the laws of Moses counts for nothing in the eyes of God, neither does the elaborate performance of religious rituals: 'For Christ ends the law and brings righteousness to everyone who has faith', Paul told the church at Rome. It was a statement of pure theology that was to recur as a *leitmotif* throughout the following two millennia. Paul even tried to rewrite Jewish history to some extent by arguing that it was not the ritual of circumcision itself that had justified Abraham in the eyes of God but his earlier obedience to God's commands. Abraham's circumcision, which Jewish tradition had seen as the seal of his covenant with God, was for Paul a later (and really rather unimportant) acknowledgement of the righteousness that was already his by virtue of his faith in God.

The God of the Damascus Road is also much less actively engaged in the world than Israel's God had been. Yahweh strides through the early books of the Old Testament like a divine action man, striking down his adversaries, scattering the enemies of Israel, and issuing commands backed up with blood-curdling threats against those who ignored them. In Paul's letters, God is much less visible. It is as though he is the director and producer of the drama of human salvation, arranging the scenes and controlling the action while the resurrected Christ occupies centre stage as the principal actor. Paul was clear, of course, that it was God who justified people and saved them but he did it through the stupendous mystery of the death and resurrection of Jesus. Paul's God is not one who forces himself upon us or wills us to obey him. He is a God of divine mercy who knows us, understands us, and forgives us. For our part, we have to summon up the will or the imagination to die to sin with Christ and to rise with him incorruptible, never to die again. For 'as in Adam all die, so in Christ all will be brought to life'.

The author of John's gospel, however, told a rather different story. His was a story about a God who came to earth in human form.

Chapter 6
The God Who Came to Earth

John's gospel stands apart from those of Matthew, Mark and Luke. It is generally thought to have been written later than theirs and certainly later than the letters of St Paul. Some New Testament scholars think it may not have been written until the first decade of the second century, though others favour an earlier date. Although the author is unknown, the last chapter of the gospel all but identifies him as John, the disciple of Jesus: 'It is this same disciple [whom Jesus loved] who vouches for what has here been written . . . he it is who wrote it.' This was certainly the view held by some of the founding fathers of the early Christian Church, but there are grounds for questioning it. It strains the imagination to suppose that a document as sophisticated as the fourth gospel could have been written by someone who is described in the Acts of the Apostles as an 'uneducated layman' and who would, at the time, have been at least eighty years old.

John's gospel differs sharply from the synoptic gospels of Matthew, Mark and Luke in a number of striking respects – differences that, as we shall see, became of critical importance to the early Church as it tried to hammer out its core beliefs about the human Jesus and his relationship to God. In the synoptic gospels Jesus often speaks in parables; in John he does not. In the synoptic gospels there are many stories of Jesus casting out devils; in John there is none. In the synoptic gospels Jesus typically refuses to give any signs of his status or authority; in John he gives many. In the synoptic gospels Jesus is reluctant to say who he is; in John he is often the principal subject of his long conversations with his disciples (the 'I am' statements). In the synoptic gospels there are numerous references to Jesus' teaching about the kingdom of God; in John there is only one. In the synoptic gospels Jesus makes extensive use of simile ('the kingdom of God is like . . . '); in John there are no similes and Jesus speaks in lengthy discourses that are stylistically rounded and theologically profound. It is, of course, possible that Jesus talked and taught in these two different ways, and that while the synoptic gospels have captured one half of his style, the author of John's gospel has picked up the other; but it is not an explanation that many find convincing. Rather, the theologically sophisticated words that are put into Jesus' mouth in the fourth gospel are now commonly seen as the later reflections of an unknown but spiritually cultured author.

Because of these differences between John's gospel and the other three, the question arises of why it was written. There are several possibilities. One is that its author may have been writing particularly for Greek-speaking readers in the Middle East who would have been quite comfortable with the idea of a god inhabiting, or even becoming, a human being – the Word made flesh, as the gospel puts it. Others have suggested that the gospel was written as a Christian rejoinder to the Gnostic tendencies that were infiltrating the infant Church and seriously threatening its emerging beliefs about the nature of God. As we shall see, the Gnostics regarded God as a perfect spiritual being, and they rejected any suggestion that he could have lived on earth in a human body. John's insistence that the eternal Word became flesh in the person of Jesus is a weighty rejoinder to the heresy of Gnosticism, for throughout his gospel he repeatedly stresses the divine symbiosis between the Father and the Son. By emphasising Jesus' absolute equality with God, John can be seen as laying one of the early foundation stones in what was later (after centuries of theological disputation) to become the Church's settled doctrine of the Holy Trinity.

The relationship between Jesus and God is set out at the very start of John's gospel, where the opening verses introduce a concept that would have been familiar to both Jewish and Greek audiences: the Word, or *Logos*. Jews would have recognised it as the creative Word of God through which, according to the creation stories in Genesis, the world was formed ('God *said*: let there be . . . '), and Greeks would have understood it as the order and harmony behind all things. According to the prologue in John's gospel, the Word had not only been with God from the beginning of all things, he had actually become incarnate in the human Jesus. Jesus was not merely the mouthpiece of the Word, he *was* the Word. 'So the Word became flesh; he made his home among us, and we saw his glory, such glory as befits the Father's only Son, full of grace and truth.' It would be difficult to over-estimate the importance of this verse for the Church's early beliefs about the complex relationship between Jesus, the Word and God: the Word, who had been with God from the beginning, became human in the person of Jesus and lived in a specific place and time in the history of the world.

It was to explain and justify this dramatic claim in the opening verses of John's gospel that the rest of it was written. The text is organised around seven miracles that Jesus is said to have performed; and to ensure that the reader does not miss them, the first two (the wedding at Cana-in-Galilee and the healing of the official's son) are conveniently labelled 'first' and 'second'. Thereafter the numbering runs out but the structure remains. The other five miracles are the healing of the crippled man at the Pool of Bethesda, the feeding of the five thousand, the walking on the water, the curing of the blind man and the raising of Lazarus. Six of the seven miracles are accompanied by a 'discourse' explaining the meaning of the event, followed by a statement in which Jesus reveals himself as the pathway to its fulfilment. For example, the miraculous feeding of the five thousand on the Galilean hillside is followed by a sermon about the bread of eternal life and, later, by Jesus' assurance that whoever believes in him will never lack spiritual food or drink.

John's purpose in setting out these miraculous signs and noting their significance was to reveal Jesus Christ as the divine Son of God, sent by the Father in heaven to bring eternal life to those who believed in him. It was all made possible by a powerfully stated yet ultimately enigmatic three-way union between the Father, the Son and each individual believer. The first part of the union, between the Father and the Son, is one of the outstanding themes of the gospel. In striking contrast to the synoptic gospels, where Jesus almost invariably refers to himself as the Son of Man, in John's gospel he speaks repeatedly of God as the heavenly Father and himself as the divine Son. Evidence of this ethereal yet inseparable union between Father and Son is scattered generously throughout the gospel. Indeed, so close are they that at times they actually merge into one another: 'The Father and I are one'. There cannot be a closer relationship between two people than this – an absolute equality of being between God and Jesus in which their unity penetrates to the very depths of their being. One is a mirror image of the other: 'I am in the Father and the Father [is] in me'. There is nothing in Matthew, Mark or Luke that matches the depth and symbiosis in John's words.

The enigmatic relationship between the Father and the Son in John's gospel extends also to those who believe in Jesus, for they too are caught up in the unity of the Father and the Son to form a mystical trinity: 'May they all be one; as you, Father, are in me, and I in you, so also may they be in us.' John carries this union between Jesus and his followers to dramatic lengths in the metaphor of bread. When the people of Israel were wandering in the wilderness on their way from Egypt to Canaan, God had sent manna from heaven for them to eat. A psalmist called it 'the bread of angels'. Now Jesus is offering them 'bread from heaven . . . that brings life to the world.' This bread, however, is no mere processed grain, it is the very body of Jesus himself: 'I am the living bread which has come down from heaven . . . Whoever eats my flesh and drinks my blood dwells in me and I am in him.' A union between two persons, one divine and one human, can scarcely get more darkly enigmatic than this, and it is no surprise that it led to a fierce argument among the Jews about the meaning of Jesus' words.

It was, moreover, not only the Jews who could enter into this symbiotic relationship with Jesus. So too could non-Jews. John writes that: 'There are other sheep of mine . . . I must lead them as well, and they too will listen to my voice.' Jesus had alien sheep to tend, the Gentiles among John's readership, and he had to ensure that there would be 'one flock and one shepherd'. Yet so swiftly does John rearrange his metaphors that the shepherd who is prepared to die for his sheep is also the lamb that is sacrificed for the sins of the world. Although the phrase 'the Lamb of God' appears only twice in John's gospel, it is a striking and significant image that has no parallel in the synoptic gospels and only a faint echo in the letters of St Paul. Some half a century earlier, in his letter to the Romans, Paul had made an oblique reference to Christ as the Passover lamb. It is only in John's gospel, however, that the full implications of the sacrificial metaphor are drawn out when John the Baptist points to Jesus and announces to those around him: 'There is the Lamb of God who takes away the sin of the world'.

By describing Jesus in this way, the author of John's gospel was tackling the burning problem of sin and salvation in a way that must have been instantly recognisable to any Jewish reader. In using the language of expiation, he was providing a ready-made context in which to understand the nature of Christ's death – the Jewish ritual of animal sacrifice in the temple at Jerusalem. Through the words of John the Baptist, Jesus is presented to the crowd as the sacrificial scapegoat, the lamb to be slaughtered in atonement for sin; but not just any lamb and not just any sin. This lamb was the Lamb of God, God himself, and the sins for which he died were the sins of all mankind throughout eternity. When the author of John's gospel looked at Jesus he saw not only the incarnate *Logos*, the Word made flesh, but also the sacrificial lamb offered up to die as an atonement for the whole of human sinfulness. It was a vision that mixed Greek and Jewish ideas in a heady cocktail of high theology – a vision that not only fuelled a great deal of theological thinking in the early Church but also caused it some dreadful headaches as the centuries went by.

Here, then, is John's complex image of Jesus. He is the eternal Word who came and dwelt among us, 'the Lamb of God who takes away the sins of the world', the Son who is in the Father as the Father is in him, the divine man who offers his flesh to be eaten and his blood to be drunk as an assurance of eternal life. Is this, however, the same person as the Jesus of the synoptic gospels, the Jewish rabbi who tramped the dusty highways and byways of Galilee and taught the people in simple but telling stories drawn from the lives of housewives, farmers and fishermen? The differences between Matthew, Mark and Luke on the one hand and John on the other are difficult to explain away. Is it credible that Jesus talked and behaved in two dramatically contrasting ways, one of which has been captured by the writers of the first three gospels and the other by the author of the fourth? Whereas the synoptic authors broadly depict Jesus as a radical Jewish teacher and healer seized with the imminent arrival of the kingdom of God and wanting his hearers to share the urgency of the moment by confessing their sins and turning to God, John gives us a more sophisticated Jesus who displays dimensions that are absent in Matthew, Mark and Luke. In the synoptic gospels we probably get as close as we are likely to come to the real, historical Jesus; in John's gospel, by contrast, we may have something rather different, an inspired theological interpretation of his significance in God's great scheme of redemption and salvation.

Whether the dialogue in the fourth gospel is read as the authentic words of Jesus or as an imaginative interpretation of God's nature, it does bring out an aspect of the Christian God that is absent from the synoptic gospels. John's God is an enigmatic God who goes about his business in ways that can hardly be explained through ordinary human language. In the person of the Word, he enters into a mystical union with Jesus Christ, and the two then enter into an equally mystical relationship with each individual believer in which the body of Christ himself becomes the staple necessities of human life: bread, wine and water. There are few parallels in human experience with this blend of the human and the divine in which each becomes the other. The God of John's gospel can hardly be explained in anything approaching a rational way, but the gospel's author is clear that he can be embraced in faith as the Word who became flesh and took his place in human history. It is a view of God that was to cause a great deal of anguish to the early Church as it tried to express the ineffable mystery of the incarnation in words and phrases that could define the core beliefs of the new faith and convince prospective converts of their eternal truth.

Chapter 7
The God of Dogma and Heresy

The Christian Church began as an almost exclusively Jewish enterprise. There was little awareness among Jesus' earliest followers that they were founding a new Church, much less a new religion; rather, they saw themselves as a sort of ginger group within Judaism to call people back to a new relationship with God through faith in him. After all, this was, apparently, what Jesus had instructed them to do when he told them *not* to 'take the road to Gentile lands'. Their new relationship with God was still to be set within the traditional framework of Jewish salvation history and still to be centred on the temple in Jerusalem. Even after his resurrection, when Jesus had (according to Matthew's gospel) been living among his disciples in Jerusalem for forty days, some of the apostles were still thinking of him as the messianic leader who would restore the fortunes of Israel. 'Lord', they are recorded as asking him in the Acts of the Apostles, 'is this the time at which you are to restore sovereignty to Israel?' Instead of answering them directly, Jesus simply replied that it was not for them to know the dates or times of God's deliverance.

The fledging Christian faith, however, did not remain for long as an obscure sect within Palestinian Judaism. In the religious hothouse of the Middle East, where Judaism was mingling with the pagan religions of the Roman Empire and competing against an exotic menu of local cults and practices, it made steady progress in the face of severe opposition and ridicule. Under a succession of brutal Roman emperors, including Nero, Trajan and Hadrian, the strange new 'way' of Christianity became the focus of a vicious and sustained campaign of persecution. Christians were accused of practising cannibalism by eating the body and drinking the blood of Jesus and of shutting themselves away in secret enclaves. They were made scapegoats for all that went wrong. Writing towards the end of the second century, the Carthaginian priest Tertullian (*c.* 160-225) observed in his *Apologeticum* that 'the Christians are to blame for every public disaster and every misfortune that befalls the people. If the Tiber rises to the walls, if the Nile fails to rise and flood the fields, if the sky withholds its rain, if there is earthquake or famine or plague, straightway the cry arises: The Christians to the lions!'

In spite of (or perhaps because of) the persecution, the new faith not only gained a foothold within Judaism, it also began to spread among non-Jewish (Gentile) people. Indeed, one of the earliest disputes to engage the fledgling Church was whether, in order to become Christians, Gentile men had first to convert to Judaism and demonstrate their commitment to the Hebrew faith by accepting circumcision. St Paul, the self-appointed apostle to the Gentiles, would have none of it. Gentiles, he insisted, must be admitted to the faith as Gentiles or not at all: all they had to do to be saved by the grace of God was to believe in the risen Christ. It mattered not whether they happened to be born Jew or Gentile, and the idea that they should be circumcised before they could be admitted to the circle of believers was, for Paul, preposterous. Writing to the Church in the ancient region of Galatia at a time when the case was still being argued for Gentiles to be circumcised, Paul blew his top: if that was what they believed, well then, let them go the whole hog and remove the disputatious organ in its entirety! Here was the beginning of the split between the old religion and the new, between the ancient faith of the Jews and the new way of the Christians. From now on, Jesus was proclaimed by the Christian community less as the long-awaited Messiah of the Jewish people and more as the Saviour of the world. Here, too, were the beginnings of a separate cult as circumcision and the sacrificial rites of the temple in Jerusalem gave way to baptism and the Church's celebration of the last supper. Yahweh, the God of the Jews, was opening up to the Gentiles – but not on Jewish terms.

As the Christian Church began to expand into new places and to gain new converts, a variety of beliefs emerged about the relationship between God, Jesus, the Word and the Holy Spirit that were gradually to coalesce into the defining creeds of the faith. It was a long and difficult period of theological strife as propositions were advanced and debated before being either accepted into the growing body of orthodox Christian doctrine or rejected as heresy. Indeed, some four hundred years were to elapse between the death of Jesus and the final authoritative statements of the Church about the nature of God, in the course of which a great many words were spoken, lives were lost, and bargains were struck. The creedal statements that finally emerged in the fourth and fifth centuries – statements that set out the defining beliefs of the Christian Church – had all the hallmarks of compromise born of the attempted reconciliation of propositions that were logically irreconcilable. They were, though, good enough to hold the Church together for a further six hundred years until the first great schism in the history of the faith saw the Eastern and Western Churches part company in the eleventh century.

The difficulties began to emerge at an early stage in the history of the Church as bishops and theologians reflected upon, and tried to put into words, their new understanding of God in the light of the life, death and resurrection of Jesus. Two foundational beliefs became dominant. The first was that God, by his very nature, was far above the human experiences of suffering, passion, change and death, and the second was that God had come to earth and lived a human life in the person of Jesus. So far so good, but between these two beliefs lay a chasm of contradiction. If God had become incarnate in the human Jesus, and if (as was self-evidently the case from the gospel narratives) Jesus had suffered and died, then it followed that God must also have suffered and died during his time on earth. The two beliefs could not logically coexist. *Either* God had not been incarnate in Jesus *or* he had experienced the human suffering of Jesus and had died on the cross. It was in struggling to reconcile this fundamental contradiction that the early Church embarked upon a series of heroic battles against an array of heretical proposals, finally arriving at a set of statements about the nature of God and his relationship to Jesus that would settle the problem once and for all in the unalterable doctrine of the Holy Trinity.

The first of these two foundational beliefs – that God, *being God*, was above the human experiences of suffering, passion, change and death – was about as far removed from the God of the early Old Testament as it was possible to get. In the first five books of the Bible, Yahweh had been involved with his people up to his elbows, exhorting them, punishing them, loving them, threatening them, saving them and even killing them. He was a God of deep and mixed emotions who could be angry and vengeful as well as just, merciful and forgiving. He could also change his mind, as he showed in his dealings with Noah, Abraham and Moses. Why, then, was the committed, passionate and sometimes indecisive God of the Pentateuch replaced by the serene and passionless God of the early Church? Part of the answer is that, in order to make headway in the Greek-speaking regions of the Middle East beyond the boundaries of Jewish Palestine, the early Christian evangelists had to work with the new cultures and traditions they were encountering. By early in the second century, the Church fathers had adopted many of the prevailing Greek ideas about God as the foundation upon which to build the edifice of the Christian faith. In particular, they found much that they could turn to their advantage in Plato's idea of God as ultimate perfection.

In his *Dialogues* written some four hundred years before the birth of Jesus, the Athenian philosopher Plato (427-347 BC) had espoused the idea of God as the 'demi-urge' or intelligent cause behind everything that was orderly and structured in the world. Plato was an idealist, and his God was a perfect being, immortal, transcendent, unchanging, and beyond all passion and suffering. He reasoned that if God is the most perfect and elevated being that can possibly be imagined, then he must surely embody the most perfect attributes imaginable – and these do not include such belittling human experiences as suffering and death. God must be above these mortal imperfections or he would not be God. It was, therefore, to Plato's serene and immutable God that many of the early Church fathers looked in order to advance their message in the Greek-speaking world. Others, however, were alarmed at this radical departure from Christianity's Jewish heritage. The conflict was not only between Greek and Jewish images of God, but also (by extension) between those who wanted the new faith to harmonise with the philosophical ideas of the Greek-speaking world and those for whom religion and philosophy were separate spheres of human experience, with no necessary points of contact between them.

The clash between these two perspectives was nowhere contested more fiercely than between Clement of Alexandria (c. 150-216) and Tertullian of Carthage (c.160-225). The theologians of Alexandria in Egypt were liberal and progressive; those of Carthage in Tunisia were traditional and conservative. Clement, a convert to Christianity who taught at the Catechetical School in Alexandria, sought to present the Christian faith not only as the fulfilment of Hebrew scripture but also as compatible with the philosophies of classical Greece. Clement's God had moved a long way on from the petulant and committed Yahweh of the early Old Testament: he was now a constant and perfect deity, a stranger to pain, suffering and change. Such Hellenistic sympathies were, however, anathema to Tertullian, the conservative counterpart to Clement down the coast in Carthage. For him, the influence of Greek philosophy on the development of Christian theology was greatly to be deplored. He famously asked: 'What has Athens to do with Jerusalem?' Why should the coat of Christian doctrine be cut from Greek rather than Jewish cloth? What can philosophy contribute to the knowledge of a God who is as far above the thoughts of man as the heavens are above the earth? In Tertullian's view, the reality of God's being and the fullness of his nature had been uniquely revealed in his mighty acts of creation and salvation in the Old Testament, and no amount of pandering to fashionable Greek ideas could add to or change that revelation.

The second foundational belief of the early Christian Church was that God had come to earth and lived a human life in Jesus of Nazareth. Christians believed this to be true from a very early time, and by the end of the first century, if not earlier, they had begun to worship Jesus in the same way that they were worshipping God. From there it was but a short step to believing that Jesus was, in a profound sense, God himself. After all, the author of John's gospel, which may have been in circulation by the very early years of the second century, had gone out of his way to stress the intensely symbiotic relationship between the Father and the Son. Jesus was not merely a man whose heart was filled with the love of God, not merely one whose life was lived in total obedience to God, not even someone chosen and elevated by God for a purpose unparalleled in human history. He was God himself – and had been from the moment he drew his first human breath in the manger at Bethlehem. There had never been a time in his earthly life when Jesus had not been God.

Here, then, were the seeds of the conundrum that was to torment the bishops and theologians for decades as they struggled not only to make sense of it for themselves but also to explain it to potential converts. How could a changeless and passionless God have been incarnate in a human being who had experienced all the sufferings that attend the human condition and who had died a human death on the cross? How could God have remained aloof from his time on earth if, as Jesus had reportedly told his disciples in John's gospel, 'the Father and I are one'? Surely it must follow that if the Son had suffered and died, then so too had the Father; but that was impossible, for he was above suffering and death.

The solution to the problem, to jump ahead a little, was worked out in the final version of the Nicene Creed in 381 and the Formulary of Chalcedon in 451. The road to Chalcedon, however, was a rocky one, and those who trod it were often ambushed by assorted gangs of heretics seeking to resolve the inconsistency by denying one or other of the two foundational beliefs. The slow and painful evolution of Christian teaching about God over the four hundred years that followed the death of Jesus was as much a process of rejecting propositions that were unacceptable to the Church as of incorporating those that suited. As one heresy after another was named and shamed, the boundaries of orthodoxy became ever more clearly defined until, by the time the final polish was applied at the ecumenical conference of Chalcedon in the middle of the fifth century, the Trinitarian faith of the Church was revealed in all its majestic contradiction.

Early attempts to resolve the problem of an unchanging God who had suffered and died a human death drew upon the insight in John's gospel that it had been the Word of God (the *Logos*) rather than God himself who had come to earth in the person of Jesus. 'So the Word became flesh; he made his home among us, and we saw his glory.' John's invocation of the Word was taken up by a group of early Christian theologians, known collectively as 'the apologists', who saw it as a way of squaring the circle. If it had been the Word rather than God himself who had taken human form in Jesus, then it must have been the Word, not God, who had suffered and died on the cross. It was a solution of sorts, but it raised an obvious new question: if Jesus had been the incarnation of the Word rather than of God, what was the relationship between the Word and God? After all, the author of John's gospel had gone out of his way to stress that what God was, the Word was also. Did this not rather undermine the arguments of those who sought to make a clear distinction between God and the Word? If God and the Word were the same, and if the Word had been incarnate in the human Jesus, then the problem remained that God must have suffered and died with him.

It was here that the apologists took the argument into imaginative new territory. Justin Martyr (103-165), who was teaching in Rome in about 150 and who was well schooled in both the Hebrew scriptures and Greek philosophy, devised an ingenious solution, elements of which were to persist in the Church's thinking for a long time. Justin proposed that although the Word was of the same *substance* as God, he was not actually God himself. Rather, the Word was somewhat less than God, in the same sense that a flame torch is less than the fire from which it is taken while still being of the same flame-like substance. God, the creative power behind all things, could thus remain in his divine perfection in heaven while the Word did the suffering and dying through his incarnation in Jesus.

Another of the apologists, Athenagoras (*c.* 133-190), a Greek philosopher from Athens who converted to Christianity in the latter years of the second century and then became an ardent proponent of the new faith, took Justin's argument one stage further. There were, he posited, three distinct and separate beings: a God who was Father, a Son who was his Word, and a Spirit. In Chapter 24 of his *Treatise on the Trinity*, Athenagoras declared that the Son was 'the Intelligence and Reason and Wisdom of the Father, and the Spirit an effluence as light from light'. In trying to visualise God as three entirely separate beings, each with its own nature and functions, Athenagoras was beginning to anticipate the Church's eventual teaching about the Holy Trinity, though he all but fell into the trap (which was to ensnare many others after him) of implying that, because the Father, the Son and the Spirit were separate beings, there were actually three Gods, not one.

Others took a different line to the embryonic Trinitarianism of Justin and Athenagoras, trying to reconcile the two foundational beliefs by abandoning one or other of them. They reasoned that if two statements were logically incompatible, at least one of them *must* be wrong: either the belief that God was above suffering and death or the belief that God had been incarnate in Jesus. On one side of the divide were those who accepted that God had come to earth and lived a human life in Jesus, but who concluded from this that God must therefore have suffered and died on the cross. A persistent proponent of this view was Praxeas, a Christian who was active in Rome and Carthage in the first decade of the third century. A contemporary of Tertullian of Carthage and a persistently painful thorn in his side, Praxeas held fast to the traditional Jewish belief in a single God, and he was also open to the idea of his incarnation in Jesus. Yet in arguing that God was an undivided being who was embodied in the human Jesus, Praxeas was led inexorably to the conclusion that God must have suffered and died with him. Tertullian responded by angrily accusing him of 'crucifying the Father'. It came to be known as the heresy of *patripassianism*, the doctrine of the suffering of the Father that lasted for a long time before being finally snuffed out at the end of the fourth century. As we shall see, though, it reappeared in a different guise in the latter part of the twentieth century – by which time nobody knew or cared whether it was any longer a heresy.

A contemporary of Praxeas in Rome was an African priest called Sabellius. Born in Lybia or Egypt and active in the early years of the third century, Sabellius became the leader of a group of African Christians (known as the Sabellians) who believed, like Praxeas in Rome, that God and Jesus were one and the same. There was, they claimed, nothing in the Bible that referred unequivocally to a fragmented God in which Father, Son, Spirit and Word were separate beings. There was no hint in the Old Testament of Yahweh sharing his divinity with others, and John's gospel had stressed the absolute unity between God and the Word: 'What the Word was, God was.' If there was only one God, the Sabellians reasoned, then no distinction could be made between the Father and the Son: if the Son had suffered and died, then so had the Father. It was easier for Sabellius and his followers to accept the heresy of *patripassianism* than to deny the unity that existed between the Father and the Son. Sabellius was excommunicated for his efforts by Pope Calixtus I in 220, but his ideas lived on and remained a potent threat to the Church's evolving doctrines until well into the fourth century. As we shall see, Sabellianism surfaced again in the wake of the Council of Nicaea in 325 which, by over-emphasising the unity between the Son and the Father (' . . . light from light, God from God, true God from true God . . . '), opened the way again to those who argued that if the Son and the Father were as close as all that, then the Father must have suffered and died with the Son.

To the conservative Tertullian in Carthage, the teachings of Praxeas and Sabellius were dangerous heresy. It was utterly unthinkable that the almighty God could die, let alone at the hands of ruthless officials and jealous clerics. That was not the sort of thing to which the creator of heaven and earth would subject himself. There had to be a way of separating Jesus from God that preserved *both* the unity of God *and* the incarnation without falling into the heresy of *patripassianism*. Echoing the earlier idea of Justin Martyr, Tertullian proposed a solution that hinged around the distinction between 'person' and 'substance' – a distinction that was later to furnish the corner stone of orthodoxy about the Holy Trinity. He argued that 'person' is what someone *does* while 'substance' is what they *are*. Tertullian thought that such a distinction would neatly sidestep the heresy of a God who suffered. God could be two or more *persons* (such as the Father and the Word) but only one *substance* (such as godliness). It would then be possible to argue that Jesus had been the incarnation of only one of the persons of God (the Word) while still embodying the essential substance of godliness. The separate person of the Father, meanwhile, could remain unsullied by the violence of the cross. Tertullian was sure that this must be the case, for otherwise there would be no defence against the heresies being preached by Praxeas and the Sabellians about an almighty God who suffered and died on earth.

The opposite solution to the problem of reconciling the two foundational beliefs of the early Church came from those who, like Tertullian, accepted that God was a stranger to suffering and death but who denied that he had been fully incarnate in Jesus. Known as the Gnostics, they claimed to be the guardians of a 'secret knowledge' that had emanated from someone within Jesus' own close circle, possibly Judas Iscariot; and for the first two centuries of Christianity they posed the greatest single threat to the steadily emerging doctrine of the Holy Trinity. Whereas Praxeas and Sabellius had tried to square the circle by ditching the belief that God was above suffering, the Gnostics did it by rejecting the alternative belief that God had become incarnate in Jesus. They held fast to the Greek idea of God as a perfect spiritual being, far above the baseness and corruption of humanity, and they would therefore have nothing to do with what they saw as the heresy of *patripassianism*. Yet if God had *not* suffered and died on the cross, it followed that Jesus could *not* have been the human embodiment of God. At best, he could only have been a human vehicle for the heavenly messages sent by God. To equate the sublime and eternal spirituality of God with the suffering and death of a human body was, for the Gnostics, unthinkable. They held fast to the perfection of God and they accepted the suffering of Jesus, but they could only reconcile the two ideas by rejecting the incarnation.

One of the earliest of the Church fathers to throw his weight against what he saw as the dangerously false teachings of Gnosticism, especially its rejection of the incarnation of God in Jesus Christ, was Irenaeus (*c.* 120-202), a student of the martyred Saint Polycarp (69-155). Born in Smyrna in Asia Minor, Irenaeus became the Bishop of Lyons, in France, where he died during a massacre of the Christians in the city in 202. In fierce opposition to the Gnostics, Irenaeus had no doubt about the divinity of Jesus. For him, Jesus was the Word incarnate. He must, in some very real sense, have been God himself – for if he was *not*, then the cross would have no power to redeem a sinful world. Echoing the ancient beliefs from other times and places about the double efficacy of a divine scapegoat, Irenaeus thought that no mere human sacrifice could atone for the sins of all mankind. For the cross to do its work of salvation, Jesus had to be divine; and his incarnation was therefore just as important as his death and resurrection.

In pressing his case, Irenaeus made use of the contrast that St Paul had drawn in his letter to the Romans between Christ and Adam. Irenaeus believed that the life of each individual was bound up in some way with the lives of everyone else to form a mass of humanity; but the mass must have a head, a representative who could influence its destiny for better or worse. The first 'head of humanity' had been Adam; but Adam had been flawed (Irenaeus described him and Eve as 'children who wanted to grow up before their time'), and they had dragged the whole of humankind with them into a state of sin. What Adam did for his fellow human beings, Jesus had been able to undo: he was the second 'head of humanity' whose divinity enabled him to reverse the descent into sin that Adam had begun. For Irenaeus, the cross and the resurrection were the culmination of this process: only God, present in Jesus as the Word, could unstitch the tangled mess into which Adam had led humanity. Jesus had to be the incarnate Word of God or the whole scheme of salvation would fall apart. Irenaeus was, of course, then left with the enduring problem of *patripassianism*, for if God was incarnate in Jesus, and if Jesus had suffered and died, then God too must have suffered and died; but he simply avoided the issue by declaring the infallibility of the bishops in matters of doctrine. The faithful, he said, must accept the teaching of the Church without question, however difficult or contradictory the bishops' words might seem. They knew best and they had to be trusted to be speaking the truths that had been revealed to them.

Closely aligned with Gnosticism in certain respects but diametrically opposed to it in others was the less durable heresy of Docetism. The Docetists agreed with the Gnostics that the perfect and unchangeable God could not possibly have involved himself in the corrupt and imperfect world of humanity, but whereas the Gnostics went on from this to reject the full divinity of Jesus, the Docetists responded by rejecting his full humanity. Some even denied that he had been a human being at all. If Jesus had come to save mankind from sin, they argued, then he could not have been a real man, for mankind cannot save itself. At best, Jesus was God in the guise of a man – that is, he only appeared to be human while all the time remaining God. It was, at least in theory, another way out of the dilemma, for if God had never 'really' been human at all but had only seemed to be, then he could never 'really' have suffered and died on the cross but only seemed to have done so. Since (in the eyes of the Docetists) God did not have a material body, it was impossible for him to have suffered and died a human death.

Docetism was opposed with great vigour by an early bishop of Antioch, Ignatius, who may have known St Paul and some of the disciples and who was martyred in Rome in 110. In his letters to the early Christian communities in Ephesus, Rome and Smyrna, Ignatius strenuously rejected the Docetic view of Jesus as having merely appeared to be human while all the while remaining truly God. On the contrary, Ignatius insisted that in Jesus, God had entered the sphere of real human experience. He truly became one of us, a fully human being. It was not a matter (as Charles Wesley was much later to put it in his famous but Docetic Christmas hymn) of the Godhead appearing on earth 'veiled in flesh'. Jesus was human flesh and blood through and through, not merely God in a human overcoat. In the event, Docetism never troubled the Church as deeply as Gnosticism, though it lived on in one form or another for a long time before being formally condemned at the Council of Chalcedon in 451. Thereafter, Docetic ideas seem to have died a natural death – apart, that is, from surfacing obliquely and unexpectedly each Christmas in 'Hark, the herald angels sing'.

By the early years of the fourth century yet another way out of the conundrum was being proposed and resisted, this time in Alexandria in Egypt, the home of the lighthouse that was one of the wonders of the ancient world. In 318 the supporters of the local bishop, Alexander (died 326), came to public blows with those of a popular and ambitious priest named Arius (c. 250-336). The principal cause of the street fighting between the two factions was not the basic question of whether Jesus had or had not been divine but the more arcane one of whether his divinity was the same *kind* of divinity as God's. Alexander said it was; Arius said it wasn't. Arius accepted the steadily coalescing view that Jesus had been the incarnation of the Word, and he also went along with the widely held belief that the Word was in some sense divine. The issue was: in *what* sense? For if God was above all passion and suffering and change, as almost everyone except the followers of Praxeus and Sabellius now accepted, then Jesus could not have been divine in *exactly* the same sense that God was divine.

Arius came up with an innovative way out of the dilemma that had echoes of Justin Martyr's analogy of the flame two hundred years earlier. Justin had argued that although the Word was of the same *substance* as God, he wasn't actually God himself. Rather, the Word was somewhat less than God, in the same sense that a flame torch is less than the fire from which it is taken. Building on Justin's analogy, Arius argued that since the Word had been created by God, the Word (and therefore Jesus) must be less than God, for a creature can never be the equal of its creator. Jesus was divine, certainly, but not in quite the same way as God, for it was the subordinate divinity of the Word that had become incarnate in him. Here, then, was the logic of what came to be known as the Arian heresy: since the Word had been created by God, the Word could not have had the same divine status as God himself; and because Jesus was the Word incarnate, neither could Jesus have had exactly the same divine status as God. In this way, the suffering of Jesus could logically be reconciled with the eternal perfection and changelessness of God – but only by denying that Jesus was the absolute equal of God.

The idea that Jesus might have been a lesser divinity than God was too much for Alexander and his supporters, and hence the street brawls that erupted outside the cathedral in Alexandria. The issue, however, was of the greatest possible importance. It was not simply a matter of philosophical emphasis but of salvation itself. Alexander, like Irenaeus before him, believed that the death and resurrection of Jesus could only assure the salvation of mankind if he had been fully and completely God. If he had been a lesser version of God, as Arius was teaching, then there could be no salvation. The matter came to a head in 318 when Alexander summoned the bishops to a meeting at Alexandria where they promptly condemned Arius for heresy and sacked him from his post as presbyter. Arius, however, was far from finished. He wrote to the bishops who had been unable to attend the Synod of Alexandria reminding them that Jesus was the 'only begotten' Son of God. It was a shrewd point to make, for if Jesus had been 'begotten' (that is, created) by God, then he must have had a beginning. And if he had had a beginning, then there must have been a time when Jesus had not existed. God himself, on the other hand, must be eternal, with neither beginning nor end. It followed, then, that a time-bound Son who had been 'begotten' or created by a timeless God *must* be a lesser divinity – a creation of God, not God himself. Problem solved!

Unsurprisingly, the bishops were confused by all of this, and a wounding schism now threatened to tear the Church apart. By this time, however, politics had begun to influence the course of events. In 312 the Roman general Constantine had set about usurping Maxentius as Emperor. Constantine had no particular sympathy for Christianity, but he did need the favour of whichever gods might help him win his battles; and he was much taken with a vision in which he saw the Christian cross and the words: 'In this sign conquer'. This was good enough for Constantine; and so it proved, for it was while he was fighting under the Christian banner that he defeated Maxentius at the battle of Milvian Bridge and succeeded him as Emperor.

Understandably impressed, Constantine declared in the following year (313) that Christianity would henceforth be tolerated in the Empire, and although he himself was not baptised into the faith until just before his death in 337, he did ensure that Christianity was favoured over the other religions of the Roman Empire. Several important things happened during Constantine's reign as Emperor that were to change both the institutional and the doctrinal position of Christianity. The persecution of Christians ended; a new imperial capital (Constantinople) was built in the East of the Empire at Byzantium; and the intense theological struggle broke out between Arius and Alexander over the precise nature of Jesus' divinity. The dispute eventually attracted the attention of the Emperor himself, who regarded a public squabble among Church leaders as weakening the cohesiveness of the Christian glue that was supposed to be holding his crumbling Empire together. Indeed, Constantine was so troubled by the schism that he was finally driven to resolve it one way or the other. It was not a matter of orthodoxy or heresy, for in all likelihood he neither understood nor cared about the theological issues involved. What mattered was the banging together of stubborn heads to produce an agreement; and he, Constantine, was minded to preside over the event to ensure its success. His decisive action in summoning and presiding over a meeting of the bishops was crucial for the Christian Church in both the West and the East of the Empire; yet when the First Council of Nicaea met in 325 it created as many difficulties as it resolved.

Chapter 8
The God of Creeds

With all their expenses paid by the Emperor Constantine, three hundred and eighteen bishops gathered for the First Council of Nicaea, near Constantinople, in the spring of 325. The Council was convened by Constantine to resolve once and for all the question of whether the Son was the equal of the Father or whether, as Arius of Alexandria had been teaching, he was a lesser version of God. Those attending were divided on the matter when the proceedings opened. Some regarded Arius as an outright heretic and some had no idea what he was talking about; but most were reportedly engaged with the issue and ready to hear the arguments. Arius himself, having been sacked as a presbyter by the Synod of Alexandria seven years earlier, was not allowed to attend. His position, however, was presented on his behalf by his friend and sympathiser Eusebius (died 341), the Bishop of Nicomedia (in modern-day Turkey) and the probable leader of the Arian party. The opposition to Arius was led by Alexander of Alexandria, aided by his ambitious young deacon Athanasius (296-373).

The proceedings began with a call for the Arian position to be stated clearly and succinctly so that the bishops would know exactly what was at issue. To the delight of Alexander and his supporters, Eusebius responded by repeating the central assertion of Arius that, far from being the equal of the Father, the Son had been 'begotten' by the Father and could not therefore be of exactly the same divine substance as him. Though this was a perfectly fair representation of the Arian position, it was probably a tactical error to have put it quite so bluntly. A riot broke out that had to be quelled by Constantine. Eventually it was agreed that a unifying creed should be prepared by a small group of bishops to summarise 'the ancient faith of the Church', the text to be binding upon all who claimed membership of the universal Church. The result, which took about a month to formulate, was the first version of what is now known as the Nicene Creed. Most scholars see the hand of Athanasius heavy upon it.

We believe in one God, the Father almighty, maker of all things visible and invisible; And in one Lord Jesus Christ, the Son of God, begotten from the Father, only-begotten, that is, from the substance of the Father, God from God, light from light, true God from true God, begotten not made, of one substance with the Father, through Whom all things came into being, things in heaven and things on earth, Who because of us humans and because of our salvation came down and became incarnate, becoming human, suffered and rose again on the third day, ascended to the heavens, and will come to judge the living and the dead; And in the Holy Spirit.

The wording was deliberately crafted to slam the door on Arianism once and for all by emphasising the absolute parity that existed between the Father and the Son. In particular, the introduction of the word 'begotten' was designed to deal a mortal blow to the Arian heresy. Arius had argued that, since Jesus was the 'only begotten' Son of God, he must be of a lesser divinity than the Father who created him, for a creature cannot be the equal of its creator. The bishops turned this argument on its head, declaring that precisely because Jesus *was* 'begotten' by God, he could not possibly have been created or made. Somehow, the bishops managed to persuade themselves that to be 'begotten' was the absolute opposite of being 'created'. And just in case any among their number still had lingering doubts about the matter, the Creed went out of its way to stress that Jesus was 'of one substance with the Father … God from God, light from light, true God from true God, *begotten not made*' (emphasis added). Jesus was not made by God and he was not subordinate to God. He was begotten from God – that is to say, he *was* God.

With all but two of the attending bishops signing up to the statement, some of them possibly under the threat of banishment by Constantine if they failed to do so, the new Creed should have been an arrow through the heart of the Arian heresy. Constantine then ordered the bishops to condemn Arius and his supporters as heretics and he later banished them to Illyria, in what is now a western region of the Balkans. It was an extraordinary moment even in the midst of extraordinary times: here was a not-yet baptised Roman Emperor ordering a meeting of most of the bishops in Christendom to sign a highly ambiguous statement of their faith. The result was to prove little short of catastrophic, for once the dust had settled on the Council of Nicaea, the awful realisation gradually dawned that in trying to avoid the Scylla of Arianism, the bishops had steered dangerously close to the Charybdis of the even older heresy of *patripassianism* (the Father suffers) that had been promoted by Sabellius and Praxeas.

The heresy of *patripassianism* could only be countered by showing that the Father and the Son were *not* the same – for it was only by demonstrating their separateness that God could have been spared the suffering and death that Jesus experienced. Yet here were the bishops declaring precisely the opposite. Jesus was, according to the new Creed, 'of one substance with the Father'. (The word *homo-ousios* in the original Greek is conventionally translated as 'consubstantial' or 'of one substance'). Jesus was 'God from God, light from light, true God from true God'. What was this if not Sabellianism by the back door? Indeed, Bishop Marcellus of Ancyra (died *c.* 374), a participant at Nicaea, actually proclaimed the Creed a triumph for Sabellianism. For his honesty, Marcellus was condemned a few years later by the Council of Constantinople in 336 and expelled from his see; but towards the end of his life he was allowed to return to Ancyra (modern-day Ankara) and minister quietly to the small congregation that still supported him.

Faced with the unwelcome prospect of renewed controversy within the Church, Constantine now had second thoughts about which side to support, and in 332 he summoned Arius back from exile and restored him to his former position as a presbyter. He also ordered Athanasius (who by now had succeeded Alexander as Bishop of Alexandria) to accept him back into communion with the Church. Athanasius refused, and in 335 he was exiled by Constantine to the German city of Trier. In the following year Arius died a horrible death that was said by his enemies to have been God's revenge for his heresy: while urgently defecating at the back of the forum in Constantinople, his bowels and intestines were evacuated *per anum* and he died on the spot. A few months later Constantine himself died. His successor as Emperor, his son Constantius (317-361), allowed Athanasius to return from Trier to Alexandria as its bishop; but the two were soon to fall out. Like his father, Constantius saw Christian unity as a force that could hold the fragmenting parts of the Roman Empire together, and with this in mind he instructed the Council of Sirmium in 358 to replace the term *homo-ousios* (of one substance) in the Nicene Creed with *homoi-ousios* (of similar substance). This would, Constantius hoped, go some way towards appeasing the Arians (who were convinced that the Father and the Son were *not* of precisely the same substance) without wholly abandoning the Creed's insistence that Jesus was 'God from God, light from light, true God from true God'. He was, so to speak, almost God from God.

It was, of course, a blatant political fudge, and Athanasius would have nothing to do with it, declaring it to be outright heresy. As far as he and his supporters were concerned, the credibility of the entire gospel depended upon the fact that Jesus *was* God. Merely to be 'of similar substance' to God was not enough. Such a reactionary stance, however, was not at all what Constantius expected from the man he had restored to his bishop's seat at Alexandria. Trumped-up charges of financial impropriety were brought against him and Athanasius was forced to flee to Rome. In all, he was in exile for seventeen of his forty-six years as a bishop. Yet Athanasius managed to assemble another council of bishops, this time in Alexandria in 362. It failed to secure the support of many of the leading bishops, but it turned out to be an important staging post on the tortuous road to doctrinal consensus. The bishops who did attend reaffirmed the declaration in the Nicene Creed that the Son was 'of one substance' with the Father (*homo-ousios*), but in order to avert the charge of implicit Sabellianism, they went on to declare that the Father, the Son and the Holy Spirit were three distinct *hypostases* (or manifestations) of the one true God. Within the unity of the Godhead, the bishops declared, there were three different beings, each of which shared *exactly* the same substance as the others but each of which was entirely itself: three in one and one in three. It was an imaginative if contradictory formula that built on the earlier work of Justin Martyr, Athenagoras and Tertullian and it stuck!

By the time Athanasius died in 373 there still remained a certain amount of unfinished business from Nicaea. It was important business, too. The bishops and theologians of the fourth-century Church desperately wanted to find a doctrinal formulation that would reflect their deepest beliefs and feelings about the mysteries of the Trinity. Many ordinary Christians, however, still remained confused about it. In particular, they found it difficult to understand how (as the now-triumphant Nicene Creed asserted) a Father and a Son could be a single substance but two entirely separate and autonomous beings. It certainly offered a paper solution to the intractable problem of how God could have been incarnate in Jesus without experiencing his suffering and death; but what did it mean to say that God was a single substance made up of three separate beings?

The final resolution of the dilemma was the work of three astute theologians towards the end of the fourth century: Basil of Caesarea (*c.* 329-379), his younger brother Gregory of Nyssa (died *c.* 385), and their close friend Gregory of Nazianzus (329-389). They have come to be known collectively as the Cappadocian fathers, since they all came from churches in the Cappadocia region of Asia Minor. Their mission was finally to rid the Christian faith of all taint of Arianism and Sabellianism by establishing a clear and authoritative formulation of the relationship between the Father, the Son (in whom the Word had been incarnate) and the Holy Spirit.

The most important of the three is generally held to be Basil of Caesarea, whose distinctive contribution to the deliberations lay in his clarification of the notion of 'begotten-ness'. Arius had argued that, since the Son was 'begotten' of the Father, he must have been created by God and could not therefore be an equal of him. The Nicene Creed turned this argument on its head by declaring that precisely because he had been begotten, the Son had *not* been created. Was this not just playing around with words though? Were not human children 'begotten' – and was not that just another way of saying that they were 'made' by their parents? Basil clarified the position by explaining that the 'begetting' of divine beings and the 'begetting' of humans were very different things, and the one could not be used as an analogue for the other. Just because a human 'begetting' is always located in time, it does not follow that a divine one must also be time-bound. In the timeless world of God, something could be both begotten and eternal. Basil pointed to the analogy of the sun: the rays of the sun are begotten by the sun itself, yet there was never a time when the sun existed without its rays. So it was with the Father and the Son. Even though the Son was begotten by the Father, there was never a time when the Father existed without the Son.

The work of the Cappadocian fathers came to fruition at the Council of Constantinople in 381 (commonly known as the Second Ecumenical Council), which finally put to rest the tortuous debates about the relationship between the Father, the Son and the Word that had wracked the Christian Church for over three hundred years. By accepting the Trinitarian formula that had been brought to perfection by the Cappadocian fathers, the bishops finally set their collective seal upon the doctrinal standards that were to be adopted throughout Christendom. Henceforth, all who denied the tenets of the Creed would be placing themselves beyond the possibility of salvation. The revised Nicene Creed, agreed by the Council of Constantinople, thus became the gold standard of dogmatic orthodoxy that few dared to challenge until comparatively recent times.

> We believe in one God the Father, the Almighty, maker of heaven and earth, of all that is, seen and unseen. We believe in one Lord, Jesus Christ, the only Son of God, eternally begotten of the Father, God from God, Light from Light, true God from true God, begotten not made, of one Being with the Father. Through him all things were made. For us men and for our salvation he came down from heaven;

by the power of the Holy Spirit he became incarnate from the Virgin Mary, and was made man. For our sake he was crucified under Pontius Pilate; he suffered death and was buried. On the third day he rose again in accordance with the Scriptures. He ascended into heaven and is seated at the right hand of the Father. He will come again in glory to judge the living and the dead, and his kingdom will have no end. We believe in the Holy Spirit, the Lord, the giver of life, who proceeds from the Father. With the Father and the Son he is worshipped and glorified. He has spoken through the Prophets. We believe in one holy, catholic and apostolic Church. We acknowledge one baptism for the forgiveness of sins. We look for the resurrection of the dead, and the life of the world to come.

This revised formulation of the Nicene Creed not only expanded upon the original version of 325, it also tried very hard to expunge any lingering traces of the heresy of Arianism. It emphasised that the Son was not only 'begotten' of the Father but eternally begotten. There never had been a time when the Son did not exist, and because he had existed from the beginning of time, he could not be a lesser version of God himself. He was, quite simply, God. Arianism was dead in the water, and the Word, which had played such a crucial part in the tortuous evolution of the Creed over three centuries, was now redundant and found no place in it.

In the context of the subsequent history of Christianity, the revised Nicene Creed must be judged a success, for it provided a doctrinal standard around which the Church could unite. For a thousand and more years, no serious theologian or churchman in either the Eastern or the Western Churches could publicly doubt that God had been incarnate in Jesus. A quantum leap of development had taken place between the Jewish God of the old covenant and the Christian God of the new. He now had an authentically human face: people could look at Jesus and see not just a man who was filled with the Spirit of God, they could see God himself. At the same time, the heresy of *patripassianism* had finally been routed, for since the Father and the Son were now entirely separate persons, the Father could not possibly have suffered and died on the cross. On top of all of that, the unity of God had been preserved, for the Father and the Son were now of exactly the same substance and could not therefore be distinguished from each other. The same reasoning applied also to the Holy Spirit. It was, in a manner of speaking, a theological version of the three card trick.

The final icing was added to the Trinitarian cake in 451 when five hundred bishops met at Chalcedon, near Constantinople. This time the meeting was directed by the Emperor Marcian (392-457) and his consort Pulcheria (399-453), who had dedicated herself to a lifetime of virginity in honour of the Virgin Mary and was later canonised by the Roman Catholic Church for her devotion to the mother of Jesus. A great deal had happened in the seventy years since the meeting at Constantinople in 381, much of it directed towards clarifying the nature of Jesus' humanity. The Nicene Creed had proclaimed his full and complete *divinity*, but how, in the light of this, was his *humanity* to be understood? How was the Church to explain the coming together of a divine nature and a human nature in the single person of Jesus of Nazareth? It was a disputation every bit as rough and messy as the earlier confrontations; but eventually the bishops were able to issue a revised statement of the faith of the Church. Known as the Formulary of Chalcedon, it was intended to stand not as a new creed but rather as a clarification of certain points in the revised Nicene Creed. It was signed by the Emperor and the bishops on 25 October 451. With little pretence at rationality or logic, the Formulary of Chalcedon simply but solemnly declared the mystery of the incarnation.

> We should confess that our Lord Jesus Christ is one and the same Son; the same perfect in Godhead and the same perfect in manhood, truly God and truly man . . . consubstantial with the Father in Godhead and the same consubstantial with us in manhood; like us in all things except sin.

In plain language, the Formulary declared that Jesus Christ was *simultaneously* one hundred per cent divine and one hundred per cent human – apart, that is, from his lack of the universal human characteristic of sinfulness. Henceforth, the Christian Church was to see Jesus as a single person in whom two entirely separate natures had come together in perfect and seamless coherence. In the broad historical sweep of Christian theology, the Formulary of Chalcedon should perhaps be seen less as a solution than as a politically satisfactory way of squaring a circle that was inherently incapable of being squared. At the end of four hundred years of theological huffing and puffing, black still remained always and only black except when it was always and only white. Jesus did not merely *appear* to be God: he *was* God – wholly and completely. Nor did he merely *appear* to be human: he *was* human – wholly and completely (apart from being sinless). St Augustine of Hippo (354-430) was surely not far wide of the mark when he reportedly said that to deny the dogma of the Trinity was to lose one's hope of salvation but to accept it was to lose one's mind.

The Church now entered a period of relative stability. It had an agreed statement about God that could serve as the doctrinal test for admission to communion with the Church: God was unitary and indivisible, of one substance, yet comprising three entirely separate beings. There was the Father, God Almighty, the maker of heaven and earth; there was Jesus Christ, his only begotten Son, in whom a wholly human nature and a wholly divine nature were perfectly and seamlessly joined; and there was the Holy Spirit, the giver of life, who proceeded from the Father. Beneath the outwardly calm surface of doctrinal unity, however, a number of jagged dogmas were waiting to tear the ecclesiastical craft apart. One of the most important turned out to be the seemingly innocuous reference in the Nicene Creed to the Holy Spirit as 'proceeding from the Father'. By about the middle of the ninth century, Latin versions of the Creed were in use in the Western Church that had added the words 'and the Son'. Known as the *filioque* clause (which means in Latin 'and the son'), the provenance of this addition is unclear; but it was formally written into the Creed, as a sort of first amendment, by a meeting of Spanish bishops at the Council of Toledo in 589.

When word of the amendment reached the ears of the Eastern bishops in Constantinople they demanded its withdrawal. This was partly because they resented the unilateral action of the Western Church in changing a text that had been universally accepted as the Church's authentic teaching about God and partly because they saw it as a denial of the Holy Spirit's equality with the Father and the Son. The Western bishops refused to budge, declaring at the Synod of Aachen in 809 that the removal of the *filioque* clause would be an act of heresy. The issue smouldered on until 1054 when the Patriarch of Constantinople, Michael Cerularius (1000-1059), declared Pope Leo IX (1002-1054) to be a heretic; whereupon the pope's representatives in Constantinople entered the cathedral of Hagia Sophia, placed a writ of excommunication against the patriarch on the high altar, and stalked out. Cerularius retaliated by excommunicating Leo. What had started as a theological controversy between the Eastern and Western Churches (a controversy that was exacerbated by differing views about the authority of the papacy) finally widened into a chasm that has never since been bridged. The Eastern Church became the Eastern Orthodox Church, the Western Church became the Roman Catholic Church, and the two have barely spoken to each other since.

Chapter 9
The God of Selective Grace

Although the schism between the Eastern and Western Churches was not complete until the middle of the eleventh century, the seeds of dissension had been sown centuries earlier by two of the biggest hitters in the early Church whose teachings anticipated the increasingly divergent theological inclinations of Constantinople and Rome.

In the Eastern corner was Origen (185-232), the brilliant but modest young pupil of Clement of Alexandria who is widely considered to have been among the most influential of the early Christian theologians. In 553, three hundred years after he had died, Origen was condemned as a heretic by the Fifth Ecumenical Council at Constantinople; but since he was active well before the Nicene Creed defined the Church's formal position on the person of Jesus, the Council's judgement may seem unduly harsh. Origen accepted the orthodox view of his time that Jesus had been the incarnation of the Word, but he thought it had only been a spiritual incarnation, not a bodily one. Jesus, Origen believed, had actually had two entirely different components: a human body and a divine spirit, and it was only his human body that had suffered and died. His divine spirit, the Word, had remained entirely untouched by the bloodshed and misery of the cross. By denying that Jesus had had a human spirit as well as a human body, Origen's teaching became, so to speak, a retrospective heresy in the light of the Formulary of Chalcedon in 451 because it rejected the full humanity of Christ, body *and* spirit. There were, moreover, several other important elements in Origen's theology that were better suited to the mystical temperament of the East than to the increasingly philosophical bent of the Western Church, and he slipped out of favour with Rome. In the East, however, his star has remained bright, and he has long been regarded by the Orthodox Churches as one of Christianity's founding fathers.

In the Western corner was Augustinus Aurelius (354-430), an African bishop who knew no Greek and was thus obliged to read the Bible and the early Church fathers in rather poor Latin translations. Known now as St Augustine of Hippo, he is one of the giants of early Christian theology, effortlessly looking back to the legacy of the Greek philosophers and forward to the scholasticism of the middle ages and the Protestantism of the Reformation. It would be almost impossible to exaggerate his influence on Western Christianity, both Catholic and Protestant, though in the Eastern tradition he has tended to be seen as sailing disturbingly close to certain controversial rocks of heresy. His birth in 354 came in the middle of the period of tortuous debate about the wording of the Nicene Creed; his death in 430 occurred a mere twenty years before the matter was finally put to rest in the Formulary of Chalcedon. Theologically speaking, Augustine lived and worked in interesting times.

St Augustine of Hippo was born not far from Carthage, the great city of Roman Africa in what is now Tunisia. His parents were respectable citizens of the Roman Empire: his mother Monica (later canonised) was a Christian, and his father Patricius was baptised on his deathbed when Augustine was a teenager. At the age of twenty-eight, restless and ambitious, Augustine left Africa to carve out a career as a rhetorician first in Rome and then in Milan. Although his time in Italy was no more than fitfully productive in academic terms, he indulged himself generously in the pleasures of the flesh, associating freely with young men who boasted of their sexual exploits and who encouraged the inexperienced Augustine to take up with the woman who eventually became the mother of his son, Adeodatus. It was at this stage in his life that he uttered his famous prayer: 'Grant me chastity and continence, but not yet'.

While in Milan, Augustine dabbled with several varieties of the Christian faith and in 386 (according to his autobiographical *Confessions*) he underwent a conversion experience not unlike that of St Paul before him or Martin Luther and John Wesley after him. He later wrote that the experience had transformed him into a wholly different person, forcing him to make a radical break with his past and confront his eternal relationship with God. In the following year he was baptised into the Christian faith by Bishop Ambrose of Milan (339-397), and four years later he was ordained priest. Almost a thousand years later, in 1298, Ambrose and Augustine were declared two of the first four doctors of the Roman Catholic Church, together with Pope Gregory the Great and Jerome.

In 391, at the age of thirty-six, Augustine was persuaded against his better judgement to return to Africa as a presbyter in the coastal city of Hippo. After only five years he was enthroned as its bishop and he spent the rest of his life in that office. He was, however, never entirely at home in a relatively small community that lacked the wealth and culture of Rome or Milan, where he preferred to spend much of his time. Augustine's literary output was prodigious, much of it directed against the prevailing heresies of Manichaeism (a Gnostic sect to which he had belonged in his youth and which contained elements not only of Christianity but Zoroastrianism and Buddhism as well) and Donatism (which held that the effectiveness of the sacraments depended upon the moral character of the priest administering them). Augustine's voluminous writings are, however, full of contradictions and changes of mind. His was a circuitous pilgrimage through the Christian faith, and he later admitted to having written things in his earlier life that were clearly at odds with the views of his mature years.

Augustine's conversion in 386 had a profound effect upon his perception of God. So crushing and irresistible had the experience been that, as he was later to put it, it was not a matter of him choosing God but of God choosing him. He had done nothing to deserve the irruption of divine grace into his life; everything was down to the initiative of God. So overwhelmed was he by the holiness of God, and so miserably aware of his own wretched sinfulness, that it was to colour his entire theological outlook. There was, of course, nothing particularly new in Augustine's awareness of the chasm between the holiness of God and the sinfulness of man. The Old Testament prophets had known it, and so too had St Paul. Augustine's articulation of the gulf between himself and God was, nevertheless, stark and uncompromising. God is God, supreme and perfect; man is man, sinful and depraved; and if there is ever to be any kind of relationship between the two, it can only be at God's bidding and on his terms. To suggest that sinful humans, wanton and degenerate as they are, can ever influence the mind of God is inconceivable, and to imply that God can ever be moved in his judgements by any humanly motivated action, however good or noble it may be, is to reject his absolute sovereignty.

Augustine did not, however, have the field of theological reflection about God entirely to himself, and he was challenged in his views in about 405 when a portly British monk, Pelagius, arrived in Rome. Pelagius (born *c.* 354) was greatly disturbed by the large number of Christians he found in the city who were living indecent, even decadent, lives. Being familiar with Augustine's view that people could do nothing to save themselves, he concluded that the Christians of Rome must be sinning because they believed that God had not yet chosen them for a life of moral rectitude. These Roman Christians, Pelagius thought, were enjoying a hedonistic time while they were waiting to be saved; for if Augustine was right, it was beyond their own unaided capacities to reform their lives. Salvation was the gift of God, not the reward for human effort.

Yet Pelagius was unhappy with this conclusion, for it seemed to strip people of all responsibility for their own actions. Was it not perverse to use the autonomy of God as an excuse for people's bad behaviour? Surely, people should – and could – strive towards honesty and decency under their own steam, regardless of anything that God might or might not do to help them. Surely, those who had apparently been passed over by God should have a second chance of salvation through their own moral actions. Pelagius let rip, tearing into Augustine's view that men and women were so irredeemably mired in wickedness that they could do nothing to extract themselves from the swamp of original sin. God's grace was not the final word on human salvation, nor was it, as Augustine had been teaching, irresistible. People were free to choose whether or not to respond to God's overtures to them, and if they did respond they would be met half-way by grace coming towards them.

Pelagius was here grasping one of the prickliest nettles in the history of the Christian understanding of God. Can people attain salvation *only* because God has, for his own good and unfathomable reasons, chosen to bestow it upon them, or can people work towards their own salvation through the moral quality of the lives they lead? It was a question to which St Paul had failed to find a wholly satisfactory answer and one that was also to set theologian against theologian at the time of the Reformation. Pelagius was clear about his own position: people had been created by God with the freedom to make what they willed of their lives, and they were personally responsible for the things they did and the choices they made. If everything was down to God alone, men and women might just as well reconcile themselves to the inevitability of their inherently sinful natures until such time as he chose to pour his irresistible grace upon them and earmark them for salvation. This, for Pelagius, was to underestimate the moral capacity of people to think and act for themselves.

Augustine responded by accusing Pelagius of three heresies. Firstly, he charged that if Pelagius was right in saying that people could choose whether or not to sin, he was ignoring the ingrained nature of sin in the human personality. He was, in theological language, rejecting the doctrine of original sin, which denied that people could ever lead sinless lives. Adam had seen to that. Secondly, Augustine accused Pelagius of denying the *absolute* necessity of God's grace as a precondition for salvation. If Pelagius was right and people were able to lead good lives without the help of God, then some might be able to achieve salvation without the need for grace at all – and that amounted to an outright denial of God's sovereignty to act in ways entirely of his own choosing. Thirdly, Augustine accused Pelagius of teaching that people could steadily become more holy in their lives through their own human efforts. They could, in a manner of speaking, pull themselves up by their own moral bootstraps; and this could exclude the need for God's grace. Augustine would have none of it, insisting that people could never be good on their own: goodness always involved God, and any goodness there might be in people's lives was always the fruits of his grace. Augustine's charges stuck and Pelagius was branded a heretic by Pope Zosimus in 417.

It was now that Augustine was free to develop his own mature ideas about human sinfulness and the selective grace of God. His greatest work, *The City of God*, completed just before his death in 430, became the basis of the orthodox view of salvation in the Western Church for a very long time. At the heart of his thesis lay two central beliefs: that human beings were indelibly stained with the mark of original sin and that God had absolute power and sovereignty over people's lives. In flat contradiction to Pelagius, Augustine insisted that *everyone* except Jesus had been born corrupted by sin, and *everyone* was deserving of eternal damnation. Salvation was possible only through baptism and the gift of grace. It followed that, however much people may strive to be good, they were unable to refrain from sin. St Paul had understood this all too well when he bewailed his failure to do the good things he wanted to do and the ease with which he could do the things he despised. Only Jesus had been able to turn his back on sin because only Jesus had been the perfect man.

It is here that we get to the heart of Augustine's distinctive brand of divine determinism. If all the good and altruistic things that people manage to do are solely the result of God's gift of grace rather than the fruits of their own endeavours, then it follows that God must hold the salvation of human souls in the palm of his hand. From the entire, seething, sinful mass of humanity God must choose some people to receive grace and salvation, whether they want it or not, and he must withhold it from others, whether they merit it or not. It is not a matter of what people deserve or even what they want but of what God wills. Those who are chosen for salvation cannot refuse and those who are rejected cannot complain, for God is greater than any of them.

The key question, of course, is why God would want to choose some and reject others. It has been a thorny question for all who have espoused a theology of predestination and Augustine was no better able to answer it than anyone else. It is not for us mere mortals, he taught, to enquire into the secret judgements of God. Our calling is simply to accept, in faith, that

God has his reasons – holy reasons that are far above the comprehension of sinful men and women. It was the answer that St Paul had given in his letter to the Romans several centuries earlier when he pointed out it was not for a pot to ask the potter why it had been made in the way it was. It was also, as we shall see, the answer that John Calvin was to give to the people of Geneva several centuries later.

Augustine's God is a sovereign deity more concerned with distributing his grace in ways of his own choosing than with loving and saving everyone. He is a God who moves people like pieces on the chequerboard of salvation, assigning some to paradise and allowing others to fall into perdition. He is, moreover, unaffected by any human acts of moral courage or goodness, for were he to respond to human endeavours of this kind, he would be diminishing his absolute and divine sovereignty. Augustine's God cannot easily be reconciled with the loving and merciful Father of much of Jesus' teaching, and it was partly for this reason that his arguments met with a cautious response from the Church. Pope Zosimus may have seen fit to condemn Pelagius as a heretic in 417, but the Church did not wholeheartedly welcome Augustine's alternative vision of an autonomous God of selective grace. Instead, it tried to find a midway view of salvation that would do justice to both the sovereignty of God's grace and the freewill decisions of men and women. It came to be known as semi-Pelagianism.

A significant leader of the semi-Pelagian faction was John Cassian (*c.* 360-435), a monk of ascetic tastes who lived in southern Gaul, probably near Marseilles. Known as one of the desert fathers, he is remembered in both the Latin and Orthodox Churches for his mystical writings. At first, Cassian taught that although salvation depended ultimately on the grace of God, the process could sometimes be triggered by a human impulse or initiative of goodwill. People could, in other words, take the first steps towards salvation for themselves. In his mercy, God might then decide to respond to and help those who began to help themselves. Cassian later clarified his position, affirming the pre-eminence of divine grace over human free will, but the damage had been done. Augustine's supporters rejected any possibility of human initiative in the process of salvation, arguing that it turned grace into something less than God's unconditional gift. They charged that, in Cassian's hands, grace became something that could be earned or merited. The Church fell into line and Cassian, the ascetic monk who had sought to acknowledge human freedom and responsibility, was condemned posthumously as a heretic at the Council of Orange in 529. In the end, it was Augustine's vision of a selective God of grace that carried the day.

Chapter 10
The God of Medieval Scholasticism

Following the great schism between the Roman Catholic Church and the Eastern Orthodox Churches in 1054, Christian theology in the West entered a new and creative phase of development that has come to be known as medieval scholasticism. Lasting until about 1500, it was a period in which the first western universities were established (among them Bologna, Paris and Oxford) and a method of learning was developed that involved the rigorous reappraisal of received truths and wisdoms from the past. Following the rediscovery of Aristotle's writings in the thirteenth century, with their emphasis on classification and logic, ideas came under the demanding spotlight of reason and argument as never before. Scholasticism flourished in many areas of knowledge, including geometry, rhetoric, law and medicine; it was, however, in philosophy and theology that its methods were most creatively deployed as scholars began to turn their attention not only to the writings of the early church fathers but even to the Bible itself. Commonly known as the 'schoolmen', these early medieval scholars attempted to construct a systematic theology of the Christian faith. As it has sometimes been put, they sought to build cathedrals of the mind that could match the sudden appearance of the great, soaring gothic cathedrals of stone that were springing up across northern Europe.

It is probably true to say that, for all its intellectual brilliance and dazzling theorising, medieval scholastic theology has had a bad press. The arcane nature of some of its questions and the complexity of its conclusions have often been seen as being far removed from the compassionate gospel of Jesus of Nazareth, with its straightforward emphasis on justice, mercy and love. Against this, it has been said, only a sadly obsessive scholar would be seriously interested in knowing how many angels could dance on the end of a needle or how many different definitions of 'reason' could be found against which to calibrate the faith of the Church. Eventually, when scholasticism yielded to the new ideas of the Reformation in the early sixteenth century, the Dutch Christian humanist Desiderius Erasmus (1466-1536) ridiculed the efforts of the schoolmen as sterile, speculative and impractical. It was

an easy target for him, especially when set beside his own uncomplicated
'philosophy of Christ' with its emphasis on the importance of spiritual
reflection and charitable behaviour. Medieval scholasticism, however,
has left a distinctive mark on the evolving portrait of the Christian
God, especially through the ideas of two of its leading early figures,
Anselm and Abelard, and it paved the way for the great upheavals that
were to come with the European Reformation and, a little later, the
Enlightenment.

St Anselm (1033-1109) was born at Aosta in Alpine Italy, and after
quarrelling with his father as a young man he set off on an educational
grand tour of Europe, finishing up at the Benedictine monastery of Bec,
in Normandy. Anselm entered the community as a novice in 1060 and
rose so rapidly through the ranks that when the prior, Lanfranc, moved
to the newly established monastery of St Stephen at Caen in 1066,
Anselm succeeded him. Lanfranc remained at Caen for only a year before
being appointed Archbishop of Canterbury by William the Conqueror
in the wake of the Norman invasion of England. When Lanfranc died
in Canterbury in 1089, Anselm once again found himself following in
his mentor's footsteps, this time to Canterbury – though there was a
four-year gap before he was enthroned as Archbishop in 1093. Once
there, Anselm quickly became embroiled in national politics, battling first
with William Rufus and then with Henry I over issues of ecclesiastical
freedom. He was forced to spend several years in exile in France, a
pattern that was repeated in the career of a later sainted Archbishop of
Canterbury, Thomas Becket. Anselm eventually returned to Canterbury
in 1107, two years before his death in 1109. He was not only a monk
and an archbishop but a statesman and politician as well. He was, too, an
important philosopher and theologian who is now recognised as one of
the outstanding figures in medieval scholasticism.

Anselm took seriously the question, much discussed by the
schoolmen, of whether faith and reason could ever be in harmony with
each other, and he concluded that they could. Both had a part to play in
the Christian life though the order in which they were to be exercised
was critical. Faith had to come first and reason second. If we start to
enquire honestly about God from a position of faith, Anselm argued,
then reason will strengthen our faith by showing our enquiries to be
philosophically sound. As he famously declared in his tract *De Veritate*:
'I do not seek to understand that I may believe, but I believe in order
to understand. For this I also believe, that unless I believe, I shall not
understand.' It became the methodological gold standard of academic

theology for five hundred years before it was turned on its head by the contrary reasoning of the Enlightenment. Whereas the medieval schoolmen were content to believe in order that they might know, the rationalists of the Enlightenment needed to know before they could honestly decide what to believe. Nevertheless, it is worth observing that Anselm's method would not allow an intellectually sloppy belief in God, unexamined in the hard light of reason and logic. Not for him the unthinking recitation of theological platitudes. 'The correct order is to believe the deep things of the Christian faith before undertaking to discuss them by reason. But we are negligent if, having come to a firm faith, we do not then seek to understand what we believe.' It still seems a warning worth heeding.

Two of Anselm's important contributions to the evolving portrait of God in the early middle ages were his 'ontological proof' of God's existence and his 'satisfaction theory' of the crucifixion. The ontological proof (or proofs, for there were two) came to him suddenly during an evening service at the monastery at Bec in 1076 and were set out in two books that he wrote over the next two years: *Monologium* and *Proslogium*. They were never intended to convert those who did not believe in God's existence, but rather to confirm the faith of those who did believe by reassuring them of the philosophical acceptability of their position. Anselm's arguments have intrigued and infuriated philosophers down the ages. They still do – though as we shall see, Immanuel Kant (1724-1804) demonstrated to his own satisfaction in the eighteenth century that the ontological proof was no proof at all and should be dropped from the list of philosophically interesting questions.

In *Monologium*, Anselm argued that unless God existed, there would be no way of judging different degrees of goodness in the world. It could not be said that A was better (or greater or more virtuous) than B unless there existed an absolute standard of goodness or virtuosity against which such a judgement could be calibrated. This absolute standard, Anselm proposed, was God. In arguing in this way, Anselm was not going very much farther than most other philosophers or theologians of his day. God's existence was not a problem for them: it was something they simply took for granted. Much of the early medieval world could only be understood and explained if God was assumed to be real, and that included people's ability to recognise different degrees of goodness. Anselm, however, was all too aware of the deficiencies in this argument, not least that people can make perfectly sensible comparisons between things even when they have no knowledge of absolute values. One bowl of water can be felt to be hotter than another without knowing what a temperature of absolute zero is like. It is only if you want to know how much hotter one bowl is than the other that a baseline is needed. By the same token, murder would be judged by most people to be a far more serious offence than petty theft without needing to invoke God as the measure of absolute morality. God may be useful in making and enforcing moral judgements but he is not essential; and the fact that people can make such judgements is no assurance of his existence.

In *Proslogium*, then, Anselm turned to a different way of proving God's existence. The first step in his long and labyrinthine argument is that people can only deny God's existence if they already have a mental image of what God is like. Anselm regarded it as logically impossible to deny the existence of something that nobody has ever imagined or conceived of. To do so would be nonsensical. To take a trivial example, the existence of unicorns can only be denied if people have at least a rough idea of what a unicorn is like – a sort of horse with a twisted horn projecting from its forehead. Without this pre-existing image, it would be meaningless to say that unicorns do not exist. Likewise, the existence of God can only be denied if people already have an image of what he is like.

The second step in the argument is that, whatever people's image of God may be, it must be greater than anything else that could possibly be imagined. That is what it means to be God. At the start of *Proslogium*, Anselm wrote: 'There must be a being which is better, and greater, and higher than all other existing beings.' Anselm did not actually say what he meant by 'better' or 'greater' or 'higher', but that does not matter very much. For him, God reflected certain qualities (omnipotence, justice, mercy, love, and so on), and to say that God was greater than anything else was simply to say that in God these qualities existed at the highest imaginable level of perfection. The final step in Anselm's argument was that, if people have an image or an understanding in their mind's eye of what God is like, there must be something even greater than the image – for an image can only exist if it has derived from a higher reality. People can only imagine something to be good or terrible or beautiful if behind the image is a reality that gave rise to it in the first place. Therefore, Anselm concluded, there must exist, both in imagination and in reality, something that is greater than anything else that can be imagined. And this is God.

It is not too difficult to see why Anselm's ontological proof has never been the hit with Christian audiences that he might have hoped – even though philosophers have argued over it for centuries. The text of *Proslogium* is hideously complicated to follow, conjuring the existence of God out of a maze of words and assumptions that are themselves highly abstract. What, Christians might want to ask, is the point of such intellectual wizardry unless it leads them to a real experience of God in their lives? To ask this, however, is largely to miss the purpose of the exercise, which was not to make new converts but to assure the faithful of the reasonableness of their belief in God in the light of the rigorous intellectual standards of the day. Faith, for Anselm, always came before reason. His ontological proof had less to do with evangelising the faith than confirming its philosophical reasonableness.

The same could be said of Anselm's second major contribution to the evolving portrait of God in the early middle ages, his 'satisfaction theory' of the crucifixion. The issue here was both simple and profound: in what sense could it be said that the cross had secured the salvation of human souls? How, to put it in theological language, had Jesus' death atoned for human sin? Both St Paul and the author of John's gospel had addressed the same question and had come up with different answers. Paul believed that atonement occurred whenever sinners died with Christ and rose again with him in their spiritual bodies; the author of John's gospel thought it happened when Jesus died on the cross as the sacrificial lamb for the sins of all mankind. Centuries later, Pope Gregory the Great (540-604) enunciated the entirely new doctrine that Jesus' death had been a ransom paid to Satan for releasing mankind from his sinful grasp. It involved the rather gruesome imagery of a fishhook. The cross, Gregory proposed, had been God's fishhook with which to ensnare Satan, and Jesus had been the bait. Satan had fallen for it, taking Jesus' life as the ransom for giving mankind back to God; but in the process he had been caught on the divine fishhook where he has presumably dangled ever since. Meanwhile, God reversed the sacrifice of Jesus by raising him from the dead.

Anselm was unhappy with Gregory's theory: he thought that it denigrated God by placing him in a position where he was obliged to negotiate with Satan, and it insulted Jesus by regarding him as no more than a pawn in a wider strategy of salvation. Whatever view was taken of Jesus, he was plainly more than mere bait on a fishhook. Anselm's alternative explanation of the atonement was set out in another book, *Cur Deus Homo* (*Why God Became Man*), written in the 1090s while he was Archbishop of Canterbury. It was an argument that emphasised the honour and justice of God. Where Gregory had depicted the death of

Jesus as a ransom offered to Satan, Anselm audaciously saw it as a ransom paid to God. God, he argued, was so incomparably just and majestic that humanity was eternally indebted to him for its abject sinfulness; and unless the debt was paid, people would be for ever alienated from him. Yet so deeply was mankind enslaved by sin that it could not possibly pay the debt itself; so God in his infinite mercy had provided a perfect substitute that would, by satisfying his own offended honour, allow him to save humanity from hell. That substitute was Jesus. As Anselm expressed it, the smear of sinful humanity upon the honour of God was so great that, although man alone was responsible for it, God alone was able to redeem it – and he did it through the death on the cross of his only begotten Son. That is why it was absolutely necessary for Jesus to be both divine and free from sin. Only the voluntary death of a perfect human being who was also divine could adequately atone for God's offended honour and reconcile mankind to him.

Anselm's satisfaction theory of the crucifixion held greater appeal than Gregory's earlier doctrine of the ransom paid to the devil; but one of his near contemporaries, Peter Abelard, found serious fault with it. A towering but hugely controversial figure in medieval scholasticism, Abelard (1079-1142) was only a generation younger than Anselm but his outlook was very different. Born near Nantes in Brittany, he is probably known less now for his philosophical writings than for his steamy correspondence with his lover and wife, the beautiful and intelligent Heloise. The story is full of pathos. In 1117 (eight years after Anselm's death) Abelard took lodgings in the Parisian house of Fulbert, a canon of Notre-Dame and the uncle of Heloise. Abelard, now approaching middle age, became the young girl's tutor and then proceeded to abuse his position of seniority over her by first seducing and then impregnating her. At first Heloise refused to marry him, selflessly arguing that, as one of the outstanding philosophers of his day, his work should not be jeopardised by the cares and concerns of marriage and fatherhood; but after their child (named Astrolabe) was born, they secretly became man and wife. Fulbert, possibly thinking that Abelard had cast off his niece after she took herself off to a convent, paid a gang of thugs to break into his lodgings at night and castrate him. Humiliated and full of remorse, Abelard retreated to the monastery of St Denis, at the same time persuading Heloise to become a nun. Then began the passionate correspondence between them that still ranks among the world's greatest testimonies to romantic love. Heloise blossomed into one of the most literate women of her age, living the exemplary and pure life of an abbess.

Abelard was one of the brightest stars in the firmament of medieval scholasticism, but also one of the most insufferable. Hugely intelligent, a brilliant speaker, a gifted poet, an able musician – he had it all. Possibly the greatest logician of the middle ages, he passionately advocated the application of reason to the study of religious faith, and he developed new doctrines that were remarkable both for their subtlety and their challenge to orthodoxy. Abelard's quick wit, sharp tongue, perfect memory and boundless self-confidence made him unbeatable in debate, and the force of his personality impressed itself vividly on all who met him. There were, though, many who found his self-assurance verging onto arrogance and his intellectual brilliance overbearing. He had enemies as well as admirers.

Like Anselm before him, Abelard saw it as important to demonstrate the seamless consistency between Christian revelation and philosophical reason. His method came straight from the textbook of medieval scholasticism: in *Sic et Non* (*Thus and Not*), published in 1120, he set out 159 propositions from classical Christian theology and proceeded to examine each one critically in the light of reason and logic. He took nothing for granted. An enlightened thinker before the Enlightenment, Abelard observed that it was by doubting that he came to examine and by examining that he came to the truth. These words could not have been voiced by Anselm a generation earlier, but they might well have been uttered by René Descartes five hundred years later.

One of Abelard's doubts settled upon Anselm's satisfaction theory of the crucifixion. It failed to convince him, for although it had a great deal to say about God, it had almost nothing to say about man. The theory stressed the besmirching of God's honour through the sinful behaviour of mankind, but it failed to consider the position of the sinner. Abelard was sure that the redemptive power of the cross was greatest when it was directed towards humanity, not towards God. The crucifixion was not a matter of satisfying God's wrath but of using the selfless death of Jesus to lift mankind to a higher moral plane. God already loves us, Abelard said, and he shows his love by identifying himself with the sufferings of humanity; he does not need to go to tortuous lengths to bring us within the ambit of his love, for we are already there. The tragedy is that we do not always realise this and continue to live in fear of God. Instead of reveling in his love, we fear his wrath and this, Abelard taught, diminishes our potentiality as human beings. The cross can overcome this fear by inspiring us to appreciate God's love and to love him in return. 'The purpose of the crucifixion', Abelard wrote in his *Commentary on the Epistle to the Romans*, 'was to pour charity into our hearts. In this manner a new motive is infused into our actions which accordingly becomes meritorious.' It is a theory of the crucifixion that has come to be known as the 'moral influence' theory.

Abelard's analysis of the crucifixion has a surprisingly modern ring about it, for it is essentially a psychological explanation. The cross 'works' not because it brought about an objective and everlasting change in the relationship between God and man but because of its symbolic force in inspiring people in each new generation to lead better and more loving lives. The cross, for Abelard, was a symbol – and like all symbols, its power is wholly dependent upon the effect it has upon the mind and the will of those who look upon it. At best, the Christian who views the cross in reverence and humility can draw from it the encouragement to persevere in the life of faith, knowing that God already loves him and is imploring him to return that love. Take away such reverence and humility and all that is left is the cruel execution of a religious trouble-maker. It was an argument that had echoes of the earlier Pelagian belief in the capacity of people to pull themselves up by their own moral bootstraps, looking to God for encouragement but not expecting a life-changing infusion of grace. Unsurprisingly, Abelard's ideas were not well received in high ecclesiastical places, and the Church threatened on several occasions to subject him to its disciplines, but no serious charges against him were ever upheld and he died, at peace with the Church, at Chalôn-sur-Saône in 1142. In 1817 his remains and those of Heloise were transferred to the cemetery of Père la Chaise, in Paris, where they now rest side by side.

Medieval scholasticism unveiled a new face of God, reflective of the intellectual concerns of a serious-minded group of European scholars rediscovering the philosophical problems and methods of ancient Greece. It is quite a surprise to follow the twisting path of Anselm's ontological proof and realise that he was writing about the same God as the God of Abraham, the God of Psalms or the God revealed in Jesus. Philosophical rigour had become the order of the day, and if theology was to lay claim to being the queen of sciences in the new universities of France, Italy and England, it had to prove its credentials in the cockpit of scholarly debate. Not for the first time, ordinary Christians must have been left wondering why reason and logic had anything to do with the revelation of God's truth – just as, almost a thousand years earlier, Tertullian of Carthage had been left wondering why Athens had anything to do with Jerusalem. What use is a God who *must* exist in order to satisfy an abstruse philosophical argument like the ontological proof?

For all their intellectual brilliance, however, Anselm and Abelard and the other schoolmen of the time were never indulging in mental gymnastics for their own sake. Their purpose in seeking to establish a philosophical coherence to the Christian faith was never an end in itself, nor was it intended to supplant faith as the motive force of Christian living. Even in this first flush of Western rationalism, the subjective experience of God must have remained paramount for ordinary Christians; and if that experience was lacking, then no amount of verbal wizardry could conjure it up. Many people must have been more willing to trust their own intuitions about God than Anselm's idea of him as a philosophical necessity. Anselm and Abelard, we feel, would have understood and approved of this. For them, the salvation of Christian souls remained the most important task of the Church, and they were merely furnishing evidence of its seriousness by confirming the existence of God and explaining the mechanisms of atonement.

Nevertheless, medieval scholasticism began to identify a tension between the hearts and the minds of the faithful that has remained a central feature of religious experience ever since. No longer would it be possible for the faith of thinking Christians to be grounded exclusively upon sentiment and emotion. No longer could the Church ignore its responsibility for justifying its teachings in intellectually coherent ways. No longer could the reality of God be commended solely on the warm and glowing feelings that he kindled in the heart, whatever might or might not be happening in the head. An unthinking faith was a faith built on sand. Belief in God, as Anselm stressed, is the bedrock of faith, but if such belief is not supported by intellectual conviction, it is shallow and unstable. Medieval scholasticism became, therefore, an important staging post in the development of Christian theology, paving the way for the intensification of the contrast between heart and mind in the wake of the Reformation and the Enlightenment.

Chapter 11
The God of Reason and Revelation

A hundred years after Anselm and Abelard exited the stage of medieval scholasticism, Thomas Aquinas (1225-1274) entered it. Arguably the most influential theologian in Western Europe between Augustine and Luther, Aquinas was born into an aristocratic Italian family in Roccasecca, Italy, and joined the Dominican order while studying philosophy and theology at Naples. Later, while continuing his studies in Paris and Cologne, he started to immerse himself in the recently discovered writings of Aristotle, beginning what was to become a life-long project of reconciling Christianity with Aristotelian philosophy. Aquinas' output of philosophical and theological writing was prodigious: his great work *Summa Theologica*, written between 1265 and 1273, contained a lifetime of thought and experience of God; but he abruptly stopped writing it a year before his death because, as he put it, 'all that I have written seems like straw to me'. That is not, however, how his work has been viewed by the Roman Catholic Church: Aquinas was canonised in 1323 and proclaimed the ninth Doctor of the Church (with the honorific title *Doctor Angelicus*) in 1567. His mature writings were formally recognised in 1879 when Pope Leo XIII (1810-1903), a long-time fan of Aquinas, incorporated them into the official theology of the Catholic Church in the papal encyclical *Aeterni Patris*.

There are some obvious affinities between Aquinas in the thirteenth century and Anselm in the eleventh. Both were committed to the aims and methods of scholasticism and both were inquisitive about the relationship between faith and reason. Neither saw any necessary conflict between the two. Whereas Anselm held faith to be a necessary prelude to understanding God, however, Aquinas was content to keep faith and understanding in separate compartments. For Anselm, faith in God was the *only* way of understanding his divine and perfect nature. 'The correct order', he wrote, 'is to believe the deep things of the Christian faith before undertaking to discuss them by reason.' Aquinas, by contrast, thought it perfectly possible to discover something about the nature and attributes of God without necessarily having any faith in him at all.

Aquinas posited two different realms of human perception: a natural realm and a supernatural realm. They corresponded roughly to what the 1879 papal encyclical *Aeterni Patris* described as the 'separate domains' of philosophy and revelation. At the natural level, it was entirely possible for people to reflect on the person of God and the destiny of the human soul without any divine inspiration at all. They could do it, so to speak, by remaining in their armchairs by the fireside, reading and thinking. After all, the philosophers of ancient Greece had been well able to arrive at an understanding of God simply by following the pathways of reason and logic. They had had no need of grace or revelation to reach their conclusions. Yet there remained, for Aquinas, grave dangers in failing to progress from the natural to the supernatural realm, for salvation was possible only for those who committed themselves to the higher level of faith. It was one thing to know about God as a philosophical idea; it was an entirely different matter to accept and respond to him in one's life. Only if people were willing to make the transition from understanding to faith – from philosophy to revelation, as *Aeterni Patris* put it – could they be saved. That required them to respond to the direct revelation of God through the actions of the Holy Spirit and the teachings of the Church.

The natural and the supernatural realms in Aquinas' scheme of things are distinguished by the words that characterise them. To the natural realm belong such properties as reason, logic, common understanding, philosophical wisdom and the natural order of things. In the supernatural realm are incarnation, grace, revelation, faith and salvation. The two realms correspond roughly to the distinction that was later to be made between beliefs *about* God and belief *in* God. How is it possible, however, to believe certain things *about* God without taking the further step of believing *in* him? How can an intelligent person discover the existence and perhaps even something of the nature of God by relying solely upon reason and logic? It was here that Aquinas achieved lasting renown in his famous 'five ways' (*quinque viae*) of proving God's existence without invoking the necessity of prior faith.

Aquinas' five ways are formally described as a cosmological argument: that is, an argument based upon people's experience of the world or cosmos around them. In its focus, it differed somewhat from Anselm's ontological proof, for whereas Anselm had argued that it was logically *impossible* to deny the existence of God, Aquinas merely tried to establish that it was *unreasonable* to do so. All the evidence that people needed to satisfy themselves of God's existence was, he argued, contained within the familiar experiences of everyday life. As it happens, Aquinas was not the first to appreciate the power of the cosmological argument in one or other of its several forms, nor was he the last. Before him Plato and Aristotle had also invoked its merits, and after him René Descartes (1596-1650), Benedict de Spinoza (1632-1677) and John Locke (1632-1704) were each to revisit it. The twentieth-century anthropic principle, that the multitude of systems needed to support life on earth are so finely tuned and inter-connected that they could only have come about through a deliberate act of creation, can also be seen as a modern version of the cosmological argument.

The five limbs of Aquinas' formulation of the cosmological argument are similar in structure, each showing a different aspect of God's nature revealed in the cosmos. The first two, which are commonly grouped together, can be taken as templates for the others. They are known as the argument from motion and the argument from cause. Aquinas' starting point was the assumption that everything in the world was either moving or resting. If an object was moving, then its motion must have been caused by something else, for nothing can move itself. The cause of this movement, whatever it might have been, must itself be in motion, for otherwise it could not impart motion to any other object. Something must therefore have caused it, too, to start moving in the first place. And that thing's motion must in turn have been caused by something else; and so the chain of causation goes on, rather like a tumbling wall of dominoes after the first one has been pushed over. Eventually, however, there must be an end to the chain of cause and effect: something must have caused the original domino to fall in the first place. Something must exist that is the cause of all movement in the world – something that has not itself been moved by anything else. If it has been moved by something else, then we would not have gone far enough back along the chain. This point of origin, Aquinas declared, is God. He is the 'unmoved mover' – the cause of all movement without himself being moved by anything else. He is (to pursue the admittedly crude analogy of the dominoes) the Great Domino that, entirely by itself, sets all the others in the wall tumbling to the ground. The Great Domino must therefore, by definition, be greater than any other domino in the cosmos, for it alone has the power to start the cascade.

The remaining limbs of Aquinas' argument are similar in structure, seeking through the same kind of reasoning to explain the existence of goodness and beauty in the world and the purpose of life. The fifth limb, the argument from design, may well have seemed much more fanciful in Aquinas' day than it does to us today, familiar as we are with the theory of the 'big bang' that brought the universe into being some thirteen billion years ago. Aquinas assumed that everything in the world has the potential *not* to exist. At one time, therefore, there must have been a state in which nothing existed at all. Because all sorts of things self-evidently *do* exist in the world, something must have conceived of them in the first place and then caused them to come into being – and this 'something' must itself have existed from the very beginning, for otherwise it could not have brought about the existence of everything else. This, Aquinas declared, is God – the one who himself existed before all things and without whom nothing would now exist. In modern parlance, he is the one who lit the blue touch-paper that started the 'big bang'.

Aquinas' cosmological argument is, like so much of medieval scholasticism, a product of its time; but viewed through modern eyes, fault can fairly easily be found with it. Two obvious objections have commonly been raised. Firstly, the argument is logically unsustainable because it contradicts itself. If, as Aquinas assumed, the movement of everything in the world is caused by something else, then by definition there cannot be an 'unmoved mover' or an 'uncaused causer'. Alternatively, if there really is an 'unmoved mover', then by definition it cannot be true that all movement is caused by something else. A lot of the wind can be taken out of Aquinas' sails simply by asking the traditional schoolboy question: what caused God to come into existence? A God who created the unimaginably vast spaces of the universe could only have come into being through the creative actions of something even more powerful than himself. Who or what was that? If it is retorted that God is so supreme that he is the one thing in the universe that does not need to have had a cause, then the cosmological argument ceases to be a proof and becomes merely an assertion that cannot be tested.

Secondly, even if there had been an original mover, and even if this original mover is what we understand by God, it does not follow that he must still exist. There is no *necessary* reason why, having set the planets spinning on their orbits in the first place, God should have stayed to watch their progress. He could have packed up and left, perhaps to repeat his great act of creation in a parallel universe elsewhere. Even if the original mover does still exist, there is no necessary reason why he should be the biblical God of the Judaeo-Christian tradition any more than he should be the God of the Muslims, the Sikhs, the Buddhists or the Hindus (for they also believe in a divine creator).

In spite of these well-known critiques of Aquinas' cosmological argument, it did at least establish the possibility of asking intelligent questions about God without actually having a belief in him as a saviour.

The cosmological argument takes place at the level of the natural realm and it uses the secular tools of reason, logic and the properties of the physical world (to the extent that they were known in the thirteenth century). Moreover, if Aquinas' reasoning is accepted, it allows people to reflect not only upon the possible *existence* of God but also his *nature*. The God of the cosmological argument must be the closest thing that the human imagination can come to absolute existence, for he does not need anyone or anything to bring him into being or cause him to act. God simply *is* – and that is just about all that can be said of him. Surprisingly, God then becomes a being with only one essential function: to be the origin of all that exists and all that moves in the world. The only essential task that falls to the Great Domino is to knock down the first domino in the wall. After that, the process acquires its own momentum; and even if the Great Domino chooses to stay and watch the spectacle, there is nothing further for it to do. It is here, of course, that the analogy of the dominoes breaks down, for the Christian narrative would assert that it is only the continuing involvement of the Great Domino that prevents the ordered cascade of all the other dominoes from collapsing into chaos.

All of this may seem a tortuous and esoteric route to God, far removed from the vengeful God of the early Old Testament and the loving God of the New. Can the 'unmoved mover' of Aquinas' cosmological argument really be the God of Abraham, Isaac and Jacob? Can he really be the God who led the Israelites out of captivity in Egypt and gave them a land flowing with milk and honey? Is he really the God who was uniquely revealed in Jesus' life of sacrifice and service? Aquinas must have been aware of such questions, for he never claimed that people could enter into the mystery of God or experience the fullness of his grace by remaining exclusively in the natural realm. If men and women wanted to know the God who had revealed himself in human history, they had to journey from the natural realm of logic and reason to the divine realm of revelation and salvation. And this, Aquinas believed, involved grace, faith and imagination. Salvation may begin in the natural realm as people start to ask questions about the world around them, but if it is to come to fruition, it must always end in the supernatural realm.

Thomas Aquinas died in Paris in 1274, a few decades before the period in Western Europe that is known as the Renaissance, or rebirth, of classical ideas in art, literature and learning. It included some of the most influential figures in Western civilisation. Aquinas still had another ten years to live when Dante Alighieri (1265-1321) was born in Florence, the Tuscan epicentre of the early Renaissance. Dante's epic poem *The*

Divine Comedy, completed shortly before his death, tells of the imaginary journey that he made to hell, purgatory and paradise in the company of Virgil and Beatrice. Drawing on rich sources of literature, history, mythology and theology, Dante laid out a panorama of the human soul that has profoundly shaped Western images of judgement, salvation and the after-life.

An exact contemporary of Dante was the Florentine painter and architect Giotto di Bondone (1267-1337), who did for the visual arts what Dante did for the written word. The two may well have known each other, and Giotto may even have painted Dante's portrait. Giotto is important in the development of Western art for breaking with the flat, stylised pictures of pre-Renaissance art and creating solid figures located in real space and displaying real human emotions. His religious paintings must have had a profoundly humanising effect on those who saw them, contrasting dramatically with Aquinas' almost abstract world of intellectual gymnastics. The exchange of looks between Jesus and Judas in Giotto's fresco of the betrayal in Gethsemane, in the Arena Chapel in Padua, could hardly be farther removed in impact and emotion from the metaphysical God of the schoolmen. Here is human drama at its most intense, played out on a cosmic stage. However confusing it may be to trace the path of Anselm's or Aquinas' reasoning, there can be no mistaking the universal look of guilty opportunism in Judas' eye. In profound contrast to the scholasticism of the medieval world, Giotto's work reveals a direct, visceral and deeply religious understanding of human nature.

As it unfolded in the fourteenth and fifteenth centuries, the Renaissance became a glorious celebration of the power and creativity of the human spirit. It was, however, not the kind of secular humanism that later characterised the Enlightenment of the eighteenth century. People still believed in God as a matter of course and they accepted the teachings of the Catholic Church as a matter of obedience; but they also needed a God who could rejoice in the artistic genius of supremely gifted men. Augustine had offered a darkly pessimistic view of humanity, mired in sin and incapable of raising itself above the swamps of degradation into which Adam had plunged it. That is not, however, how it must have seemed to the citizens of late fifteenth-century Florence, Rome or Venice as they feasted their eyes on the dazzling achievements of the human imagination in their streets, churches and cathedrals. When Leonardo da Vinci, Botticelli, Michelangelo, Raphael, Alberti, Bramante, Brunellesco, Donatello and Piero della Francesca burst upon the cultural scene with artistic and architectural skills unsurpassed since the high points of the Greek and

Roman civilisations, there must have seemed no limits to the capacities of the human mind and spirit. It was all done to the glory of God, of course, but nobody pretended that it was done by God. Man had now become God's partner in creation: a reasonable, rational and above all *human* being. Nobody exemplified the new spirit of Christian humanism more eloquently than Erasmus of Rotterdam.

Desiderius Erasmus (*c.* 1466-1536) is one of the great luminaries of European learning. Dutch, Catholic and a free-thinker, he laid the intellectual foundations for what has come to be known as liberal theology – a way of thinking about God that owes more to reason and common sense than to either the dogmas of the Church or the mind-games of the medieval schoolmen. Erasmus was not against God as such, merely the distorted images of him that were commonplace on the eve of the Reformation. Whereas Anselm had declared four hundred years earlier that he needed to believe before he could understand, Erasmus instinctively reversed the order. He may not explicitly have said that he understood in order to believe, but he could well have done. By refusing to be shackled or awed by ecclesiastical authority or ancient doctrines, he was a hugely important bridge between the old world of the medieval mind-set and the new world of enlightenment and reform. As historians are wont to point out, Erasmus laid the egg that Luther hatched.

Erasmus was born in Rotterdam, the second illegitimate son of Roger Gerard, a priest, and Margaret, a physician's daughter. He was educated at a school run by the Brethren of the Common Life that fostered a monastic vocation among its pupils. In 1485 he entered an Augustinian monastery near Gouda where he castigated his superiors as 'barbarians' for discouraging him from studying the classics. In 1492 he was ordained a priest and happily escaped the suffocating confines of the monastery by accepting the post of secretary to the Bishop of Cambrai, a wealthy city in northern France and one of the great European centres of church music. Erasmus later studied theology at Paris but soon became a wandering scholar of Europe, observing the patterns of religious and social life, reading the Bible, studying the early church fathers, and developing a style of discourse closer to the classical art of rhetoric than to the logic of scholasticism. In 1505 he arrived in England, where he met and became much influenced by his immediate contemporaries Sir Thomas More (1478-1535) and John Colet (1467-1519). Erasmus wrote one his more famous works, *In Praise of Folly*, while staying in More's house in London. His tours of the English cathedrals in the company of Colet, especially a visit paid to Canterbury Cathedral in *c.* 1512, disgusted him with their repulsive displays of relics, icons and other symbols of what he saw as little more than superstitious veneration. The Catholic Church, he believed, had become no better than a secular power, devoid of moral or spiritual authority and interested mainly in protecting its own ecclesiastical interests.

In contrast to the gaudy rituals and venal trappings of eve-of-Reformation Catholicism, Erasmus placed the simple teachings of Jesus of Nazareth at the centre of a reasonable faith. In his *Handbook of a Christian Knight*, published in England by William Tyndale in 1503, he urged his readers to 'inject into their vitals' the moral and spiritual teachings of Jesus, believing them to be as close as people could get to the true nature of God. He even hoped that his uncomplicated 'philosophy of Christ', offering a humane and reasonable guide to righteous living, might unify Christendom through its restrained approach to contentious dogma and ostentatious rituals. Prayer and learning were, for Erasmus, the only proper tools for discerning the moral pathways to salvation, and he peremptorily dismissed as folly many of the other tools and techniques favoured by the Catholic Church, including pilgrimages, the worship of relics, prayers for the souls of those in purgatory, and self-promoting acts of charity and penance. These were for him the marks of a blind obedience to an authoritarian Church. Instead, Erasmus wanted people to think for themselves and come to their own conclusions. As he once put it, every milkmaid and peasant should read the Bible. Unsurprisingly, Erasmus was repeatedly denounced by orthodox Catholic theologians.

Erasmus distanced himself from both Augustine and his near contemporary Martin Luther in the great debate about faith or works as the royal road to salvation. Augustine, following St Paul and needing to react against the heresy of Pelagianism, had allowed no scope for any human input to the process of salvation, regarding it as the unmerited gift of a gracious God who had the sovereign freedom to decide whom he would save and whom he would not. Erasmus, by contrast, saw this as inflexible and unreasonable, arguing (as Pelagius had done almost twelve hundred years earlier) that because people had been created with free will, it was wrong to absolve them from responsibility for their own actions. It was not good enough to load all the blame and all the responsibility onto God. God took the initiative in offering his grace, certainly, but people were free to choose for themselves whether to accept or reject it; and if they opted for rejection, God did not force himself upon them. Erasmus called it 'co-operative grace' in which God weighed the measure of faith in everyone and worked with it, however great or small it was. As we shall see, this brought him into sharp conflict with Martin Luther, who by now was pursuing an uncompromisingly Augustinian path. For Luther, humans were mere horses ridden by either God or Satan, with God deciding the jockey's colours. It was too bad if people wanted to change their rider, for there was nothing they could do about it. Erasmus protested. 'Let us agree', he wrote to Luther in his polemical work *De Libero Arbitrio*, 'that we are justified by faith provided we admit that the works of charity are necessary for salvation'.

Desiderius Erasmus died in Basel in 1536. It is said that he abjured the last sacraments and that his dying words (in Dutch) were 'Lieve Got' – dear God. It could be said that Erasmus' God sits more lightly with humanity than the God of medieval scholasticism. He has no need to be discovered through philosophical proofs and theorems, for he has revealed all that people need to know about him in the teaching of Jesus. Nor has he any need to be heavy-handed or authoritarian, for he is a God of invitation, not of imposition. Through the eyes of Erasmus we see the face of a God who loves people, wants their moral good, and desires to save them. It is not the face of a God who demands elaborate ecclesiastical ceremonials and rituals presided over by men who claim an exclusive and esoteric authority to do so. Indeed, Erasmus once castigated the priesthood as fleas in God's overcoat. Erasmus' God is a God of reason and moderation, several degrees removed from extremes of doctrine and from what he called the 'insane quarrels' of warring clerics. Had he lived long enough, Erasmus might have looked with smiling approval upon the *via media* carved out by Queen Elizabeth I for the English Church in the late sixteenth century, but that still lay some way into the future. Europe had yet to be torn apart by the Reformation.

Chapter 12
The God of the Reformers

By about 1500 an elaborate understanding had grown up in Western Christendom of the divine order of things. It was a hierarchical picture, both topographically and organisationally. The earth and its inhabitants, which God had created in six days, lay at the centre of the cosmos with the heavenly bodies revolving around it. Of that there could be no doubt: Psalm 93 attested that 'the earth is established immovably' and the author of Ecclesiastes had declared majestically that 'the sun rises and the sun goes down; then it speeds to its place and rises there again'. Common sense as well as biblical authority confirmed the truth of this earth-centred view of the cosmos. People could see for themselves that the sun rose each day in the east, travelled south across the sky, and set in the west. To believe that the earth was circling the sun would have been to deny the evidence of their own eyes as well as to question the authority of the Bible and the teaching of the Church.

Above the earth were the heavens. Heaven was a real place beyond the clouds where the sky was the deepest blue by day and the stars shone like jewels at night. It was the dwelling place of God and his hosts. In the late medieval worldview, beings could move up and down between heaven and earth. The Old Testament story of Jacob's dream at Bethel, in which he saw the angels of God ascending and descending a stairway stretched from earth to heaven, was a tangible expression of the traffic that took place between the two. The New Testament likewise bore witness to journeys made between heaven and earth. The angel Gabriel descended from heaven to earth to announce the conception of Jesus to Mary, and at the end of his earthly life Jesus was bodily 'lifted up' from the top of the Mount of Olives before disappearing from the disciples' view, engulfed in cloud on his way to heaven. The culmination of St Paul's empyrean drama of human salvation would come when the trumpet sounded and the faithful, living and dead, would all rise up to meet Christ in the clouds.

Somewhere beneath the surface of the earth was hell. It was a fiery place of torment and punishment, known not only to Christianity but to other faiths as well. Hell, like heaven, was not an earthly place, for the earth was plainly not on fire; nor was hell merely a metaphor to indicate a state of spiritual separation from God. Hell was a real place of great pain and desolation, but whereas heaven was above the plane of mortal life, hell was below it. Souls ascended into heaven but they descended into hell. Even Jesus, according to the First Letter of Peter, had descended into hell in the three days between his crucifixion and his resurrection. Wisely, the early Church fathers declined to specify its precise location. St John Chrysostom (347-407) observed that 'we must not ask where hell is, but how we are to escape it'; and St Augustine of Hippo (354-430) taught that 'the nature of hell-fire and the location of hell are known to no man unless the Holy Ghost made it known to him by a special revelation'. St Gregory the Great – who was Pope between 590 and 604 and who sent the other St Augustine on his epoch-making mission to Canterbury in 597 – wrote: 'I do not dare to decide this question. Some think hell is somewhere inside the earth; others believe it is under the earth.' There was no doubting whether hell existed, merely where it was.

The hope of heaven and the fear of hell were huge preoccupations for people in late medieval times. The possibility of imminent death through infection or accident was an ever-present reality, and since Christ might return at any moment to separate the righteous from the wicked and send them on their respective ways, the transition from this life to the next was a matter of deep and daily practical concern. Divine judgement could come, as Paul had warned the early Christians at Corinth, in the twinkling of an eye. It was a favoured theme of painters and sculptors until at least the end of the seventeenth century, offering abundant scope for their most vivid fantasies and imaginings. European cathedrals, churches and art galleries are replete with examples. The sumptuously carved West front of Orvieto Cathedral in Umbria and Michelangelo's painting of the last judgement in the Sistine Chapel in Rome are but two of the many sensational artistic representations of what the day of reckoning might bring for Christian souls, one way or the other.

Nobody could be certain what heaven and hell might look like, but the artists of the Renaissance seem to have worked within a common set of conventions. At the centre of their representations of the final judgement was Jesus Christ, the Son of God, seated in majesty on his throne and flanked by his disciples. Above and around the seated Christ was heaven, a paradisiacal place of beauty, tranquillity and order where angels sang, clouds rolled gently by and winged and naked *putti* played their trumpets.

The great company of those who had already arrived in paradise were sometimes massed in the background ready to greet the newcomers, some of whom were depicted as naked bodies emerging from their tombs in readiness for their journey to heaven. Below the seated Christ was hell, a place of great terror, chaos and fire where diabolical beasts with fearsome jaws were waiting to seize the damned and drag them screaming into the roaring inferno. Sometimes the journey to hell took people across the River Styx: in Michelangelo's terrifying depiction of the last judgement in the Sistine Chapel a group of miserable and naked sinners are being ferried across the river by the vicious-looking Charon before being dumped unceremoniously on the other side, there to await their unimaginably awful fate.

A few impeccably virtuous souls might go directly to heaven, and religious art in the late medieval period contains some notable examples of the apotheosis of such saints as they are carried bodily upwards to heaven. Others might go directly to hell. Most, however, were assigned to purgatory, where the souls of those who had died in a state of grace could be made ready for heaven. Even those whose lives on earth had been models of Christian rectitude might expect to spend time in purgatory, for none could be entirely free of moral blemish. Unwelcome though the prospect of purgatory might be, it did at least offer the hope of final salvation in the fullness of time, and there was much that people could do to help themselves before the arms of death embraced them. They could participate in the sacraments, go on pilgrimages, give alms to the poor, and carry out works of charity. They could enlist the help of saints, martyrs and, most notably, the Virgin Mary herself to intercede with God on their behalf. They could venerate relics, buy indulgences, and engage in other exercises of penance for their sins. Even after death, all was not lost for those whose souls were waiting in purgatory. Wealthy people could leave money in their wills for chantry chapels to be built in churches or cathedrals where private priests were hired to say daily prayers for their souls. If this was too expensive, the relatives and friends of the dead could offer up prayers for their loved ones to shorten their time in purgatory. It was also prudent to make gifts of money to churches, convents and charities.

At the apex of the whole schema was God the Father – the 'unmoved mover' of St Thomas Aquinas' theology who had brought everything into existence and who reigned in glory in heaven with the Son and the Holy Ghost. Beneath God in the heavenly hierarchy were the hosts of heaven: seraphim, cherubim, thrones, dominions, virtues, powers, principalities, archangels and angels. Each had specific functions to perform. The elaborate hierarchy of heaven was mirrored on earth, with kings (anointed by God) at the apex of the pyramid of secular power followed by princes, lords, governors, priests and all the other offices of medieval feudal society. Command and patronage flowed down, obedience and taxes flowed up. At the very bottom of the pile were the peasants who had nobody to command and nothing to patronise except the dog.

Superintending the whole system in Western Christendom was the Roman Catholic Church. For over a thousand years until Martin Luther (1483-1546) nailed his ninety-five theses to the great door of Wittenberg Cathedral in 1517, Catholicism had exerted a cultural stranglehold not only over theology and doctrine but also over the fate of souls. By 1500 the Church had become an elaborate and often fearsome vehicle for the proclamation of truth and the suppression of dissent. God may have been at the apex of the entire structure, but his voice on earth was the papacy; and the full weight and majesty of papal judgement fell on all who were foolish enough to challenge that voice. Never far away was the Inquisition, the tribunal established by the Vatican to root out heresy and disobedience in all its manifestations. As we shall see, even scientists of the stature of Copernicus and Galileo, who revolutionised our understanding of the universe by showing the sun to be at the centre of the solar system, incurred the wrath of the Church for daring to challenge its teachings. As for ordinary folk, their lives were a perpetual struggle to avoid consignment to the flames of hell.

This, broadly, was the religious and ecclesiastical context in which Desiderius Erasmus came to a fundamentally different vision of God: not as an absolute monarch who demanded impossible standards of behaviour and who communicated through an authoritarian ecclesiastical structure but as the source and encouragement of a wise and reasonable way of living based upon the moral teachings of Jesus. Erasmus has been described variously as the intellectual father of Protestantism, the midwife of the Reformation, and the provider of the egg that Luther hatched. Whatever the metaphor, he laid the intellectual and moral foundations on which the European reformers were soon to build. Such was Erasmus' instinctive non-conformity, however, that he never actively collaborated with any of them; and his relationship with Luther, which at first was close, deteriorated as Luther began to put clear water between himself and his erstwhile mentor. Luther wrote in 1525 that his liking for Erasmus declined from day to day, complaining that he (Erasmus) valued human free will more highly than the grace of God. 'The times are now dangerous', Luther observed in his tract *De Servo Arbitrio* with Erasmus plainly in his sights, 'and I see that a man is not a more sincere or a wiser Christian for all that he is a good Greek or Hebrew scholar'. It was a defining moment. The baton of protest and reform had, for the time being, passed from the Low Countries to the northern regions of Germany where it was to erupt into a movement that changed the face of Western Christianity forever.

Martin Luther was born at Eisleben in Saxony in 1483. He entered the University of Erfurt in Thuringia to train as a lawyer, and one day in the summer of 1505, while walking home from his studies, he was caught in a terrible storm. In fear of his life, he cried out to his patron saint: 'Help me! I shall become a monk!' Soon afterwards Luther sold his law books and entered the Augustinian monastery in Erfurt where, in spite of the spirituality surrounding him, he developed an almost neurotic anxiety about the state of his soul. If, as the thrust of Catholic doctrine had taught him, he had to secure his own salvation by good works, self-denial, prayer and pious exercises, how could he ever be sure that he was trying hard enough? How could he know that he was pleasing a God of infinitely demanding expectations? Luther yearned for a gracious God but found only one who demanded an impossible schedule of spiritual exercises and good works. Depression set in which turned quickly into a melancholic despair of ever being able to please God. Michael Mullett, in his biography of Luther, quotes him as saying that: 'Although I lived a blameless life as a monk, I felt that I was a sinner with an uneasy conscience before God. I could not believe that I had pleased him with my works. Far from loving that righteous God who punished sinners, I actually hated him.'

In 1511 Luther travelled to Rome hoping for enlightenment, but he found there nothing but squalor, immorality and spiritual apathy. In the following year he began teaching in the University of Wittenberg, and it was there, between 1513 and 1518, that he had a series of spiritual crises while sitting in his tower-room preparing his lectures on St Paul's letter to the Romans. Matters came to a head in 1517 when a travelling salesman arrived in Wittenberg selling indulgences to those who sought to shorten their time in purgatory. The catchy little number that accompanied his sales pitch informed his customers that 'as soon as the coin in the coffer rings, another soul from purgatory springs!' For Luther it was the last straw. Full of anger at both the corruption of the medieval Catholic Church in putting a price on God's grace and the nihilism of the theology that allowed it to be done, Luther stormed to Wittenberg Cathedral and nailed his ninety-five theses onto its main door.

It was one of the most celebrated acts of protest in history, scathing in its analysis and passionate in its exposition. After all his struggles, Luther had finally realised the futility of trying to grasp the grace of God by his own paltry and sinful efforts. If this was how salvation worked, he would stand forever condemned: no amount of effort on his part would ever put him right with God. Luther's protest was not only against the immorality of the trade in indulgences (though that was a recurrent theme throughout the theses) but the entire system of Catholic theology that underlay it. It was a system in which personal merit and endeavour had become the central prerequisites for salvation, and people had to add their own efforts to the grace of God if they wished to be saved. It was a system, too, in which faith had come to mean faithfulness to the teachings of the Catholic Church and works of love had come to mean the buying of indulgences and the saying of prayers for the dead.

To Luther, these were monstrous perversions of the truth about a God of grace. If, he asked rhetorically in his eighty-second thesis, the salvation of people's souls was more important than anything else in heaven or earth, why did not the pope simply liberate all the imprisoned souls in purgatory? It was not, however, until two years after posting his theses on the door of Wittenberg Cathedral that Luther finally plumbed the scriptural depth of his position; and he found it in St. Paul's letter to the Romans. Paul had written that the righteousness of God was powerfully at work in the gospel of Christ: 'for as scripture says, whoever is justified through faith shall gain life'. This was the key for which Luther had been searching since the dark days of the monastery in Erfurt: he now knew, with every fibre of his being, that God justified – or saved – people through faith *and faith alone*. Justification was not, as the prevailing Catholic doctrine put it, a matter of progressing steadily towards perfection, aided by good works, spiritual exercises and a dollop of grace from God. It was a once-and-for-all act of absolute and unmerited grace on the part of God whenever people responded to Christ in faith.

If justification was immediate, sanctification might take a little longer. Luther realised that people could still be sinners in the process of becoming sanctified long after they had been justified by their faith in

Christ. That was only to be expected, for as Luther humbly observed, 'it is not I who am good and righteous but Christ'. Those who knew they had been justified by their faith would want continually to express that faith by repenting their sins and doing good works. For Luther, however, these were the *consequences* of justification, not – as Catholic teaching had it – the *prerequisites*. Salvation was the freely offered gift of a gracious God, available to all who placed their faith in the gospel of Christ. It was not to be earned, much less bought through indulgences, chantry chapels and all the rest. It could only be accepted in humility and faith. Here, then, was the first of the three central pillars of the Protestant Reformation that Martin Luther erected: salvation by grace through faith alone. *Sola fide.*

The second pillar was the authority of scripture. In opposition to much of the thrust of medieval scholasticism, Luther argued that God could only be known through his own self-revelation. Reason, logic and philosophy may give rise to questions about God's existence, but it was only in his revelation of himself that the answers could be found; and the only place where authentic self-revelation was to be found was the Bible. Luther held that, provided it was read in faith and guided by the Holy Spirit, the Bible contained all that was necessary for human salvation. This was not to say that the Catholic Church had ignored the Bible as a source of divine revelation, but it did not give it the absolute pre-eminence that Luther thought it should have. In the Catholic tradition, other resources such as the teachings of the Church and the infallible pronouncements of popes could also be of value in matters of Christian life and faith. Of these, however, Luther was contemptuously dismissive: scripture alone could furnish the knowledge of God's grace and stimulate the faith to respond to it. *Sola scriptura.*

The third of the central pillars of the Protestant Reformation, further emphasising its break from the prevailing Catholicism, was that of the priesthood of all believers. It flowed naturally from Luther's insistence upon salvation by grace through faith: for him, all who responded to Christ in faith were priests of God, whether ordained or not. Luther never belittled the value of ordained priests as pastors and teachers, but he did deny their possession of any spiritual superiority separating them from those they served. He also rejected their claim to be necessary mediators between God and his people. Anyone, according to Luther, could approach God directly in prayer if they did so with sincerity and faith. It did not require the intervention either of a priest or of the saints to assure people of God's forgiveness of their sins or the efficacy of their intercessions.

The division that Martin Luther opened up between his own vision of God and the prevailing teaching of the Catholic Church has sometimes been characterised as the divide between the 'theology of the cross' and 'the theology of glory'. Luther came to the theology of the cross through a growing awareness of his absolute dependence on the grace of God at every twist and turn of life. For him, as for St Paul and St Augustine before him, there was nothing that people could do to rescue themselves from the mire of sin into which they had fallen, other than to approach God in prayerful penitence. They could not find God by reason or argument, nor could they find a living faith in him through the kind of cerebral gymnastics so beloved of the medieval schoolmen. They certainly couldn't do so by buying indulgences to finance the popes' pet building projects in Rome. Only the gift of faith and the supernatural grace of God, revealed in the Bible and mediated through the cross, could do for men and women what they could not do for themselves. It was God, and God alone, who justified sinners. Despise your sins, Luther was saying, and God will shower you with grace. Give God your good works, the Catholic Church was teaching, and he will crown them with glory. For Luther, the more the virtue of man was stressed, the less the graciousness of God was heeded. Merit counted for nothing, faith for everything. 'I am not good and righteous' he said, 'but Christ is'. It was to become a central motto of the Protestant Reformation.

Chapter 13
The God of Predestination

Towering though Martin Luther's influence over the European religious scene in the early sixteenth century unquestionably was, his legacy to Christian theology was piecemeal rather than systematic. He never wrote an organised account of Protestant theology and he did little to turn the new ideas of Protestantism into a blueprint for social reform. It was left to theologians working elsewhere in Europe, especially the Swiss-based reformers Huldrych Zwingli (1484-1531) and John Calvin (1509-1564), to furnish the new Protestantism with a coherent programme of thought and action for the Reformed Churches that were springing up in several European countries. The new Reformed theology was based firmly on the three central tenets of Luther's Protestantism: salvation by grace through faith, the supreme authority of scripture, and the priesthood of all believers; but in the hands of Zwingli and Calvin it became inextricably interwoven with the idea of God's absolute sovereignty over people's salvation or damnation.

Huldrych Zwingli was born at Wildhaus in the Swiss canton of St Gallen in 1484, the year after Luther's birth. He studied at the University of Basle, a major centre of humanist scholarship, and in 1506 at the age of twenty-two he was appointed pastor of Glarus, a small town near Zürich, where he became politically active and was much attracted to the humanist writings of Erasmus. In 1516 Zwingli left Glarus for the important pilgrimage centre of Einsiedeln in the canton of Schwyz where he was appointed preacher at the Catholic Abbey, and in 1519, two years after Luther nailed his theses to the cathedral door at Wittenberg, he moved again to Zürich as 'people's priest' in the Great Minster. It was here that the humanist preacher and politician reinvented himself as an autocratic teacher and enforcer of the new Reformed faith. In the twelve years that he spent in Zürich, Zwingli imposed his own particular brand of biblical authority and civic order first upon the city, then upon the canton of Zürich, and eventually (albeit with mixed success) upon the country as a whole. In the hands of Zwingli, the Bible was not only the word of God, it also doubled up as the handbook of local government.

Zwingli's rise to prominence was aided by the political and ecclesiastical conditions in Switzerland at the time. Public morality was at a low ebb and many of the clergy were seen as more caring of their concubines than of their congregations. Zwingli threw himself into the political and ecclesiastical fray, relying on the authority of the Bible for the reforms that he was championing. When this brought him into conflict with the Catholic hierarchy's insistence on the equal authority of the traditions and teachings of the Church, Zwingli responded by redoubling his efforts against time-honoured Catholic views on such doctrines as the veneration of saints, salvation through good works and the real presence of Christ in the bread and wine of the communion. By Easter 1524 indulgences and pilgrimages had been abolished in Zürich and the sacraments of penance and extreme unction had been rejected. Pictures, statues, relics, altars and organs had been destroyed and chalices melted into coins. These, Zwingli believed, were not at all what God wanted. In 1525 a new Reformed liturgy of Holy Communion was introduced to replace the Mass.

As the breach with Rome became an unbridgeable gulf, the cantons of Switzerland had to choose sides. Six remained true to the Catholic tradition but the remainder adopted the new Reformed theology. Matters came to a head at Berne in the winter of 1528 when, supported by Joachim Vadian (1485-1551) in St Gallen, Sebastian Hofmeister (1476-1533) in Schaffhausen and John Oecolampadius (1482-1531) in Basle, Zwingli swept the board at an ecumenical conference with representatives of the Catholic cantons. Emboldened, he drew up a military campaign against the remaining Catholic cantons to force them into acceptance of the new doctrines. Loyal to the old order, a Catholic army declared war on Zürich and the opposing armies met at Kappel, near Basle, in October 1531. The Catholic soldiers, led by Hans Jauch, decisively overpowered the beleaguered troops from Zürich, and Zwingli was killed in the fighting. His plan to impose the new Reformed theology throughout Switzerland by force had failed.

In spite of his ultimate downfall, Zwingli left a considerable legacy, in part because of the simplicity of his theology. Compared to Luther, who pronounced upon many things, Zwingli's teaching was largely dominated by a single theme: anything that was not permitted by the Bible should have no part in Christian belief or practice. For him, the Bible was the literal word of God; and even though it needed to be read with care and diligence, it nevertheless contained everything necessary for the Christian life. To hold such a high view of scripture was no more than might be expected of one who was deeply committed to the ideals of the Reformation. Zwingli, however, carried the doctrine of *sola scriptura* farther than Luther was prepared to go, insisting that because the entire Bible was the literal word of God, no part of it carried greater authority than any other. Every verse had an equal weight with every other. It was a simple theology, verging onto fundamentalism, which was to form the background to the harsher strains of Protestantism that grew up in the wake of Zwingli.

At the heart of Zwingli's programme was a belief in God's absolute sovereignty over the whole of the created order. If God is God, then nothing else can be greater or more powerful than him, and nothing can have any dominion over him. Because of his unique and unsurpassable greatness, God must exert his control over every nook and cranny of creation, and everything must embody his divine essence. If, moreover, God is sovereign over *everything*, it must include the salvation of people's souls. To put it bluntly, God must hold the power to decide who is to be selected for everlasting life in heaven and who is to be rejected for an eternity in hell. In the theological jargon of the day, God must 'elect' or 'predestine' some people for paradise and others for perdition, and there is nothing they can do to make him change his mind. If people were indeed able to influence the mind of God, then his absolute omnipotence would crumble to dust. It was not an original idea: the antecedents of Zwingli's thoughts about divine predestination can be traced back through St Thomas Aquinas and St Augustine to St Paul, especially to Paul's letter to the Romans. Each in his own way had argued that God chose some people to receive the gift of saving grace and others to be denied it. Not only that, those who had been chosen for salvation would be unable to resist the gift: they could no more decline the offer of God's grace than those from whom it had been withheld could earn or demand it.

Whereas Augustine and Paul had been reluctant to confront the harsher implications of predestination, Zwingli had no such hesitations. Augustine, for example, had had little to say about the unfortunate souls who were *not* predestined by God for salvation, implicitly assuming that they simply fell beside the wayside and had to fend for themselves as best they could. Zwingli, however, accepted the inescapable logic that if God had actively predestined some people for eternal life, then he must actively have predestined others for eternal rejection. It was not simply a matter of their falling accidentally by the wayside, as Augustine had supposed: they were there because it was what God willed. Augustine had been lost for an adequate explanation of the paradox of a gracious God who raised some to heaven and cast others into hell. Following St

Paul, he merely noted in his book *On Providence* that 'the reason why one person is assisted by grace and another is not . . . must be referred to the secret judgements of God'. Zwingli put his own particular gloss on the problem: even if sin and evil were the result of God's own freewill actions, he could not be held responsible for them because, being God, he was not accountable to anyone for anything. Just as an absolute monarch, being above the law of the land, could never be guilty of any crime, so God, being above the moral law of the universe, could never be open to a charge of injustice. It was an unquestioning acceptance of the absolute and unaccountable sovereignty of God to display his majestic power in whatever ways he pleased.

John Calvin (1509-1564) belonged to the next generation after Luther and Zwingli. Relatively little is known of his early life. He was born at Noyon in Picardie in 1509, the son of a lawyer and the grandson of a bargee on the River Oise. Calvin was a bright boy who did well at the local Collège des Capettes before going to Paris to continue his studies. By 1527 his education as a humanist lawyer with a civic conscience was largely complete, and two years later he had a sort of conversion experience. It was not as dramatic as Paul's, Augustine's or Luther's, but it left him convinced that God had taken his failures and weaknesses and transformed them into tools of obedience and mission. By 1531 Calvin was back in Paris where he rubbed shoulders with some of the leading figures of the Reformation; but it was a dangerous time to have Protestant sympathies in Catholic France, and when Calvin's close friend, Nicholas Cop, was forced to flee Paris in disguise after delivering a Lutheran sermon, Calvin decided that he too had better leave. His travels took him first to Strasbourg, where he met Thomas Cranmer's friend Martin Bucer (1491-1551), and then to Basle, where in 1536 he published the first edition of his great work, *The Institutes of Christian Religion*.

By the summer of the same year (1536) Calvin was on the move again, this time on a journey that brought him to the half-French, half-Swiss city of Geneva. Intending to stay there for only one night, Calvin remained more or less continuously for the rest of his life. It is said that a leading Protestant preacher in the city, Guillaume Farel (1489-1565), was so persuasive in urging Calvin to stay that, as Calvin himself later confessed, he was terrified into submission. Calvin must have seen the potentiality for Geneva to become the same kind of urban theocracy that Zwingli had created in Zürich, and he set about the task with zeal and commitment. Geneva, a large city of some 15,000 inhabitants, was ready to respond to his potent mixture of politics and religion, for even by the mid-1530s Protestantism had already gained a substantial foothold in the city. Catholicism had largely been defeated, altars desecrated, and images broken. The Catholic Mass had been outlawed, priests had been imprisoned, and citizens were fined for not attending Protestant sermons. In May 1536, just before Calvin's arrival, Protestant troops from Berne had entered the city and Geneva had taken a corporate oath to live 'by the holy law of the gospel'. Calvin's timing was thus impeccable. The Reformed Churches in Geneva were ready for him, accepting his teachings as though they were infallible. His extraordinary hold over his followers had begun.

In 1537 Calvin and Farel presented the city magistrates with a series of measures designed to bring order and discipline to church life. Holy Communion had to be taken four times a year and defaulters were reported. A moral censorship was established, punishable for those who broke it by excommunication. Children were to learn a junior catechism written specially for them by Calvin himself: some think it was among his best writing. Those who dared to criticise Calvin were shunned, along with others who gave loud parties. A scandal occurred in 1553 when Calvin ordered the arrest of the Spanish Catholic theologian and physician Michael Servetus (1509-1553) for denying the doctrine of the Holy Trinity, which he thought was more a Greek than a biblical concoction. Servetus, who had studied medicine in Paris and Lyons and was the first to describe the function of pulmonary circulation, had argued that he was merely seeking to return to the faith of the first apostles, none of whom, so he claimed, had heard of such an extraordinary idea. Had this been Servetus' only crime his life might have been spared but he compounded his offence by questioning some of Calvin's own favoured doctrines on God and infant baptism. The autocratic reformer hit back, publishing a detailed rebuttal of the Spaniard's arguments and asking the City Council of Geneva to burn him at the stake. Zwingli's successor in Zürich, Heinrich Bullinger (1504-1575), agreed. 'Let the world see,' he declared, 'that Geneva wills the glory of Christ'. Calvin later claimed to have tried to mitigate the sentence of death on Servetus, but the evidence is otherwise. He disputed with him on the day of his execution and he watched as he burned to death in October 1553. Consigned to the flames with Servetus were almost all the known copies of his major work, *The Restoration of Christianity*.

In the following year a pamphlet circulated in Geneva under the title *Should Heretics be Persecuted?* It is sometimes described as the first modern plea for religious tolerance; but the man who was later to succeed Calvin in Geneva, Theodore Beza (1519-1605), responded with a loud and violent 'yes!' Under first Calvin and then Beza, Geneva was preached into submission to the will of a Protestant God, being at one time described by the Scottish Presbyterian John Knox as 'the most perfect school of Christ since the days of the apostles'. The Bible doubled up as a code of law and people's moral failings became civic crimes. Die-hard reformers now saw Geneva as Protestantism's answer to Rome, though at precisely the time that Popes Paul III and Julius III were enjoying the artistic fruits of their patronage of Raphael and Michelangelo, Calvin was transforming Geneva into a citadel of joyless and colourless rectitude. It may have been a city without crime, but it was also a city without theatres and entertainments. Beneath the hard and disciplined eye of its social and ecclesiastical architect, the only art that was allowed was music – and that not instrumental. Calvin's God did not approve of fun.

Like Luther and Zwingli before him, Calvin saw God as the providential source of all that happened in the world. For him, history and nature were the surfaces on which God etched his grand designs. Nothing ever happened, or had ever happened, by godless chance: everything, including even the sin of Adam and Eve, had been anticipated and ordained by God. It was not, of course, for mere mortals to understand God's reasons, but the tragic events in the Garden of Eden must somehow have allowed his glory to be released and revealed. The cataclysmic disobedience of Adam and Eve had all been part of the divine plan.

Calvin's views on predestination are said to have been influenced by an observation attributed to St Augustine, who had puzzled over the fact that people responded to the gospel of Christ in different ways. Some accepted it, others rejected it. The reason, Augustine had concluded, was that God willed it thus. It was God who selected those to whom the gospel would be preached, and it was God who decided how they would respond. In Augustine's opinion it was useless to ask why God would want to behave like this, for to do so would be to 'penetrate the sacred precincts of divine wisdom'. It was Augustine's certainty about the absolute freedom of God to act in ways of his own choosing that gave Calvin the key to his doctrine. 'Predestination', he declared in *The Institutes of Christian Religion*, 'is God's eternal decree by which he determines what he wills to become of each man. For all are not created in equal condition; rather, eternal life is fore-ordained for some, eternal damnation for others. Therefore, as any man has been created to one or the other of these ends, we speak of him as predestined to life or to death'.

As if to anticipate the criticisms that he knew must come his way, Calvin observed that there was nothing new about this. Divine predestination had been happening throughout recorded time. The people of Israel had been chosen by God and the rest of humanity rejected. Isaac and Jacob had been chosen as the patriarchs of the Jews while Ishmael and Esau had been discarded. Mary had been chosen as the mother of Jesus and other Jewish women of childbearing age passed over. St Peter had been chosen as the rock on whom the Church was to be built and the rest of the disciples overlooked. Throughout the ages, God had always gathered his elect together, whether Jew or Gentile, to the exclusion of others. As for those who were cast aside, Calvin was as sure as Zwingli had been before him that they were eternally damned. Calvin had no doubt that God condemned some people to everlasting rejection as a sign of his supreme authority over human souls.

Obvious objections can be raised against such a bleak and compassionless view of God. Does it not make him a capricious and tyrannical God, much like the God of Abraham and Moses? Why should the loving God revealed in Jesus want any of his creatures to spend an eternity in hell? Why should people bother to lead upright and sober lives if their eternal fate has already been decided? Such questions were simply batted aside by Calvin. The mind of God, he declared, is secret and unfathomable and it is not for man to question or challenge it. In any case, it is precisely by meekly accepting the will of God in their lives that people are made humble and grateful. Theodore Beza, Calvin's successor in Geneva, went even farther: when people expressed their concern about the fate of those whom God had capriciously tossed into hell, he is said to have replied that they could at least take comfort in the fact that they were there for the greater glory of God.

John Calvin's legacy was to prove, in the long run, much more pervasive and enduring than that of either Luther or Zwingli. Whereas Lutheranism became confined largely to Luther's home country, Calvinism profoundly affected the development of Protestantism across large swathes of Europe and North America. Within a short time of Calvin's death in Geneva in 1564, varieties of Calvinism had spread into Scotland, Holland, Hungary and large parts of what is now Germany. Presbyterianism was, at least initially, a Scottish version of Calvinism brought to Scotland by one of Calvin's most fervent admirers, John Knox (1505-1572). In the seventeenth century, Puritanism in England owed more to Calvinism than to any other strand of Protestantism, and those who found religious life too restrictive in England set sail for the New World, there to establish godly communities on the model of Calvin's Geneva. American Presbyterianism and Congregationalism each adopted Calvinist theology, and it was to Calvin rather than to Luther or Zwingli that they looked for their inspiration. Although Luther is rightly remembered as the one who lit the blue touch-paper of the Reformation, it was Calvin who changed the course of post-Reformation Protestantism, touching the souls of millions of his followers with his distinctive but dour amalgam of rectitude and election.

To every action, however, there is a reaction, and in this case it came early in the seventeenth century in the shape of a bitter feud between two professors of theology at Leiden University in Holland. One was Francis Gomarus, a hard-line supporter of Calvin and Beza, the other was Jacob Arminius, a Protestant of more moderate leanings. The legacy of their confrontation was to constitute an important new face of the God of Protestantism.

Chapter 14
The God of Prevenient Grace

By the time John Calvin died at Geneva in 1564 the split between Roman Catholic and Protestant beliefs and practices had become an unbridgeable divide in Western Christendom. The Ecumenical Council of Trent, which met intermittently between 1544 and 1563 during the reign of three popes (Paul III, Julius III and Pius IV), had set the face of Catholicism firmly against the doctrines that the Protestant reformers had assiduously crafted and enforced. To many Protestants, Trent was the reactionary knee-jerk of a papacy anxious to salvage something from the intellectual and religious storms that were raging across Europe. In reaffirming the Catholic Church's traditional stand on such matters as original sin, the transubstantiation of the bread and wine, the veneration of saints and the sale of indulgences, the magisterial declarations of the Council of Trent were seen by its detractors as a desperate attempt by the Vatican to maintain its traditional hold over the faithful. Protestant representatives had been invited to the Council and a few had attended some of the sessions, but as the influence of the recently formed Jesuits waxed in the debates, that of the Protestants waned, and the Council ended up as an almost exclusively Catholic gathering. It was a major staging post in what has come to be known as the Counter-Reformation.

The tensions between traditional Catholicism and the new Protestant theology were everywhere to be seen in the work of the Council. Where Luther and Calvin had insisted on the supreme authority of the Bible, Trent continued to reserve a large measure of authority to the Church. Where the Reformation leaders had taught a doctrine of salvation based upon the faith of the believer and the grace of God, Trent upheld the value of good works and spiritual exercises in securing a place in heaven. Where Luther had protested violently against the trade in indulgences, Trent commended their efficacy in shortening the time of souls in purgatory. Where Protestants were proclaiming the priesthood of all believers, Trent upheld the singular position of the ordained priesthood in mediating between God and man. Against the austere aesthetic of Reformed theology, with its distaste for icons and decoration, Trent embraced the exuberance of colour and imagery in worship. It could only have been in a Roman church, Santa Maria della

Vittoria, that the artistic director of the Counter-Reformation, Gianlorenzo Bernini, was able to give sculptural expression to the ecstasy of St Theresa of Avila, swooning in unmistakeably sensual pleasure as her body is about to be pierced with a cherub's golden spear. God may have been a Catholic or he may have been a Protestant but he could scarcely have been both, so different were the images of him that each side was promoting.

There is a sense, then, in which the Reformation ended in disarray, with Western Christendom divided and Europe in a state of cultural fission. Theological warfare turned into military conflict as Protestant and Catholic states locked horns in sectarian battles that were to last until the middle of the seventeenth century. Not only that, Protestantism itself was splintering in ways that few might have dreamed possible during the height of Zwingli's and Calvin's influence. In England, Puritanism was beginning to challenge the middle-of-the-road theology of the Church that had been brokered by Queen Elizabeth I and engineered by Richard Hooker. In Scotland, the distinctive brand of Protestantism imposed by John Knox was so unyielding that Elizabeth's dynastic rival, the Catholic Mary Queen of Scots, is said to have feared his prayers more than all the armies of Europe. In North America, Puritan immigrants who had failed to establish theocracies in England of the kind that Zwingli and Calvin had created in Switzerland were struggling to establish a Christian commonwealth in the mosquito-infested swamps of Virginia. In Holland, the Dutch Reformed Church was challenged over the doctrine of predestination as a more moderate form of Protestant theology, Arminianism, sprang up.

Out of this post-Reformation ferment, new denominations appeared and new forms of Christian expression were born. Methodism and its several offshoots arose out of a marriage between Pietism and Arminianism. Deism came to be seen by many as the natural theological soul mate of the Enlightenment, and the Unitarian Church became its most obvious ecclesiastical home. The Baptist Church emerged out of a union between Puritans and the Dutch Anabaptists. All of these fissions and groupings had their origins in the legacy of the Reformation in the sixteenth-century theological debates that had been set in train by Erasmus, Luther, Calvin, Zwingli and others. Among the more important of them for the longer term future of Protestantism was the bitter conflict that erupted between two Dutch academics, Francis Gomarus (1563-1641) and Jacob Arminius (1560-1609), at the University of Leiden.

The feud between Gomarus and Arminius was sparked by an extreme form of Calvinism espoused by the son of a prosperous Burgundian family, Theodore Beza (1519-1605). He was born in the pilgrimage town of Vézelay, the resting place (so it is claimed) of the relics of St Mary Magdalene and one of the traditional starting points of the pilgrimage route to Santiago de Compostela. Ten years younger than his mentor John Calvin, Beza arrived in Geneva in 1548 where he converted to the new Reformed faith. He held academic appointments as professor of Greek in both Lausanne and Geneva before being chosen by Calvin to be the rector of the newly instituted Academy of Geneva in 1559. His success in establishing the Academy as an internationally acknowledged centre of theology and classical learning was accompanied by his rapid rise in the ecclesiastical hierarchy. When Calvin died in 1564, Beza succeeded him as the leader of the Reformed Church in Geneva, and it was then that he entered his most productive period as a theologian of stature and influence. His most important work, *Tractationes Theologicae* (1570), set out an uncompromising version of Calvinism, known as 'supralapsarianism', against which Arminius was soon to react so fiercely. By the time Beza died in 1605, the confrontation between Arminius and his opponent Gomarus was already in train.

The squabble over supralapsarianism may seem to modern eyes little more than an arcane philosophical storm in a Protestant teacup. There is an obvious sense in which it echoed the ultimately sterile debates about the existence of God that had reverberated around the universities and seminaries of medieval Europe several centuries earlier. At the heart of the confrontation lay a question about the order in which God had decided (or, to use the terminology of the day, decreed) to do things. There was general agreement among Calvinists that, at some point in the process of creation, God must have made two decisions: to create mankind and to save some people while rejecting others. The question was: in what order did he take these decisions? Did he first decide to create mankind, knowing that people would fall into sin, and then to institute divine election as the method of separating the saved from the lost, or did he do it the other way round?

Beza was sure that he did it the other way round. He taught that God *first* decided that he would save some and reject others, and *then* he allowed Adam and all his descendants to be tainted with the mark of sin. Having taken these two decisions – in that order – God then provided the mechanism of salvation for sinners through the death and resurrection of Jesus. Because only some of those who had sinned would be saved, it followed that Christ did not die for everyone. He died only for the elect – only, that is, for those who had already been chosen for everlasting life. The complete doctrine was known as supralapsarianism, which translates roughly as divine election 'before the fall of mankind into sin'. The doctrine of Christ dying only for the elect was known as 'limited atonement'. Those Calvinists who opposed it, known as 'infralapsarians', thought that God's omnipotence was most fully revealed in creation, not in his acts of predestination. (Infralapsarianism translates roughly as divine election 'after the fall of mankind into sin'). Both groups were Calvinist and both agreed that all of God's actions reflected his absolute, eternal and immutable will. It was 'simply' a matter of timing, but in it lay the seeds of what was to become a major schism in European Protestantism.

Beza's God was, if anything, an even harsher and more judgemental deity than Calvin's. He was a God who threw human freedom and responsibility out of the window of salvation and replaced them with an autocratic selectivity, assigning some souls to heaven and dispatching others to hell. And he did so not because of anything that people themselves may or may not have done, but simply because it was part of his divine plan for the world. It was the ultimate mark of his supreme power and authority over his creation. Sooner or later, someone was bound to emerge from the ecclesiastical ranks of European Protestantism to challenge such an unforgiving God; and the task fell to the Dutchman Jakob Hermanzoon, usually known in the English-speaking world as Jacob Arminius.

Arminius was born at Oudewater, in the south of Holland, in 1560. It was a time when the Dutch were struggling to cope with their Catholic inheritance and the aggression of Catholic Spain. The Spanish government under Philip II was waging a fierce campaign of religious persecution against the infiltration of Protestantism into Holland, and the Spanish Inquisition was set to become a major instrument of repression and tyranny. An academically brilliant youth, Arminius was sent to Geneva in 1581 by the merchants' guild of Amsterdam to study Calvinist theology at the feet of Theodore Beza. In 1586 he visited Italy, causing rumours to circulate in Amsterdam and Geneva that he had fallen under the spell of the Jesuits. Arminius was recalled to Amsterdam where he was cleared of any suspicion of Jesuitical tendencies and appointed a preacher to the Dutch Reformed congregation in the capital. For the next fifteen years, aided by a booming voice and an intimate knowledge of the Bible, Arminius' reputation as a Reformed preacher grew and spread. Indeed, when Professor Dirk Koornhert (1522-1590) of Leiden University was moved publicly to describe Beza's God as 'a tyrant and an executioner', Arminius took on the task of rebutting him. It was, however, to prove a watershed in his religious life, for the more he probed the God of the supralapsarians, the less Arminius liked what he was seeing. Such an extreme form of Calvinism became, for him, anathema to the generous and charitable instincts of his mind and spirit; and far from confounding Koornhert's supposedly heretical views, he eventually found himself agreeing whole-heartedly with them.

As his preaching and writing became ever more critical of Beza's theology, Arminius found himself the target of those who interpreted his rejection of the more extreme forms of Calvinism as a covert sympathy for Catholic doctrines. Yet his career continued to prosper, and in 1602 he was appointed to the prestigious post of professor of theology at Leiden University. There he was forcefully, even vehemently, opposed by the second professor of theology, Francis Gomarus. A graduate of Cambridge University, Gomarus was an unyielding supralapsarian who gathered about him a group of supporters (known as the Gomarists) intent on undermining Arminius and his supposedly Catholic sympathies. The bitter feud between the two professors soon escalated into a national confrontation, forcing the Dutch provinces to side with one or the other. Theology became as much a topic for public discussion as local taxes and law and order, and people supported Arminius or Gomarus with all the fervour that now goes into supporting Dutch football teams.

Yet far from being soft on Catholicism, much of Arminius' teaching was a model of Protestant – even Calvinist – orthodoxy. He subscribed to the main pillars of Protestant theology, especially the supreme authority of the Bible and the priesthood of all believers. He held that salvation depended upon the grace of God and that it could be grasped only through faith in Jesus Christ. This was mainstream Protestant theology that could hardly have upset the Gomarists. It was when Arminius began to question the more extreme claims of supralapsarianism that the trouble started. In particular, he rejected the core belief of Beza and his followers that people were chosen by God for heaven or hell whatever they may or may not have done in their lives. For Arminius (as it had been centuries earlier for Pelagius) it was false to see men and women as no more than passive lumps of clay in the hands of God, pre-programmed by him to behave in ways of his own choosing and dispatched after death entirely according to his pleasure. Arminius believed that people had a measure of freedom and moral obligation of their own, and they should rightly be called to account for their actions. Salvation was by no means as cut and dried as the more extreme versions of Calvinism were making it out to be.

Reasonable though this position might seem, it was anathema to the supralapsarians, for if the saving effect of God's grace could be influenced, even to the tiniest degree, by the behaviour of abject sinners, then it robbed him of his absolute sovereignty. Yet if that was bad, worse was to come. For in rejecting unconditional election, Arminius also set aside the Calvinist doctrine of irresistible grace: he did not accept that, when people were confronted by the saving grace of God, they had no choice but to accept it. As far as Arminius was concerned, people were perfectly able to decide for themselves whether or not to respond to God's overtures in their lives. Indeed, the Bible was full of those who had freely chosen one way or the other. If, as Arminius believed, people had been created with the freedom to choose the way they lived, that must include the freedom to accept or reject the grace of God. They had a real choice. Arminius accepted that without grace there could be no salvation; but if people chose to turn away from the path of grace and salvation, they were free to do so and take the consequences.

Arminius was, however, careful not simply to fall back on the old Catholic beliefs about the value of good works, pilgrimages, indulgences and all the other manifestations of meretricious piety against which Luther and the other Protestant leaders had strenuously fought. By endorsing the traditional Protestant teaching that people were saved only through the supernatural and enabling mercy of God in Christ, Arminius held fast to the hallowed Protestant formula of salvation through grace and faith. Yet this grace, Arminius thought, came into the lives of sinners before they responded to it. He gave it a name, 'prevenient grace', and having recognised it in their lives, people were free to accept or reject it. If they accepted it and allowed it to work in their lives, then prevenient grace became 'justifying grace', and all that was needed to get from one to the other was faith in Jesus Christ. Good works and all the rest were of no avail. It was, it might be said, Pelagianism updated for the seventeenth century.

Jacob Arminius was feeling his way towards a more sympathetic God than the unsmiling, autocratic God of the supralapsarians – a God who was still recognisably Protestant but who allowed people to be themselves and who worked *with* them rather than against them. Yet that is not how it was seen in early seventeenth-century Holland. Arminius and his supporters were out of tune with the religious ethos of the day, and they paid the price. In 1609, in the midst of a public inquisition into his theology by Dutch religious and political leaders, Arminius died. After his death his followers gathered together their objections to the supralapsarianism of Beza and Gomarus and published them in the form of a document that came to be known as the 'Remonstrance'. They themselves were dubbed 'Remonstrants'. The document set out their opposition to five of the most fundamental elements of extreme Calvinism, including unconditional election, limited atonement and irresistible grace. For their pains, many Remonstrants were jailed pending the outcome of a national synod (the Synod of Dort) convened by the

Dutch Reformed Church to examine their claims. Meeting at Dordrecht between November 1618 and May 1619, the Synod condemned the Remonstrants as heretics. Some two hundred of them were ejected from their churches and a further hundred were exiled or imprisoned.

Not only did the Synod of Dort condemn the Remonstrants, it also upheld the strict principles of Calvinism as the doctrinal standards of the Reformed Church. They came to be known (appropriately for Holland) as the TULIP doctrines. 'T' stood for total depravity: men and women were mired in their own sinfulness and could do nothing to help themselves. 'U' stood for unconditional election: only the unconditional grace of God, offered to whomsoever he chose, could bring people to salvation. 'L' stood for limited atonement: Christ died not for all, but only for those whom God had already predestined for salvation. 'I' stood for irresistible grace: people were helpless when confronted by the saving grace of God and had no choice but to accept it. And 'P' stood for perseverance: those who had been chosen by God would persevere unfailingly on their path to salvation, not through their own efforts but because God had decreed that they would. TULIP was supralapsarianism, if not in a nutshell, then at least in a flower bulb.

In the end, everything that Arminius and the Remonstrants had resisted was endorsed by the Synod of Dort as the official doctrine of the Dutch Reformed Church. Arminianism was effectively dead in the Netherlands. Elsewhere, however, it was to become a major theological force in European and American Protestantism. In England it took root and flourished, becoming a permanent option within the Anglican tradition, and in America too it was to shape the faith of many people. As we shall see, the conflict between Arminian and Calvinist views of predestination and limited atonement was also to play a distinctive part in the emergence of Methodism in the eighteenth century. Two different faces of God were now to be seen in the Protestant world. One was the face of a glorious but autocratic and selective God who displayed his power and his majesty by choosing some people for salvation and others for perdition; the other was the face of a universal and forgiving God who invited everyone to take him into their lives but who never rode roughshod over their freedom to reject him. In one narrative, Jesus died only for those whom God had predestined for salvation; in the other, he died for all. In the long term, the latter was to become the more abiding image, though it was to undergo several further transformations as Protestantism progressed in both Europe and America.

Chapter 15
The God of the Gaps

Although the Reformation brought change and innovation to the doctrines and practices of Western Christendom, many aspects of popular religious belief were probably unaffected by the work of the great reformers. Beneath the surface storms of theological conflict that re-sculpted the formal religious face of Europe in the sixteenth century, the deeper waters of traditional faith flowed much as they always had done. Given the slow pace of cultural change in the late medieval world, this is hardly surprising. With the vantage of hindsight, the sixteenth century can be seen as the start of a huge and irreversible shift in European culture from a religious to a scientific understanding of the natural world; but it would not have seemed like that at the time. Faithful Christians, Protestant as well as Catholic, still looked to the Church for a coherent account of why things were as they were, and ancient beliefs and superstitions still dominated the lives of ordinary people even as scientists of the stature of Copernicus and Galileo were revealing their astonishing ideas to a sceptical and resistant Church.

This sixteenth century was an age when magic and superstition still permeated the fabric of daily life. Spirits, demons, angels and bogeymen were everywhere in the world. Martin Luther repeatedly ascribed his various diseases, including chronic constipation, to 'the devil's spells', declaring that 'Satan produces all the maladies which afflict mankind, for he is the prince of death'. God, too, was continually at work in the world, and life for many people was a daily battle between the good and evil forces that surrounded them. People instinctively signed themselves with the cross to protect them from danger and they habitually invoked the help of the saints to ease their passage through life. Sometimes their invocations were heeded, at other times not; but there was rarely any doubting the potency of these occult powers. The failure of a prayer to be answered was as likely to be interpreted as a sign of God's displeasure as of the natural processes of cause and effect. Bad weather, infertility, stillbirths, poor harvests, madness, plague and pestilence – all these and more besides could spring from dark forces at work in the world and all might be alleviated by prayer, penance and other ecclesiastically sanctioned actions.

136

Rock of Ages?

Holy relics were greatly prized, for they exuded enormous potency. Objects that had been intimately associated with a saint, such as his clothes, hair, blood or bones, could transmit their sacred power to those who revered them, amplifying the prayers of the faithful and increasing their efficacy. Relics that could actually be touched or kissed might generate yet more spectacular results. Even a handkerchief stained with the sweat or nasal secretions of a saint could sometimes work wonders. The more celebrated the saint and the more exalted the relic, the greater the effect; and pilgrims travelled great distances throughout medieval Europe to worship at the shrines of the most popular saints. In reality, a belief in the power of saintly relics was little more than the ancient principle of associative magic imported into a Christian context; but if people truly believed in the potency of holy artefacts, then many seemingly miraculous or supernatural cures must have occurred through what is now understood as the placebo effect.

The most powerful association of all was with Jesus himself, and relics that were believed to have been in physical contact with him, such as thorns from his crucifixion crown, fragments of his cross or the shroud in which he had been buried, were of unsurpassable holiness. To offer prayers to God in the presence of such awesomely sacred objects was associative magic at its most intense. Even the words of Jesus could bring hope to those who believed in their saving power. At rogation-tide, when fields and livestock were blessed for their fertility, parishioners read passages from the gospels over their crops and pregnant women bound their stomachs with papers scribbled with prayers and verses from the Bible. It was not just the words of Jesus that were available: in spite of the protestations of Luther and Zwingli, many people continued to believe that the communion bread became Christ's physical body as the priest raised it heavenwards and, to the tolling of the sacring bell, declared to the parish that the saviour was among them. 'This *is* my body, broken for you.' So sacred were the communion elements that some parishioners wore gloves while washing the cloth on which they had lain, fearing directly to handle objects that had been in contact with Christ himself. Others, more boldly, were given to storing the consecrated bread in their mouths for later use as a charm against misfortune or even to rid their gardens of caterpillars.

Many of these beliefs and rituals relied upon what we now know to be false assumptions about cause and effect in the natural world. Charms and talismans cannot protect against misfortune and a piece of bread left in the garden, even one that has been consecrated by a priest, cannot prevent an infestation of caterpillars. If the true cause of something is unknown, however, there is a kind of logic in attributing it to unseen forces at work in the ether. Why shouldn't good health, large families and plentiful harvests be seen as the benevolent work of God? Why shouldn't plague, drought and pestilence (and even, as Martin Luther evidently believed, constipation) be seen as the malevolent work of the devil? After all, that is how they were commonly understood in biblical times. From here it was but a short step to believing that the bad things in life could be prevented and the good ones encouraged by pleasing God and fighting the devil. If the intercessions of a saint could tip the balance in favour of the supplicant, then it made good sense to visit his shrine and enlist his help. Faith, pilgrimage and healing were all tied up together in the medieval imagination.

There are countless examples from all over medieval Christendom. The early thirteenth-century windows in Canterbury Cathedral, though much depleted by the actions of iconoclasts across the ages, depict dramatic stories in coloured glass of the healing powers of Canterbury's miracle-working saint, Thomas Becket. Mediating the grace of God among the sick and the wounded, St Thomas restored the gouged-out eyes of a felon, cured epilepsy and leprosy, healed industrial injuries, resuscitated a boy who had drowned in the River Medway, rescued workmen from a collapsed trench, helped the lame to walk again, and dispensed an array of other miraculous cures. With such a proven track record to his name, it made good sense for the sick and the lame to visit Becket's shrine; and many pilgrims, for many different reasons, doubtless left Canterbury feeling better than when they arrived. Times have changed, though, and a modern visitor to Canterbury Cathedral who fell and broke a leg would certainly not expect the chaplains to dally in prayer at the site of St Thomas' shrine. Indeed, if an ambulance equipped with all the necessary technology failed to be summoned forthwith, an expensive claim for negligence might be lodged against the Dean and Chapter.

It is clear from these brief examples that something very important began to change in the intellectual climate of Europe at about the time of the Reformation. Whereas God had been a vital factor in explaining a great many things in the late middle ages, he gradually ceased to be a force as people's knowledge of the natural world increased apace. For the last three hundred years our understanding of the cosmos has been driven by scientific evidence, not ecclesiastical dogma, and even though there remain many gaps in scientific knowledge, few scientists now believe that the supernatural power of a deity will prove to be the answer.

Acts of God in the twenty-first century have been relegated largely to the small print of insurance policies. People may still instinctively appeal for supernatural help when things go wrong, but more from a sense of frustration than in genuine expectation of a divine solution. When the car breaks down, a muttered prayer of pleading may be made that it will miraculously start again; but few believe that God can do a better job of it than a motor mechanic. The internal combustion engine has to be understood in terms of mechanical engineering, not the power of God; and if it were otherwise, the world of engineering would be a totally chaotic and unpredictable place.

This fundamental shift in human understanding about the natural world, which began in earnest in the sixteenth century and gained momentum in the seventeenth and eighteenth centuries, has come to be known as the period of the Enlightenment. It had the effect (among many other things) of eroding the authority of the Church by enhancing the status of science. In astronomy, medicine, physics, anatomy and many other areas of human knowledge, statements about the ways in which things worked came to be accepted as true less because the Church said they were than because the new sciences were proving them so. In sharp contrast to the traditional but ultimately unverifiable pronouncements of ecclesiastical authorities, scientists were going about their business by observing natural phenomena, formulating hypotheses to explain them, and testing them by means of controlled experiments that others could replicate. Findings that could not be shown to be wrong would provisionally be accepted as true, but always with the reservation that the apparent truths of today could become the proven falsehoods of tomorrow. Crucially, the difference between science and religion was not only one of method (experimentation versus authority) but also of mind-set: the default position of science, that truth is always provisional, was alien to the Church.

The seismic change from ecclesiastical authority to scientific verification did not happen overnight. Even before the impact of the Enlightenment, the Church had often tried to suppress whatever challenged its dogmas and to silence those who asked awkward questions. An interesting early example is that of the Franciscan monk William of Ockham, who was born in 1280 or 1290 in the village near Guildford from which he took his name and which in turn gave its name to the principle that he enunciated – Occam's Razor. It was a principle of parsimony in explanation: if something could adequately be explained in terms of its immediate physical causes, then it was unnecessary to look for supernatural ones. The best explanation was the one that invoked the fewest and most plausible assumptions. If the fall of a rock down a mountainside could be explained through a combination of soil erosion and wind, there was no point wondering whether it had been pushed by an angel. The Church, however, instinctively saw things differently: in William's day it was liable to claim both a natural *and* a supernatural explanation for events and happenings. To argue, as William of Ockham did, that it was unnecessary to invoke the presence of supernatural forces when a perfectly natural explanation would suffice, was to challenge the intellectual hegemony of the Church; and in 1326 he was condemned as a heretic by a papal court in Avignon.

A little over a hundred years after the death of William of Ockham, Nicolaus Copernicus (1473-1543) was born at Thorn, in Poland. Trained as both a lawyer and a doctor, he practised medicine at the episcopal court at Heilsberg, in East Prussia, where he became interested in astronomy and worked assiduously on a study of the motion of heavenly bodies. By 1530 he had completed his great work, *De Revolutionibus Orbium Coelestium*; but because of his fears about its reception by the Catholic Church, it was not until 1543 that it was first published under the name of a young Lutheran from Wittenberg University, Georg Rheticus (1514-1574). The work was dedicated to Pope Paul III. In *De Revolutionibus* Copernicus claimed, in flat contradiction to the teachings of the Church, that the sun was a stationary body at the centre of the solar system with the earth moving in orbit around it. It was a scandalous claim, for it meant that the earth – God's supreme creation – was not, after all, the centre of everything. Copernicus well understood the magnitude of what he was doing, noting in the preface to the first edition of *De Revolutionibus* that: 'there will be babblers who, although completely ignorant of mathematics, nevertheless take it upon themselves to pass judgement on mathematical questions and, badly distorting some passages of Scripture to their purpose, will dare to find fault with my undertaking and censure it.' He added that: 'I disregard them even to the extent of despising their criticism as unfounded.' Copernicus' confidence (some might say arrogance) was justified: he had arrived at a profound truth about the heliocentric nature of the solar system long before the theoretical evidence for it was provided by Isaac Newton (1642-1727).

Although Copernicus began the demolition of an intellectual system that had been consecrated by a thousand years of universal acceptance and ecclesiastical approval, he did not incur the displeasure of the

Catholic Church until after his death. It was the work of two of his scientific successors, Giordano Bruno (1548-1600) and Galileo Galilei (1564-1642), which finally provoked the Church into a reaction against the new science. Of the two, Bruno was by far the inferior scientist, though his punishment was much more severe than Galileo's. Born near Naples in 1548, five years after Copernicus' death, Bruno was ordained a priest and admitted to the Dominican order; but he was an outspoken critic of the theological orthodoxies of his day, and four years after his ordination he was formally charged with heresy. Thereafter Bruno became something of a European nomad, visiting a number of Italian cities as well as Toulouse, Lyons, Paris, London and Geneva (where he is said to have flirted with Calvinism). He seems to have attracted controversy wherever he went, defending the heliocentric theories of Copernicus and suggesting that the universe may contain an infinite number of worlds, all of which could be inhabited by intelligent creatures. This was not to the Catholic Church's liking, and in 1591 Bruno was arrested in Venice on multiple charges of heresy and tried by the Inquisition. He recanted his views but was sent to Rome in 1592 for a second trial. Found guilty, he was imprisoned and interrogated for eight years, and when he refused to recant for a second time he was declared a heretic and burned at the stake in Rome in 1600. A statue now marks the place of his death in the Campo de' Fiori.

Bruno's near contemporary Galileo Galilei, the devout Catholic genius from Tuscany, ranks as one of the truly great scientists in world history who in the course of a staggeringly innovative career made fundamental contributions to the study of motion, astronomy, the strength of materials and the scientific method. His insistence that the book of nature was written in the language of mathematics redirected the course of science away from the narrative arguments of philosophy towards the quantitative methods of observation and experimentation. In 1613, Galileo produced telescopic evidence that vindicated Copernicus' heliocentric view of the solar system and paved the way for a general acceptance that the earth, spinning on its own axis, did indeed orbit around the sun. Three years later the Catholic Sacred Congregation of the Index of Forbidden Books, controlled by Cardinal Robert Bellarmine (1542-1621), ordered Galileo to renounce his Copernican views. (Bellarmine had earlier affirmed not only that the earth was at the centre of the universe but also that hell was at the centre of the earth). Galileo declined to repudiate his evidence or to recant his position, and it was then that the Congregation placed a ban on Copernicus' great work

De Revolutionibus Orbium Coelestium, at least until certain corrections had been made to its heliocentric passages. These were duly done, and the Congregation allowed the amended work to pass into the public domain, but it was not until 1758 that the original text of *De Revolutionibus* was removed from the Index of Forbidden Books.

As for Galileo, he was summoned to appear before an Inquisition in Rome in 1633 where he was sentenced to indefinite house arrest. Many influential Europeans, outraged by his treatment, pressed unsuccessfully for his release, and even after his death near Florence in 1642 his supporters continued to campaign for his rehabilitation. In 1734 the Vatican allowed his remains to be moved from its modest grave to a suitably imposing mausoleum in the Church of Santa Croce in Florence, and within a short space of time it relaxed its rule forbidding discussion of the motion of the earth. Nevertheless, some of Galileo's writings remained on the Vatican's Index of Forbidden Books until 1835. It was not until the 1870s that the documents relating to his conflict with the ecclesiastical authorities were released. A further hundred years were to pass before Galileo was finally rehabilitated by Pope John Paul II in an address to the Pontifical Academy of Sciences in 1992.

The confrontation between Galileo and Bellarmine has often been depicted as the archetypal conflict between the rationality of science and the authority of the Catholic Church in the sixteenth and seventeenth centuries. Galileo's courage in speaking and writing about his findings was met with humiliation and punishment by an ecclesiastic hierarchy bent on defending its dogmatic teachings through the exercise of its power over human souls. Eventually, however, observation and experimentation necessarily replaced ecclesiastical authority, and the scientific method became the accepted gold standard for understanding the natural world. In the process, the Church lost much of its control over the intellectual paradigms of Western civilisation.

There is a good deal of truth in this traditional telling of the story; but the gradual ascendancy of scientific enquiry over religious dogma was far from swift or smooth. For all that science achieved between 1600 and 1800, the Catholic Church clung onto its prerogative to explain the natural world for a great deal longer than that; and the Protestant Churches also weighed into the fray from time to time. When Charles Darwin (1809-1882) published his groundbreaking book *The Origin of Species by Means of Natural Selection* in 1859, the ecclesiastical opposition to his theory of evolution through natural selection was led not only by Catholics but also by senior Anglicans and Methodists. The Methodist

Church, in particular, erupted in pious indignation over the suggestion that the beauty of nature might be the result of naturally occurring processes rather than the creative imagination of God, and it condemned Darwin as though he were the anti-Christ. As we shall see, echoes of this particular confrontation between faith and science still reverberate in fundamentalist circles, especially (but not exclusively) in the southern states of America.

It is also too simple to see the rise of science as the death knell of popular religion – at least in the short-term. The increasing momentum of the Enlightenment during the eighteenth century coincided in England with a striking religious revival as evangelical preachers took the simple gospel of Christ to the people and converted them in huge numbers. The founder of Methodism, John Wesley (1703-1791), is an interesting example of the complex relationship between religion and science at this time. On the one hand, Wesley was a hugely successful evangelical preacher, convinced of the reality of heaven and hell and given to casting lots to divine the will of God. Yet he was also intensely interested in the scientific debates of his day. He was well informed about pharmacy, physics, botany, metallurgy, zoology, astronomy and much else besides. His two-volume *Compendium of Natural Philosophy* is a remarkably comprehensive description of what was known about the natural world in the mid-eighteenth century and his *Primitive Physick*, published anonymously in 1747, laid down rules for healthy living that still seem eminently sensible.

If Wesley, the intelligent and well-read graduate of Oxford University had no difficulty in holding a religious and a scientific view of the world in constructive tension, the ordinary worshipper in the pew was unlikely even to have realised there was an issue at stake. Many people in Wesley's day still inhabited a universe controlled and manipulated by unseen forces. They still believed in ghosts, evil spirits and angels. More than four hundred years after William of Ockham expounded his principle of parsimony in explanation, escapes from death and other disasters were still commonly attributed to divine intervention, and close shaves were taken to be a warning from God. Far from putting paid to religion, including even the more irrational and superstitious aspects of popular religion such as casting lots to divine the will of God, the Enlightenment seems to have left ordinary people largely untouched.

In the long run, however, the Enlightenment unquestionably set in train the intellectual revolution that was to see the replacement of the religious supernaturalism of the medieval world with the scientific rationalism of the modern world. In the process, the power of occult forces gradually ceased to be an adequate explanation of why things happened as they did. The supernatural face of God, which had been highly conspicuous from earliest times, was steadily departing the limelight as the acceptance of miracles and divine interventions began to erode in educated circles.

If a new face did emerge from the intellectual upheavals of the Enlightenment, it was the face of the God of the gaps. Reluctant to abandon their belief in a God who had created the universe and who held its innermost secrets in the palm of his hand, many Christians yearned for a set of truths about God's creative power that would remain forever beyond the inquisitive minds of rationalists and scholars. They thought they had found them in the gaps in human knowledge that science had not yet explained – and hopefully never would. Science might be able to account for a great deal, they thought, but it could never penetrate the mind of God himself. It could never unravel the mystery of life itself. Black holes of human ignorance, impenetrable by the light of science, would always remain where God could dwell secure; and it was from those eternal gaps in scientific knowledge that he would continue to choreograph the dance of the cosmos.

Yet this was at best a short-term solution to the threatening encroachments of science, buying time for God only for as long as it took the scholars to turn their inquisitive gaze towards the gaps. The God of the gaps was always likely to be a fragile God, destined to shrink as the missing pieces in the jigsaw of human knowledge were patiently assembled. It was bad theology as well as bad science, for there was never going to be a future for a God whose credibility depended upon the limitations of science. That, though, is far from the end of the story. The Enlightenment may have placed a discreet veil over one of the faces of God, but it opened the way for others to emerge. If God could no longer be defended with any great conviction as a supernatural force at work in the world, that merely redirected the divine quest towards other aspects of his nature – aspects that could withstand the critical gaze of secular scholarship and still offer hope and meaning to faithful believers. In the process, philosophy returned to the stage of theological discourse for the first time since medieval scholasticism as some of the finest intellects in seventeenth-century Europe began to think and write about God. Among them were René Descartes, Blaise Pascal and John Locke, together with the polymath scientist, philosopher and theologian, Isaac Newton.

Chapter 16
The God for Enlightened Times

Although the Enlightenment began the long process of destabilising popular belief in a God who intervened at will in the natural world, it by no means betokened the end of a God of faith. Religion is far too deeply ingrained in the human imagination for that. It did, however, prompt the search for new images of God that could withstand the revelations of science while still providing meaning and purpose in people's lives. Philosophy now re-entered the debates, joining science in exploring the boundaries of a credible God for enlightened times; and as the medieval world slowly gave way to the modern, a distinctively new way of thinking about God, Deism, emerged in Britain to take its place alongside the broad theology of Anglicanism and the increasingly evangelical proclamations of the English Dissenters.

Prominent among those in the vanguard of intellectual discourse about God in seventeenth-century Europe was the French philosopher René Descartes (1596-1650). Born a generation after Galileo, Descartes epitomised the rationality that came to be seen as a defining characteristic of the Enlightenment. He was, like Galileo, a Catholic and he believed, like Galileo, that the natural world should properly be read in the language of mathematics. He questioned, however, traditional views about the relationship between faith and reason. St Anselm, a leading early figure in the world of medieval scholasticism, had declared that without belief there could be no understanding: 'I do not seek to understand that I may believe', Anselm had said, 'but I believe in order to understand.' Descartes was inclined to reverse the order: without understanding, there could be no firm basis for belief. Understanding was a prelude to faith, not a consequence of it. Descartes' insistence on the need for a rational understanding of God did not lead him, however, to reject religion entirely. Rather like St Thomas Aquinas four centuries before him, he thought that reason was perfectly able to generate whatever religious truths may lie at the heart of morality, whether or not people chose to accept them. Indeed, God could be known more certainly than almost anything else in existence; but the route to divine understanding was coherent thought and analysis, not blind faith or mystical insight.

Descartes' process of rational reflection about God began with his famous insight into his own consciousness. Perplexed with the question of whether he could be certain of anything, even his own existence, Descartes finally realised that the answer lay in his ability even to think about the matter. Since he was able to reflect upon his own doubt, it followed that he must exist, for without his own existence there could be nothing for him to reflect about: 'I think, therefore I am' (*cogito ergo sum*). Even if he could not be certain of anything in the world outside himself, Descartes was sure about the reality of his own thoughts and reflections. Here was firm ground that no amount of philosophising could spirit out of existence. Here was the basis from which an intelligent search for God could proceed.

The form of Descartes' search for God had echoes of an even earlier medieval theologian than Aquinas. In his first attempt at an ontological proof of God's existence, published in *Monologium* in 1076, St Anselm had argued that people would be unable to recognise different degrees of goodness unless there existed an absolute standard of goodness against which such a judgement could be calibrated. This absolute standard, Anselm had proposed, was God. Descartes avoided the central problem in Anselm's ontological proof by recasting it as a matter of contrast rather than degree, arguing that people could only grasp the concept of *imperfection* if they already had some kind of inner understanding of what *perfection* was. This intuitive appreciation of perfection, Descartes proposed, is what people mean when they talk about God. God must, though, be more than just a mental picture or an intuitive appreciation, for it would be a contradiction in terms to suppose that 'perfection' does not automatically include existence. If, therefore, God can properly be perceived in the human imagination as absolute perfection, then he must also exist in reality. Existence cannot be separated from the image of a perfect God any more than the sum of two right angles can be separated from the internal properties of a triangle. For Descartes, God's existence was as obvious and self-evident as this basic mathematical truth. As he wrote in his *Meditations* on the existence of God: 'It is at least as certain that God, who is this perfect being, is or exists, as any demonstration of geometry can possibly be.' Crucially, though, the evidence lay in the internal reasoning of the human mind, not in revelation or experience.

The somewhat abstract God of Anselm and Aquinas was never likely to appeal very much to the popular imagination: he was more a God for cerebral philosophers than for red-blooded sinners, and he had seemingly little in common with either the engaged and committed God of the early Old Testament or the incarnate God of the New. Descartes'

God, likewise, was as much an abstraction as a living being – a God who could be encountered through calm and rational introspection rather than engagement with the imperfections of the human condition. He was the archetypal God of the Enlightenment, acceptable to those who felt comfortable with the rational outlook of the times. Others, however, wanted something altogether different, and among them was France's other great seventeenth-century philosopher and mathematician, Blaise Pascal (1623-1662). When it came to religion, Pascal was ruled by his heart, not his head. For him it was emotion rather than reason that held the key to belief and therefore to salvation.

Blaise Pascal, physicist, mathematician and theologian, was a sickly but precocious child who became one of the outstanding natural philosophers of his age. Born at Clermont-Ferrand in the Auvergne, he was a generation younger than Descartes. By the age of eleven he had worked out the first twenty-three of Euclid's 115 propositions for himself, and by sixteen he had published a paper on geometry that Descartes refused to believe could have been written by one so young. In the course of his short life (he died at the age of thirty-nine) Pascal built a digital calculator and a hydraulic press, laid the foundations of binomial theory upon which Isaac Newton was soon to build, and set out the basis of probability theory. Yet for all that Pascal shared Descartes' rationalism, he found God through channels that Descartes deemed unnecessary. Indeed, Pascal went out of his way to be dismissive of Descartes, describing him as 'useless and uncertain'. In his unfinished *Pensées*, Pascal said of him that: 'in his whole philosophy he would like to do without God; but he could not help allowing him a flick of the fingers to set the world in motion; after that he had no more use of God.'

Pascal's family was not particularly devout, but in 1646 they converted to Jansenism when Pascal's sister Jacqueline entered the Jansenist convent of Port-Royal-des-Champs in Paris. Jansenism was, at its simplest, Calvinism for Catholics, closer to the severe Protestantism of Calvin, Zwingli and Beza than to the kind of resurgent Catholicism promoted by the Council of Trent. Opposed particularly by the Jesuits, it emphasised original sin, divine grace and predestination. Partly through his sister's passionate advocacy of Jansenism, Pascal threw his lot in with the sect; and on a dark night in November 1654 he had a mystical experience of the revelation of God not unlike that of Augustine, Luther or Wesley. He recorded it in a 'memorial' that was stitched into his doublet and not discovered until after his death in 1662. It was entitled *Fire*: 'God of Abraham, God of Isaac, God of Jacob, not of philosophers and scholars. Certainty, certainty, heartfelt, joy, peace. God of Jesus Christ. God of Jesus Christ. My God and your God, thy God shall be my God. The world forgotten, and everything except God. He can only be found by the ways taught in the gospels . . . O righteous Father, the world had not known thee, but I have known thee. Joy, joy, tears of joy . . . I will not forget thy word.'

If Descartes' God was the product of the intellectual processes of the mind, Pascal's God sprang from the emotional processes of the heart. His was a God of revelation, not of philosophy, a God to be experienced rather than understood. This made him, for Pascal, a shadowy God about whose existence he could not be certain. If the reality of God depended solely upon his inward recognition of him, what if he was mistaken in his perception? What if it had not been the God of Jesus Christ whom he had encountered on that dark night in 1654? Not for him the almost cavalier assertion of Descartes that God's being was as certain as anything that mathematics could throw up. In spite of his own deeply mystical experience, Pascal was almost overwhelmed with a sense of God's absence from the world: 'When I see the blind and wretched state of man', he wrote in his *Pensées,* 'when I survey the whole universe in its dumbness and man left to himself with no light, as though lost in the corner of the universe, I am moved to terror.' It is a confession remarkable for its modernity as well as its honesty. Not only was Pascal uncertain of God's very existence, he was open enough with himself to confront his doubts head on. He articulated the secret fear that often accompanies an outward show of religious certainty: what if I am wrong? For Pascal, doubt was ever-present and faith was a gamble.

Pascal was nothing if not ingenious, however, and he found an elegant way of persuading people to back what he believed to be the winner. If faith is a gamble, is it wiser to believe or not to believe in the existence of God – assuming that if God really does exist, the consequences of getting it wrong might be immense in the realms beyond the grave? Is there the religious equivalent of an odds-on favourite? Pascal thought there was, and it has come to be known as 'Pascal's wager'. If God does exist, then those who prefer to believe that he doesn't, and who live their lives in disobedience to his law, may enjoy an earthly life of hedonistic self-indulgence but face an eternity of remorse beyond the grave. Those, on the other hand, who choose to believe in him and who live in obedience to his law may forego an earthly life of unbridled pleasure but will enjoy an eternity of everlasting joy in the next. If God doesn't exist, then there is no life for anyone beyond the grave, and the only price paid by believers is to miss out on the life of hedonistic pleasure that they might otherwise have chosen to live.

In a situation in which nobody can be absolutely certain about the existence of God, then, the substantive choice is between, on the one hand, an earthly life of self-indulgence followed by the possibility of an eternity of remorse, and on the other, an earthly life of righteousness followed by the possibility of an eternity of joy. The rational man, Pascal believed, would put his money on the existence of God. In any case, Pascal rejected the proposition that to live in accordance with the will of God was to consign oneself to an earthly life of miserable self-denial. The life of faith and discipleship can be one of dignity and fulfilment whether or not God exists. Indeed, for reasons entirely unconnected with religion it may well be a far more rewarding life than one of selfishness and greed. Faith, for Pascal, may have been a leap, but it was not entirely a leap in the dark.

If anyone managed to bring together the differing perspectives of Descartes and Pascal, it was the English philosopher John Locke (1632-1704). Locke's was one of the most heeded voices in European philosophy, not only in his lifetime but for decades thereafter. He was to the seventeenth century what Erasmus had been to the sixteenth: an intelligent, enlightened and impartial critic of the intellectual fashions of his day. Like Descartes and Pascal, Locke was deeply interested in religious questions, and like them, he believed in God and saw himself as a Christian. He was a middle-of-the-road Anglican with an instinctive distaste for extremism or emotionalism. Theologically, Locke favoured the moderate Protestantism of Jacob Arminius above the severities of Calvinism; but he was also a man of the Enlightenment, and in his essay *The Reasonableness of Christianity*, published anonymously in 1695, he examined the central tenets of Christianity in the light of reason. The essay is sometimes described as an attempt to make the lion of enlightened rationalism lie down in harmony with the lamb of Christian traditionalism. Others put it more brutally: the lamb of traditionalism was forced to lie down and be quiet by the lion of rationalism.

In his religious writings, Locke went some way towards reconciling Pascal's subjective experience of divine revelation with Descartes' objective approach of intellectual reason. However important it may be for Christians to lead good lives, Locke noted, they were not alone in upholding the traditional Christian standards of honesty, justice and compassion. Many people of other faiths and none were doing the same. It followed, then, that to be a Christian required more than a general disposition towards righteous living: it required also a belief in the God of the Bible and in Jesus Christ as God's Messiah. This, for Locke, was the very heart of Christianity, though he seems not to have pondered too deeply the implications of Christ's messianic status. So far so uncontroversial: any devout Anglican of the time could have said much the same. Then Locke introduced a new condition into the argument, one taken straight from the textbook of enlightened thought. Nothing should be believed about God that was not entirely consistent with natural human reason. Since God had given people the ability to think for themselves, all that he revealed to them must be consistent with a human understanding of what is reasonable and rational. Anything purporting to be a revelation of God that forced people to set aside their intellectual integrity must be false, for Christianity was nothing if not the rational assent to reasonable beliefs.

Having said this, Locke's personal position on revelation and reason is not entirely clear. Privately, at least, he seems to have rejected a number of traditional Christian doctrines as contrary to his own criteria, but it is a matter of conjecture which they were. A clue may be found in his apparent approval of Socinianism – a system of Christian doctrine named after Fausto Sizzini (1539-1604) that developed in the Reformed Church of Poland in the sixteenth century and was embraced by the Transylvanian Unitarian Church. Socinianism rejected a great deal of what passed at the time for orthodox Christian theology, including the doctrine of the Holy Trinity, the divinity of Christ, and the satisfaction theory of the crucifixion. Socinians also dismissed the idea of eternal life, arguing that death was the natural and inevitable fate of every human being, however virtuous their lives may have been. To expect there to be life after death, assured through a belief in the resurrection of Jesus, was an expectation too far. Much of this, one feels, would have harmonised with Locke's search for some rational foundations of Christian belief. For him, believing in Jesus and in the things he taught about morality and virtue lay at the heart of what it meant to be a Christian. Angels, miracles, virgin births and the resuscitation of dead bodies were optional extras and definitely not for the reasonably-minded.

Another giant of the European Enlightenment, Isaac Newton (1642-1727), was an almost exact contemporary of Locke. More than anyone else, Newton reflected the complex relationship between the scientific and religious ideas of the times. Born at Woolsthorpe in Lincolnshire on Christmas Day 1642, he graduated from Cambridge University in 1665 and was immediately elected a fellow of Trinity College. When the University was forced into closure by the plague, Newton returned home to the family farm in Lincolnshire where he spent the next eighteen months working out a number of ideas that would utterly transform Western science. In mathematics, he devised binomial theory and established the principles of differential calculus. In optics, he discovered the colour composition of white light. In physics, his investigations into the force of gravity began with his famous (but possibly apocryphal) observation of an apple falling from a tree. Returning to Cambridge in 1667, Newton was appointed to the prestigious Lucasian Professorship of Mathematics at the age of twenty-six when his former teacher, Isaac Barrow, resigned it in favour of his young protégé.

Newton now turned his fertile imagination to the cosmos as he pondered the force that held the planets in their orbits around the sun. He established that the force, gravity, became stronger as bodies came nearer to each other and weaker as they moved away. By calculating the gravitational forces acting upon the centres of planetary bodies, he was able to explain the trajectories of planets through the skies, the movements of tides, and the velocity of falling objects. Newton's laws of motion, which were to pass unchallenged for more than two hundred years, laid out the foundations of modern physics. They offered a compellingly dynamic account of the cosmos, far removed from the static medieval vision of the universe as a triple-decker sandwich, with heaven above the earth and hell below it.

It might be thought that the man who came closer than any before him to plumbing the mysteries of the universe would have had little sympathy with the popular religious views of his day; yet Newton regarded himself as a devout Christian. Indeed, he was not only a scientist but a theologian also, leaving behind a corpus of theological writing unmatched in size by all but a few of his seventeenth-century contemporaries. In a series of letters to his friend Richard Bentley (1662-1742), later to become Master of Trinity College when Newton was in residence there, Newton revealed that he regarded the dynamics of the universe as evidence of God's existence. Why, he wondered, were the planets so carefully arranged in space that the gravitational attraction of the sun had not sucked them into its fiery mass? The answer, surely, must be that an intelligent and divine overseer had placed them thus. 'Gravity may put ye planets into motion', he wrote to Bentley in 1687, 'but without ye divine power it could never put them in such a Circulating motion as they have about ye Sun, and therefore, for this as well as other reasons, I am compelled to ascribe ye frame of this Systeme to an intelligent agent.' Newton observed that if the earth revolved on its axis at only one hundred miles an hour instead of a thousand, night would be ten times longer and the earth would be too cold for life to exist. Whoever had contrived to ensure such a perfect combination of circumstances could only be seen as an unsurpassably intelligent being. It was an early exposition of what has come to be known as the anthropic argument: because the systems necessary to support life on earth are so finely calibrated and inter-connected, the probability of their having arisen by chance seems infinitesimally small.

Although Newton saw the hand of God in the intricate design and perfect balance of the universe, he nevertheless rejected the idea that God had simply set the whole thing in motion and then stood back from it. Newton's God was an engaged and committed God who not only placed the planets in their orbits but held them there through gravitational forces. In an appendix to the second edition of his great work *Philosophiae Naturalis Principia Mathematica* in 1713, Newton laid bare his religious convictions. 'This most beautiful system of the sun, planets and comets could only proceed from the counsel and dominion of an intelligent and powerful Being . . . He is eternal and infinite, omnipotent and omniscient; that is, his duration reaches from eternity to eternity; his presence from infinity to infinity; he governs all things, and knows all things that are or can be done.' A God who 'governs all things and knows all things' is very close to the omnipotent and omniscient God of orthodox Christian theology.

In other respects, however, Newton was far from conventional in his religious views. Like his contemporary John Locke, he had no time for theological dogmas about salvation and sacrifice, which he equated with ignorance and superstition; and like Locke, he seems to have been drawn towards the ideas of Socinianism. In particular, Newton rejected the doctrine of the Holy Trinity as a corrupt belief imposed upon a gullible Church by Athanasius of Alexandria in the fourth century. Newton was far more sympathetic to the views of Athanasius' redoubtable but ultimately defeated opponent, the heretical Arius of Antioch, who saw the Father as the only true God and Jesus as a divine but lesser being. Newton also spurned an orthodox belief in the immortality of the soul and he thought that demons were merely the delusions or distempers of a disordered mind. The devil was nothing more than a symbol of human lust and ambition. These were dangerous beliefs to hold, at least in public, for to deny the Holy Trinity was illegal in his day and to reject the immortality of the soul was scandalous. To dismiss the reality of evil spirits was tantamount to atheism. Unsurprisingly, Newton kept his heretical tendencies a closely guarded secret from all but his most trusted friends.

Newton's wish to see Christianity purged of its dogmatic excesses (especially where they concerned the Holy Trinity) did not, however, extend to questioning the actual existence of God. In this he was a child of his time. His God was, in certain respects, the traditional God of Jewish and Christian history, revealed through the elegance of the universe he had created as well as through the moral demands he placed upon humanity. Newton's work as a scientist had begun to answer the 'how' questions about the universe but he found no scientific answers to the 'why' questions. And so even he was persuaded by the classical argument from design: a stupendously elegant universe must have been created by a wondrously intelligent being. Even Newton, one of the founding fathers of modern physics, could not fully explain the cosmos without God lurking somewhere in the background.

Out of the rationalism of the Enlightenment, captured in their different ways in the seventeenth and early eighteenth centuries by Descartes, Pascal, Locke and Newton, a formal view of God emerged in Europe and North America that flourished for a while before being swallowed up in the broader currents of liberal Protestant theology in the nineteenth and twentieth centuries. It came to be known as Deism, or natural religion. Deism is often seen as the quintessential expression of a God for enlightened times, born of the intellectual spirit of the age and bent on reinterpreting the faith in the clear and sharp light of reason and logic. Echoing Locke, it rested on the belief that nothing should be accepted that was out of tune with the dictates of human reason and the harmonies of the natural world. Order, precision, predictability, rationality – these were, to the Enlightenment mind, the outward signs of the deepest regularities of the universe; and Deists saw it as their task to disclose the nature of the divine being who had caused it all to come into being.

A famous example of eighteenth-century Deist reasoning is William Paley's celebrated analogy of the pocket-watch. A clergyman and mathematician who became Archdeacon of Carlisle, Paley (1743-1805) was well versed in Enlightenment views about the orderliness and rationality of nature. Indeed, so taken was he with the complex precision and predictability of the natural world that he likened the universe to a celestial pocket-watch; and just as a watch could not possibly have put itself together, neither could the universe. Nobody who marvelled at the immaculate intricacies of the watch could doubt the existence of the skilled and gifted watch-maker who had designed its parts, brought them together, and set them in motion. By the same token, nobody could doubt the existence of the 'divine watchmaker' who had designed the universe, brought it into being, and now sustained its unvarying regularities. Moreover, if this was true for the universe as a whole, so also must it be true for all its constituent parts as they fitted perfectly together to form a thing of unimaginable splendour, order and complexity. The intricate yet precisely functioning optics of the eye or the delicate beauty of a butterfly's wing, so perfectly adapted to their purposes, could only be the work of a master-craftsman of unsurpassable intelligence and power.

It is easy to understand the appeal of Deism at a time when science and engineering were coming of age, yet the God of Deism was largely an absentee God, sustaining the delicate mechanisms he had created but never involving himself in the misery and the ecstasy, the generosity and the sinfulness of people's life. A wonderful cosmic engineer he may have been, but he had little or no concern for the joys and pains of the human condition. Herein lay the ultimate limitation of Deism, for a God who stood apart from his creation was far removed from the traditional God of grace who so loved the world that he gave his only Son to die for its salvation. There was no place in the precisely regulated world of Deism for the blood of the cross or the cries of the damned. Anything that smacked of mystery, supernaturalism or whatever else had held generations of faithful believers in the grip of ancient myths or superstitions were banished from the sterile, orderly, regulated workshop of the divine watchmaker. What was left was sparse and somewhat austere. The God of Deism may have been the answer to intelligent questioning about the harmonies and regularities of universe, but he was hardly the answer to a wretched sinner's plea for mercy.

Two of the most prominent Deists were the Irishman John Toland and the Englishman Matthew Tindal. John Toland (1670-1722) was raised a Catholic in Northern Ireland but converted to Protestantism at the age of sixteen. In 1696 (the year after the appearance of John Locke's seminal essay *The Reasonableness of Christianity*) Toland published his own controversial book, *Christianity Not Mysterious*, in which he launched a ferocious attack on all the accretions and elaborations (mainly, in his view, Roman Catholic elaborations) that had distorted the simple message of the gospels. The sub-title of the 1702 edition of the book was: 'Shewing that there is nothing in the gospel contrary to reason, nor above it, and that no Christian doctrine can be properly called a mystery.' The only authentic Christianity, Toland argued, was one that did not violate the natural and instinctive religious sentiments of clear-thinking people. At the heart of his book lay an axiom that might have come from Locke himself: 'Whoever reveals anything (that is, whoever tells us something we did not know before), his words must be intelligible and the matter possible.' Whatever is mysterious, unintelligible or impossible cannot be part of the natural religion of reasonable people, and to expect them to sacrifice their reason in the name of Christianity is to violate the very image of God in humanity.

By arguing publicly that the Christian faith was credible only when it was intellectually reasonable, Toland stripped traditional Christianity of much that made it a dogmatic religion of revelation and faith. It was a view that got him into a great deal of trouble, for this was not yet the time for religious radicalism. In 1697 Thomas Aitkenhead, a medical student, was hanged in Edinburgh for questioning the doctrine of the Holy Trinity and denouncing theology as 'a rhapsody of feigned and ill invented nonsense'. It was to be the last auto-da-fé in Britain. In the same year, Toland's book *Christianity not Mysterious* was debated by outraged bishops in England and was condemned by a Grand Jury of Middlesex. The Irish House of Commons ordered it to be burned by the public hangman. By 1718 Toland, now a broken man, was lodging with a carpenter in Putney where he spent the rest of his days in poverty and debt before dying, largely forgotten, in 1722.

Toland's near contemporary, Matthew Tindal (1657-1733), was an English gentleman of Anglican persuasion who became a fellow of All Souls' College at Oxford and was once described as 'certainly the most learned of the Deists'. His major work, *Christianity as Old as Creation*, first published in London in 1730, came to be known as the Deists' Bible; and following its translation into German in 1741 was influential in the rise of liberal Protestant theology in the German-speaking world. Tindal held that the essential truths of Christianity had always been known to sensitive people from the dawn of time, for they were truths that had as much to do with social and personal morality as with dogma and revelation. Tindal believed that whatever honoured God and whatever was good for the generality of mankind was in tune with the will of God. So far so good: Jesus himself had said the same thing. For Tindal, however, that was just about all there was to be said. Since (in his view) it was a 'natural' religious impulse to want to love God and one's neighbour, the social ethic of Christianity could safely be accepted as the *only* true revelation from God. Everything else, on such matters as the Holy Trinity, the incarnation, the atonement and the resurrection were so far removed from any normal or intuitive meaning that they had no part to play in Tindal's understanding of natural religion. Concocted by ecclesiastical power brokers and foisted upon ill-educated people incapable of thinking for themselves, these beliefs showed only 'the petty and arbitrary God of revelation', not the 'impartial and magnanimous God of Natural Religion'.

Those who were in sympathy with the principles of Deism were hard pressed to find places of worship that embodied their beliefs about God. Finding little to cheer them in the mainstream Christian churches in the eighteenth century, they began to organise a new denomination to cater for their beliefs. Among them were disillusioned Anglicans, progressive Congregationalists and disenchanted Baptists. In 1774 the first Unitarian congregation was formed in London (the Essex Chapel) followed in 1785 by the founding of the North American Unitarian Church in Boston. A number of Churches (mainly Congregational) effectively adopted a Deist position, denying the Holy Trinity, the divinity of Jesus, eternal punishment and the atoning power of the crucifixion. But most Christians with Deist sympathies either cut themselves off from organised religion entirely or continued to attend the established churches while quietly dissenting from their public doctrines.

It is all but impossible to judge the extent to which the legacy of Deism is still to be seen today, but it might be argued that the God in whom a large proportion of people in North America and Europe claim to believe is closer to the God of natural religion than to the God of biblical Judaism or creedal Christianity. In America, particularly, the God of natural religion is recognisably the archetype of the God of civic religion, whose name springs readily to the lips of public figures and whom politicians spurn or deny at their peril. When Americans ask God to bless their country (or, for that matter, when Britons ask him to save their gracious queen), the God they have in mind may be closer to the antiseptic God of natural religion than to the fiery God of Sabbaoth or the Trinitarian God of Nicaea. It is a safe option in a religiously pluralistic world. The God of natural religion is a conservative God who keeps the world moving smoothly along morally acceptable pathways, but he is not a God who judges or punishes people, nor does he require them to believe in supernatural occurrences. He does not invite them to eat his body, drink his blood, or accept his death as a human sacrifice. By definition, nothing about the God of Deism stretches human credulity beyond its ordinary limits, for he is a God of reason and rationality.

Even as Deism was at its height, others 'isms' were being born that would reveal a fundamentally different face of the Christian God, a God who was better at warming the heart than enlightening the mind. Foremost among them were Pietism and Methodism.

Chapter 17
The God Who Warms the Heart

The history of Protestantism has been, in part, one of continuing schism and separation. Martin Luther may have set the Reformation in train with his forthright insights into faith, grace and salvation, but pure Lutheranism, if it ever existed, did not last for long. Throughout much of Europe, reformers first adopted and then adapted the spirit of Luther's protestations, creating in the process new sects and denominations that reflected their own political and theological agendas. God may be forgiven for wondering what was happening to him as new and sometimes conflicting images of him were unveiled in Switzerland, Holland, Scotland, England, Germany, America and elsewhere.

Two of the more important breakaway Protestant sects, each intended to bring about a distinctive change of emphasis in the Christian experience of God, were Pietism and Methodism. Although they were different kinds of movements, they had in common the desire for a more intimate and inspiring face of God than that of the Lutherans, the Calvinists or the Deists. Methodism began as an attempt to reinvigorate the hearts and emotions of Anglicans in eighteenth-century England, but it eventually became a separate Church with its own ministry, its own organisational structures and its own doctrinal standards. Pietism, by contrast, was never much more than a meeting of minds and spirits among German Lutherans who yearned for a more personal and inward experience of God. The Pietists never broke away, as the Methodists did, to form a separate denomination or Church. The influence of Pietism eventually spread a little beyond Germany; but unlike Methodism, which has flourished as a mainstream Protestant Church since its beginnings in the mid-eighteenth century, Pietism was largely a movement of its time.

Pietism began as a reaction among German Lutherans in the seventeenth century against what they saw as the excessively rigid views of Martin Luther, especially on matters of salvation. Above all else, Luther had wanted certainty: he needed to know, beyond any shadow of doubt, that he was justified in the eyes of God, and he desperately sought a way of grasping that knowledge. He found it in the principle, first set out by St Paul in his letter to the Romans, of justification by grace through faith: people are justified by nothing other than the grace of God, and they can claim that grace by professing their faith in the gospel of Jesus Christ. Yet although it was a formula that satisfied Luther, it failed to meet the needs of many Lutherans who came to see it as a rather abstract principle, somewhat removed from the human realities of their daily lives. As a recipe for salvation, it might be true; but many people wanted more than recipes. They wanted a God who would stir their hearts as well as tax their minds, and Luther's God failed to do this for them. By the early seventeenth century, Lutheranism was felt by many in Germany to be obsessed with the fine-tuning of doctrine in the quest of ever greater refinements of Protestant truth. Passion and emotion had largely gone out of religion as scholars jockeyed among themselves to expose each other's theological flaws and assert their own doctrinal purity.

It was against such intellectualising of the Christian faith that the Pietists reacted. They needed a God who could be 'loved by sinners and worshipped by peasants'. They believed that Luther had over-played the outward, objective truths about salvation at the expense of an inward, subjective experience of God's love and forgiveness. For the Pietists, it was less a matter of what God could do *for* people than of what he could do *within* them. They drew a much-loved distinction between 'sacramental piety' and 'conversional piety'. Sacramental piety was the outward veneer of sanctity that people acquired through baptism and participation in worship and the sacraments. Conversional piety was a living sanctification that began when Christians became inwardly aware not only of their own sinfulness but also of the love of God within them. The thin broth of sacramental piety may have satisfied the appetites of more orthodox Lutherans, but it did not satisfy the Pietists. They wanted the red meat of conversional piety.

None of this amounted to a wholesale rejection of Protestant doctrines or traditions, much less of Christianity itself. In many respects, Pietism was rather conservative in its theology. It offered, however, a new way of testing the truth of doctrinal statements, judging them less by the fame of the theologians who pronounced them than by the experiences of those whose hearts were aflame with the love and forgiveness of God. Pietism also stressed the changes that would be wrought in the lives of those who were reborn in the Spirit. They should expect and tolerate trials and temptations. They should consciously carry the cross of Christ each day. They should engage in daily self-examination and repentance. They should rejoice in the word of God and embrace the sacraments.

Their active Christianity should spill over into the world around them, meeting the needs of the destitute and challenging the privileges of the powerful. It was a heady gospel to which many disillusioned Lutherans responded with joyful enthusiasm.

The founding father of Pietism is generally regarded as the Lutheran preacher and pastor, Philipp Spener (1635-1705). Like many other Lutherans of his day, Spener felt that Lutheranism had produced a Church only half reformed. Germany, he thought, was full of professing Christians well versed in the mechanics of justification by faith but lacking in devotional fire and devoid of any real fear of divine judgement. They were casually taking the grace of God almost for granted. In 1670 Spener began to assemble small groups of believers who, like himself, were dissatisfied with such a lifeless religion. Meeting together for Bible study and prayer, he encouraged them to follow the literal meanings of the texts, freed as far as possible from any dogmatic assumptions about God. He also gave practical expression to the Protestant doctrine of the priesthood of all believers, encouraging lay people to lead prayers, read lessons, discuss sermons and generally assume responsibility for nurturing each other in the faith. Spener's success in building up an extensive network of 'cell groups' or 'house churches' got him into hot water with the Lutheran hierarchy, and he spent much of his time evading their attempts to call him to account. Wherever he went throughout Germany, however, new groups sprang up to revivify the dry and even dull proceedings of many Lutheran congregations. Spener died in Berlin in 1705 and was buried in a white coffin as a symbol of his hope for everlasting life in heaven.

Spener painted the face of God in the warm tones of human and emotional responsiveness that had been largely absent from Luther's palate. His vision of God became a beacon for his godson Nicholas Ludwig, Count Zinzendorf (1700-1760). Born into a noble Dresden family, Zinzendorf is said to have developed an unnaturally deep faith as a child and expressed the wish to train as a pastor; but he well understood the conflict between his vocation and his destiny as a hereditary count. Like many wealthy young men of his age, he embarked upon a grand tour of Europe, during the course of which he encountered Domenico Fetti's painting of the scourged Christ in a gallery in Düsseldorf. The legend beneath the painting read: 'This I have done for you. What will you do for me?' Moved beyond speaking, he vowed to offer his life to the service of God. Zinzendorf was ordained in the Lutheran Church, and like his godfather Spener he soon became an obsessive critic of its orthodoxy and its formulaic approach to doctrine.

In 1722 Zinzendorf was approached by a group of Moravian Brethren seeking permission to settle on his land at Berthelsdorf, in Saxony. The Moravian Church was one of a small number of what would now be called Protestant churches to predate the Reformation, having already been in existence for many decades when Luther posted his theses at Wittenberg in 1517. It began in Moravia and Bohemia (now part of the Czech Republic) when Jan Hus (1369-1415), the rector of Prague University, objected to the excesses of the Roman Catholic Church and used his brilliance as an orator to denounce the abuse of its power. His followers formed the Unity of Brethren, noted for the simplicity of their worship and the zeal of their missionary activities. After the Reformation, the Unity of Brethren, or the Moravian Church as it came to be known in Germany, became a mainstream Protestant Church, and when a group of Moravians led by an itinerant carpenter, Christian David, asked Zinzendorf for permission to move onto his land, their request was granted. They settled in a place they called Herrnhut (the Lord's Watch), hoping to establish there a Christian community of love, but their life together was far from smooth and quarrels broke out among them.

Intrigued by the discrepancy between expectation and reality, Zinzendorf abandoned his public life as an aristocrat and began to work with the troubled settlers. Under his leadership they evolved a set of Christian guidelines, based upon biblical teaching, which they were all expected to follow. The result was an intense experience of renewal among the group, culminating in a service in August 1727 when they felt the Holy Spirit powerfully among them telling them to 'love one another'. The experience is sometimes described as the Moravian Pentecost. Thereafter, 'heart religion' (as the Pietists liked to call it) became the ideal towards which Zinzendorf and the Moravians were constantly striving. For them, faith was a matter of experiencing God with an irresistible emotional fervour. It had nothing to do with theological propositions and very little to do with formal professions of faith. Their activities included unusual gatherings such as love feasts, song services, New Year watch-night services and Easter sunrise services.

It may fairly be said that Zinzendorf and the Moravians were inclined towards an emotional approach to their faith that bordered onto the anti-intellectual. They never, however, descended into fanaticism, nor did they entirely abandon the classical Protestant doctrines or the Christian creeds. Zinzendorf himself affirmed the Nicene Creed, though he did not hold it to be central to the Christian faith. More important in his eyes was repentance and what modern evangelical Christians would call 'a personal relationship with Jesus'. When Zinzendorf died at Herrnhut in 1760 he left behind not only a highly organised Moravian Church in Germany but also a string of Moravian communities throughout the world, especially in America. It was during one of the Moravians' missionary journeys across the Atlantic that they made a deep impression on an Anglican clergyman who was travelling with them, John Wesley. Zinzendorf came to know John and his brother Charles quite well during their several visits to Herrnhut; and although the Wesley brothers later parted company with him to establish the Methodist Church, they both retained a warm affection for the Moravians throughout their lives.

Methodism was the eighteenth-century product of a union between Pietism and Arminianism. John Wesley (1703-1791) supplied the theology, the preaching and the organisation while Charles Wesley (1707-1788) wrote the hymns. Together they made Methodism one of the most influential social and religious movements in Georgian Britain, not only changing the religious face of the nation but also attacking its social and economic evils. The Wesleys were not, like some of their contemporaries in America, hell-fire evangelical preachers with little interest in the intellectual currents swirling around them. John Wesley, in particular, was an intensely curious man in an age when there was much to be curious about; and he was as much at home expatiating upon the remedies for gout or condemning the evils of slavery as he was proclaiming the grace of God. His *Compendium of Natural Philosophy* reveals him as a true product of the English Enlightenment, interested in anatomy, biology, zoology, geology, cosmology and chemistry. So sure was he of God's role in creation that the pronouncements of the scientists held no threat for him. Quite the reverse: they were to be praised for uncovering ever more of the creative majesty of God.

John Wesley's theology was shaped by a series of experiences not unlike those of Luther and Zinzendorf. As a young student he believed that the road to holiness lay in the cultivation of spiritual discipline, and he and Charles gathered together a number of undergraduates of the same mind at Oxford University to form a 'holy club'. Characterised by their serious approach to religion and their methodical, disciplined exercises in spirituality, they acquired the nickname of 'the Oxford Methodists'. Yet just like Luther more than two centuries earlier, Wesley felt that something was lacking. He could never be sure that he was doing enough through prayer, study and good works to grasp the grace of God. Bereft of a vibrant sense of God's presence in his life, he was much more familiar with what the Pietists were dismissively calling 'head religion' than with full-blooded 'heart religion'. After an abortive, even disastrous, search for the missing spark in the British colony of Savannah, in Georgia, John Wesley finally found the assurance he craved in May 1738 as he was attending a meeting at Aldersgate in London. During a reading from Martin Luther's *Preface to the Epistle to the Romans*, Wesley famously 'felt his heart strangely warmed' and he knew beyond any doubt that Jesus Christ was his saviour. It was for him an overwhelming moment of epiphany, setting him on a life of unquenchable faith and unparalleled itinerant evangelism.

It was, then, from the Pietist heritage of Spener, Zinzendorf and the Moravians that Methodism drew one of its distinctive features: a warmed heart. Yet Wesley was much more than just a gifted evangelist, able to rouse his hearers to a frenzy of emotional fervour with his exhortations and warnings. He knew the supreme importance of a heart warmed and a life renewed, certainly, but he also knew that a warmed heart was of little lasting value unless accompanied by a clear head. Emotion by itself was not enough: there had also to be a hard theology of grace to provide a framework within which religious fervour could endure and flourish. John Wesley found it in the second great influence on Methodism, Arminianism; but it could easily have turned out differently, for in its early years Methodism also attracted others of a Calvinist disposition who wanted the movement to follow the path set out by Calvin, Zwingli and Beza.

Foremost among the Calvinist pretenders was an outstanding – even theatrical – evangelical preacher, George Whitefield (1714-1770), and it was as a result of his disputations with Whitefield that John Wesley grabbed the reins and set the tone of Methodist theology along Arminian rather than Calvinist lines. Converted at the same time when Wesley was experiencing humiliation in Savannah, Whitefield was every bit as effective a preacher as Wesley, and for a while the two worked powerfully together in harmonious tandem. Following his conversion experience in 1738, however, Wesley became increasingly opposed to Calvinist views on predestination and limited atonement; and he rapidly fell out with his erstwhile collaborator. Within a year, in June 1739, he was writing to Whitefield expressing shock at his intention to print a sermon on predestination: 'What will be the consequences but controversy? If people ask my opinion, what shall I do?' Later that year, after Whitefield went to America, Wesley published his own sermon on free grace, and from then onwards the gap between the two men became a divide. In America, Whitefield's Calvinist outlook was reinforced by the influence of hard-line evangelicals like Jonathan Edwards (1703-1768) and Howell Harris (1714-1773); and it was Harris who wrote to tell Wesley in 1740 that 'you grieve God's people by your opposition to electing love; and many poor souls believe your doctrine simply because you hold it.'

George Whitefield and John Wesley continued to be at loggerheads with each other over these fundamental points of doctrine. Wesley even went as far as to denounce the Calvinist doctrines of predestination, irresistible grace and limited atonement as blasphemous. He utterly rejected the idea that salvation was only for those whom God had predestined for it, teaching instead that *everyone* could be saved. Christ's atonement, he insisted, was universal, not limited, and to argue otherwise was an offensive denial of God's all-inclusive love. In nailing his theological colours to the mast of universal salvation, Wesley was treading firmly in the footsteps of Jacob Arminius (1560-1609), the Dutch pastor and academic who (as we have seen) had strenuously opposed the rigid Calvinism of Theodore Beza and Francis Gomarus in the very early years of the seventeenth century. Indeed, John Wesley was by far the most influential Arminian since Arminius himself, and it is largely through his explicit espousal of the Dutchman's theology that his name has been remembered.

Arminius believed that God had created men and women with free-will, knowing that they would sin and fall short of the mark; but he had also provided for their salvation in the death and resurrection of Jesus. It was not, however, the inescapable provision that the hard-line Calvinists were making it out to be. People were free to choose whether or not to believe in Jesus and repent of their sins. Salvation was *potentially* available to all even if it was *actually* granted only to those who responded in faith to the grace of God in their lives. Arminius drew a distinction between the 'prevenient grace' and the 'justifying grace' of God. The former came into people's lives before they had even recognised it; but having recognised it, they were then free to accept or reject it. They had a genuine choice. If they accepted and acted upon it, then prevenient grace became justifying grace; and all that was needed to get from one to the other was faith in Jesus Christ. It was good Protestant stuff, but not of the Calvinist variety.

Wesley took over many of the ideas of Arminius and turned them into the distinctive theological fingerprint of Methodism. He also added some embellishments of his own. He taught that people could know, with complete certainty, that they were saved. He taught that justification was a once-and-for-all acceptance by God of the repentant sinner, followed by a process of sanctification leading to a state of Christian perfection or perfect love. He taught that holy living and good works were more than just the natural responses of those who knew they were saved: they were also the volitional actions of people seeking salvation. In this respect, Wesley might be described as an eighteenth-century Pelagian, and it was this as much as anything else that set him at odds with Calvinism and that led some to accuse him of diluting the classical Protestant doctrine of justification by faith. If Christians could also be justified by their good works, then the saving power of faith alone must surely be compromised. It was much the same charge that Augustine had levelled against Pelagius fourteen hundred years earlier.

Though working from the same scriptural sources as the Lutherans and Calvinists, the Pietists and the Methodists sought – and found – a rather different God. They yearned for a God who would not merely save them in some abstract way but who would set their hearts on fire with love for him and for their fellows. They wanted a God who offered redemption to the whole of humanity, not just to those he had predestined for salvation, and who placed nobody beyond the scope of his loving grace. They wanted a God who was accessible, knowable and merciful. And the God that Philipp Spener, Nicholas Zinzendorf and the Wesley brothers found became the prototype of the God of evangelical Christians ever since. Even as Pietism and Methodism were stoking the fires of an evangelical revival in some parts of Europe, however, cultural and intellectual leaders elsewhere on the continent were beginning to draft the obituaries to the personal, heart-warming God of conversional piety – and powerful obituaries they were too.

Chapter 18
The God Who Was Fading Away

The eighteenth century was not only a time of significant revival in the religious life of northern Europe, it was also the century when thinkers and sceptics began seriously to question the transcendent God of Christian tradition. In 1729 a little-noticed event occurred in north-eastern France that brought into sharp relief the sea-change in public attitudes towards religion that was beginning to take place among both clergy and laity as they absorbed and reflected upon the philosophical and scientific messages of the Enlightenment. When Jean Meslier (1664-1729), a French country Catholic priest who had led an apparently exemplary personal and professional life, died in his home town of Etrépigny in the Ardennes region, his legacy to his astonished parish was a dramatic confession, *Mon Testament*. It was a vast work of some six hundred pages, revealing that over the course of his life he had lost his faith in God and the Church and embraced instead a bleak despair about the human condition. For Meslier, the flame of Christian hope had become a guttering candle and God a hollow shell. Disgusted by the greed and selfishness of those who used their positions of power to advance their own interests at the expense of the weak, *Mon Testament* was the anguished tirade of a disillusioned priest who had abandoned any hope he may have had of seeing a godly society on earth. Not only had the Catholic Church lost its Christian bearings, it was actually part of the problem, for its leaders were amply represented among the powerful and greedy figures in French society against whom Meslier was railing. He raged that the lust of the Church for power was 'the origin of all those pompous but vain and ridiculous ceremonies that your priests pretend to lead with ostentation in the celebration of their fake mysteries and their bogus divine worship.' He is said to have observed, tartly, that his greatest wish would be to see the last king strangled with the guts of the last priest.

Meslier's confession, which he would surely not have dared to publish before his death, came into the public domain largely through the efforts of the French philosopher François-Marie Voltaire (1694-1778), for it was Voltaire who wrote the preface to Meslier's *Testament* when it was published in its revised form in 1732 under the title *Superstition in All Ages*. 'Every honest man should have Meslier's *Testament* in his pocket', he remarked. A contemporary of John Wesley and Nicholas Zinzendorf, Voltaire may well have shared Meslier's dismay at the endemic corruption of secular and ecclesiastical powers, but whatever his personal views, he was passionately committed to the freedom of speech of those who criticised as well as supported the status quo. He was only a young child in Paris when Thomas Aitkenhead was executed in Edinburgh in 1697 for denying the reality of the Holy Trinity. We can safely say that the mature Voltaire, who famously declared that he would defend to the death the right of people to say things that he might personally detest, would have been consumed with revulsion.

Like Newton, Locke and Descartes before him, Voltaire did not reject religion, but like them, he was guided in his religious disposition by reason rather than revelation. 'It is perfectly evident to my mind', he wrote in his *Philosophical Dictionary* published in in 1764, 'that there exists a necessary, eternal, supreme and intelligent being. This is no matter of faith but of reason.' Voltaire made it clear, however, that only a particular kind of religion would meet with his approval, one that taught much morality, very little dogma and absolutely no superstition. It would, he declared, be a religion that 'did not order one to believe in things that are impossible, contradictory, injurious to divinity, and pernicious to mankind, and which dared not menace with eternal punishment anyone possessing common sense'. It would teach 'only the worship of one god, justice, tolerance and humanity'. It was the pure creed of the Enlightenment – and it excluded much that the early Church had agonised over for centuries.

Voltaire was here rejecting not the idea of God as such (he would probably have been content to be called a Deist) but only the dogma-encrusted God of Christian orthodoxy. As a source of human hope and social morality, the idea of God was indispensable in Voltaire's mind: if God did not exist, he famously proclaimed in a poem in 1768, it would be necessary to invent him. It was not to be long before others were reversing the proposition: *because* God did not exist, it *had* been necessary to invent him. Even Voltaire himself came close to conceding that God was the product of human invention: 'If God created us in his own image, we have more than reciprocated.' Like Descartes a century earlier, however, Voltaire never saw himself as an outright atheist. Quite apart from his clearly-held beliefs, it would have been social suicide at a time when atheism was still a badge of shame in Europe and caution was still needed by those who wrote about it. Indiscretions could be punished with fines, imprisonment or even worse.

Some did, however, venture a little closer towards the forbidden land of atheism, even if they still felt the need to tread with care. One was the deeply sceptical and hugely influential Scottish philosopher David Hume (1711-1776). Though a contemporary of John Wesley, he was as far removed from him in religious temperament as it was possible to get. Echoing William of Ockham almost five hundred years earlier, Hume saw no need to go beyond the objective analysis of cause and effect in explaining why things happened in the world. For him, God was no longer to be found even in the black holes of human knowledge that science had not yet penetrated, for whatever had not yet been explained would eventually be clarified without resort to supernatural assumptions about the power or intervention of God. And if, as the Deists proclaimed, God was the intelligent coordinator of the harmonies of creation, how could the manifest *dis*harmonies and evils in the world be explained? Hume saw much to reflect upon in the remorseless logic of Epicurus (*c.* 341-271 BC), the pre-Christian Hellenistic philosopher better known for his celebration of pleasure than for his views on God. Either God can remove evil from the world and will not; or being willing to do so, he cannot; or he neither can nor will; or he is both able and willing to do so. These are the only possibilities, and since the last is flatly contradicted by the evidence, it must be concluded that God either cannot or will not do anything about evil. Whichever it is, he is scarcely a God worth bothering about.

Much the same viewpoint was taken by Hume's contemporary across the English Channel, the French philosopher and man of letters, Denis Diderot (1713-1784). For many years Diderot was editor-in-chief of *L'Encyclopédie*, one of the principal literary monuments of the Enlightenment, in which he ventured to write about atheism without actually calling himself one. In fact, it was not a matter of any great moment to him whether atheists or Christians were right in their beliefs: 'It is very important not to mistake hemlock for parsley, but to believe or not to believe in God is not important at all.' Diderot conceded that God was real enough to those like Blaise Pascal a century earlier whose experiences had convinced them of his existence; but without this subjective experience, God melted away. He had no proven existence apart from the sense of reality that was triggered in the hearts and minds of those who claimed to know him. Moreover, to accept his existence merely out of a sense of philosophical necessity was pointless. Thus in a sentence or two did Diderot dismiss the claims of philosophers and theologians across the centuries from Anselm and Aquinas to Descartes and Newton who could not make sense of the world without at least the hypothesis of God.

It was, at the time, a defining step to take. Although Isaac Newton had (to his own satisfaction) eliminated the need for a superstitious God who worked supernatural miracles and was three deities in one, he still clung to the Deist belief in a God who held the universe in a constant and perfect balance. So, too, in slightly different language, did Voltaire. Now, almost a century after Newton, Diderot was rejecting the need for *any* kind of God as a necessary condition for understanding reality. In his view, there was no need to posit the existence of a divine creator at all. Everything in the natural world had its own dynamic and was governed by its own laws; and it was these that regulated the behaviour of matter, not some celestial engineer continually tinkering with the mechanism as though it were a cosmic pocket-watch.

Still, however, Diderot could not yet openly declare such subversive ideas, and he, like other radical eighteenth-century writers, found it prudent to put his thoughts into the mouths of fictional characters in a dialogue. In *A Letter to the Blind for the Use of Those Who See*, published in 1749, Diderot concocted an argument between a supporter of Isaac Newton (Mr Holmes) and Nicholas Saunderson (1682-1739), a Cambridge mathematician who had been blind since early childhood as a result of smallpox. How, Saunderson asked Holmes, could an intelligent and benign creator have brought about a world in which such dreadful things could happen to an innocent child like himself? When Holmes was unable to supply a satisfactory answer, Saunderson retorted: 'My good friend, admit your ignorance'. In a dramatic deathbed scene, the dying Saunderson rejected the idea of a providential God, arguing (a century before Charles Darwin) that species arose, evolved, suffered and faded away without any kind of divine control or intervention. His own life may have had its tragic elements, but that was the way of nature and it was fruitless to discuss it in the context of a loving God. As for Diderot, he was swiftly identified as the author of *A Letter to the Blind* and imprisoned for some months in the fortress at Vincennes, in Paris. There he was visited almost daily by Jean-Jacques Rousseau (1712-1778), whose own religious sentiments were closer to those of Voltaire than of Diderot. Instinctively a Deist, Rousseau affirmed the necessity of religion and embraced it with intense emotion, anticipating the attitude of nineteenth-century English and German romanticism towards religion and nature.

Another who, like Diderot, was cautious about publicising his views was Paul Heinrich, Baron of Holbach (1723-1789). A kindred spirit with Diderot and a collaborator with him in the production of *L'Encyclopédie*,

Holbach was born in Germany in 1723 but was raised in France where he inherited his uncle's fortune and title. His most important book *The System of Nature: or Laws of the Moral and Physical World*, published in 1770 and nicknamed 'The Atheist's Bible', marked him as one of the most scandalous thinkers of the Enlightenment. Holbach argued that belief in a transcendent God was both dishonest and despairing: dishonest because it required people to set aside their intellectual integrity, and despairing because it stunted their growth as responsible and independent human beings. People created the gods they needed, Holbach thought, and they did so mainly because they could not cope with the trials of life and the terror of death without the protection and comfort of a father figure. He saw God as nothing but the cumulative sum of human hopes and expectations, observing that religion flourished wherever there was ignorance and fear. In the fullness of time people would overcome their infantile dependence upon a divine crutch as their knowledge and understanding of the world increased. As he put the matter in *The System of Nature*: 'If the ignorance of nature gave birth to the gods, the knowledge of nature is calculated to destroy them.'

Like his collaborator Diderot, however, Holbach was obliged to publish his views anonymously or under false names, sometimes those of freethinkers who had been dead for some time. *The System of Nature* first appeared under the name of Jean-Baptist de Mirabaud (1675-1760), Secretary of the Académie Française, and its godless tenor attracted a good deal of hostility. Freedom of speech, at least in matters of religion, was still far from assured. The constraints of public opinion, however, were starting to loosen as religious sceptics began to emerge from the intellectual closets of their private thoughts. Holbach died in Paris in January 1789 a few months before the eruption of the Revolution in France that was to mark a turning point in the freedom of expression in Western Europe. By the early part of the nineteenth century, Holbach's ideas, once regarded as dangerously subversive, had become familiar to a much wider audience than the coterie of intellectuals who flocked to his radical gatherings in pre-revolutionary Paris. Atheism was gingerly becoming a permissible subject of public debate, and scientists were now adding their views about God to those of the intellectuals.

One was Pierre-Simon Laplace (1749-1827), a French nobleman and one of the outstanding physicists of his day. Laplace was intrigued by the regularities of the natural world, especially the consistency of the movement of heavenly bodies through the skies. He was the first scientist to posit the existence of what cosmologists now recognise as black holes. Rather as Diderot had conjectured, there seemed to Laplace to be fixed and definite laws that governed the behaviour of objects in the natural world, allowing predictions to be made of what might happen to them in the future. The more Laplace studied the regularities of the universe, the less random and unpredictable it seemed to be: the natural world was not, as earlier generations had assumed, an arbitrary place dependent for its existence upon the continuous interventions of God. It was a place of immense regularity, governed by constant laws that either could not or would not be overridden by the irruption of divine initiatives.

Laplace developed the idea of scientific determinism as a way of explaining the regularities of the natural world. He believed that if, at any one time, the position and speed of every single particle in the universe was known, then it should be possible to calculate its behaviour at any other moment in time, past or future. Both the history and the future of the entire universe could, in principle, be known through its unvarying regularities. In fact, Laplace's vision of an entirely ordered and predictable universe was eventually revealed as misplaced: the mutations that lie at the heart of Charles Darwin's theory of evolution through natural selection, for example, are random in their origin, and Werner Heisenberg's principle of uncertainty is central to quantum mechanics. In the eighteenth century, however, Laplace's notion of a deterministic universe commanded interest and respect even though it excluded any dependence upon divine intervention for its day-to-day existence. The story (probably apocryphal) is told that when Napoleon asked Laplace why there was no mention of God in any of his writings, the scientist candidly replied that he had no need of any such hypothesis. A scientific law cannot be a scientific law if it is valid only for as long as God chooses not to break it.

Laplace was one of a growing band of eighteenth-century scientists who saw no need to posit the existence of an interventionist God in order to make sense of the world. They were joined by philosophers of the stature of Immanuel Kant (1724-1804) and Georg Hegel (1770-1831) who, like the scientists, were rethinking the traditional God of orthodox Christian belief. Kant, who ranks with Voltaire and Hume as among the most influential thinkers of the eighteenth century, saw the Enlightenment as a time of mankind's moral and intellectual coming-of-age. His watchword was: think for yourself! Kant's achievements were remarkable for a man of limited worldly experience and unvarying habits who passed his entire life as a scholarly bachelor in his provincial birthplace of Königsberg (now Kaliningrad) in East Prussia. His daily walk round the town, at half past three every afternoon, was so punctual that people were said to be able to set their clocks by it. The German poet Heinrich Heine (1797-1856) was doubtless not the only one to remark upon the contrast between the ordinariness of Kant's outward life and the enormous impact his thinking had upon the world.

Central to Kant's thinking was the idea that there exist two different kinds of realms or worlds, intimately connected but always separated by a veil that can never be fully drawn aside. The first is the world of things as they 'really are' – that is, the everyday world as it would be seen by the pure eye of a perfect being, undistorted by human bias, prejudice or preconception. Kant called this the 'noumenal' world, and although it must really exist, we can never access it directly. Rather, we can only know about the noumenal world indirectly through our senses, for without them we would have no awareness of anything that was going on around us. Our senses, in other words, are the windows through which we view the noumenal world, but they are not the unblemished panes of glass that we casually assume them to be. Far from giving us an objective view of the world as it really is – that is, as it would be seen by the pure eye of a perfect being – our senses are continually *interpreting* the things we see to fit our preconceptions of what the world is like. They always come between us and the noumenal world, rather as a filter comes between a camera and the object it is recording. What we see may be very close to the 'real thing', but it can never quite be the 'real thing' itself.

The second world, then, is the world of human perception: that is, the subjective impressions that we have of the objects and ideas we encounter in the noumenal world. These impressions are, so to speak, the filtered images of the world that we carry around with us and that determine how we interact with it. Kant called this the 'phenomenal' world, and he used the term to include not only the ways in which we understand and interpret the noumenal world but also our emotions and beliefs about it. God, for example, might exist in some absolute (noumenal) sense, but we can never know this directly. The closest we can come to knowing God is through the feelings and beliefs we have about him. It is precisely because the God of the noumenal world cannot be known directly that so many different images of him exist, filtered through the human senses in a thousand different ways.

In *The Critique of Pure Reason*, Kant's prolix and convoluted masterpiece published in 1781, he used the distinction between the noumenal and phenomenal worlds to address the problem of the ontological proof of God's existence. It was a problem with a history. The earliest systematic exponent of the ontological proof had been

St Anselm, Archbishop of Canterbury in the late eleventh century and one of the greatest of the early medieval schoolmen. Anselm had argued that if God is a greater being than anything that can possibly be imagined, there must exist a being who is even greater than that, for existence is always greater than imagination. The God of the noumenal world (to use Kant's terminology) must be a purer distillation of truth than all the filtered images of him that have accumulated in the phenomenal world of human interpretation.

Kant's rebuttal of the ontological argument hinged around the assertion that the *existence* of something (in this case, the existence of God) cannot be inferred from whatever else may be said or thought about that thing. The existence of something in the noumenal world cannot be inferred from people's beliefs or perceptions about it in the phenomenal world. A great many things have been believed or asserted about God over the ages, including his self-revelation, his actions, his attributes, his characteristics and his supernatural qualities; and it is all too easy to assume that a being about whom so much is known *must* exist. Kant, however, satisfied himself that something does not *necessarily* exist just because it has an impressive accumulation of attributes or characteristics. For example (though the example is not Kant's), so many detailed depictions have been made over the ages of angels and unicorns that most people would easily recognise pictures of them; but angels and unicorns do not actually exist. The same reasoning can be applied to the ontological argument. The *existence* of God cannot be established merely by creating recognisable pictures of him. It may be said with Anselm that God is a greater being than anything we can possibly imagine. It may be said with Aquinas that God is the first cause of all matter and movement in the universe. It may even be said with Descartes that God is the standard of perfection by which we are aware of our own imperfections. All of these properties can be attributed to God and more besides, but none of them proves that God exists. All of them could have been invented or imagined, just as angels and unicorns have been invented. As Kant put it, existence is not a predicate. In short, Kant exposed the ontological proof of God's existence as no proof at all. Never again would it carry the same authority that it had enjoyed for almost six hundred years.

Yet to say that God's existence cannot be proved by philosophical argument is not the same as saying that he does not exist as a meaningful presence in many people's lives; and Kant was not opposed to religion *per se*. He would certainly have denied that he was an atheist. Like others before him, however, he tried to find an Enlightenment path towards God that took him through the realms of moral conscience rather than along the more traditional doctrinal pathways of salvation. For Kant, religion was about living a life in tune with what we know, rationally, to be our moral duties and responsibilities – as parents, citizens, workers or whatever. We may not be able to prove that God exists by any logical or philosophical method but we may nevertheless have moments of deep and intense awareness that transcend our normal experiences and that may be hard to explain or even describe. There is no reason why these should not be seen as God-filled moments, provided they encourage us to lead lives of moral righteousness. For Kant, then, God was a sort of moral mentor who could inspire, direct and even reward good behaviour, but he was not, and never could be, the mysterious ground of being or the saviour of the world.

Dissatisfied with the rather peripheral role that Kant accorded to God's actions in the world, Georg Hegel tried to reinstate God at the centre of human affairs and human history. Born at Stuttgart in 1770, Hegel belonged to the generation after Kant. At school, where he failed to shine, he was singled out for his 'inadequate grasp of philosophy', and when he matriculated at Tübingen University it was in theology, not philosophy. The distinction was less clear-cut then than it would be now, and his work often appears to straddle both perspectives. On graduating from Tübingen, Hegel became a family tutor in Berne and Frankfurt before being appointed to his first university post at Jena in 1801. After the Battle of Jena in 1806, when Napoleon defeated the Prussians, Hegel saw the Emperor riding past and was deeply impressed. He wrote, in *Phenomenology of Spirit*, that: 'It is a truly wonderful experience to see such an individual, on horseback, stretching over the world and dominating it'. He saw Napoleon as the historical hero of the age – the human agent of the divine 'world spirit' that lay at the centre of human history. It was a remarkable vision that shaped his later theological sensitivities. It would be a gross exaggeration to say that Napoleon was to Hegel's God what Jesus had been to the God of Israel; but the juxtaposition of divine power and human agency, working together to shape the course of world history, is interestingly similar in the two cases.

Like others before and after him, Hegel strove for an enlightened understanding of God that would avoid the extremes of unthinking emotionalism on the one hand and arid philosophising on the other. He sought a religious perspective that could hold the intellectual honesty of rational thought in a constructive tension with the mystery of divine engagement in the world. In *Lectures on the Philosophy of Religion*, published in 1827, Hegel developed the idea of God as the centralising force in world affairs, holding things together and shepherding them forward. Drawing upon one of the favoured themes of nineteenth-century European thought, he saw all the different strands of human history converging inexorably upon a utopian state of rationality and freedom – all organised and orchestrated by God. God, Hegel believed, was the 'world spirit' whose existence lay at the heart of history. In a manner of speaking, God *was* the cumulative history of the world. Hegel wrote in *Lectures on the Philosophy of Religion*: 'Without the world, God would not be God'. Indeed, he seems almost to have argued that God was conscious of himself *only* through the life of the world. God and the world go together and they grow together, for human history and human culture are the arenas in which God becomes himself.

Such a God was certainly compatible with the rationality of the times, acceptable even to those committed to a scientific outlook on life. Whereas Kant's God had been a kind of moral guardian, directing individuals in the paths of righteousness, Hegel's God was a much more active and pervasive being. He was immanent in the world and at work in all its processes. The boundaries between the creator and the creation were blurred as one seemed to merge into, and become, the other. It was a compelling vision that appeared to many to offer a natural and rational image of God that avoided the stigma of atheism (the poet Percy Bysshe Shelley had been sent down from Oxford in 1811 for publishing atheistic pamphlets) yet did not require either the acceptance of age-old dogmas about sacrifice and salvation or a belief in supernatural happenings. It was another challenge to the conventional theistic vision of God. As a result, by about the end of the eighteenth century the traditional framework of Christian consciousness had taken a considerable battering. Many of the elements in the time-hallowed system of belief remained unscathed in the hearts and minds of faithful Christians, but others had been irrevocably transformed in ways that were to exert an ever-increasing influence over the religious beliefs of ordinary people.

No longer was God self-evidently a real, transcendent being who could be talked about in a human vocabulary and who said and did the kinds of things that humans said and did – albeit on an unimaginably vast scale. No longer was it beyond question that God had single-handedly created the universe and was now sustaining its every moment. No longer were heaven and hell indubitably real locations where the souls of people were washed up after death. No longer were miracles, angels and a host of other supernatural phenomena accepted without demur as true realities. No longer could people be relied upon

meekly and reverently to accept the dogmas of the Church, unfiltered
by their own experiences and intellectual insights. No longer could the
Bible be read uncritically as factual history or accepted as the inerrant
word of God. It was a huge and dramatic change. Although it was to
be a long time before it all began to trickle down into the taken-for-
granted assumptions of ordinary churchgoers, it had certainly done so
by the middle of the twentieth century when public acceptance of a
pre-Enlightenment theology, and all that it implied about God and the
universe, had largely disappeared.

It soon became impossible for professional theologians to ignore
the intellectual impact of the Enlightenment, and by the end of the
eighteenth century a new way of thinking about God was beginning
to emerge from the universities and seminaries of Europe. Known as
liberal Protestant theology, the phrase describes a loosely connected
stream of ideas that permeated nineteenth- and early twentieth-
century European theology without entirely colonising it. It may be
no exaggeration to say that those in the vanguard of the new liberal
theology regarded their labours as vital to the very survival of the
Christian faith. Unless Christianity could reinvent itself in ways that
harmonised with the things that the Enlightenment philosophers
and scientists had been saying, it seemed to have very little future as
a mainstream faith. The objectivity of science had now supplanted
ecclesiastical authority as the key to understanding the nature of the
universe; and if Christianity was unable to hitch itself to the same key
ring, it was surely doomed. Nothing less than survival was at stake in
the minds of the liberal theologians.

Chapter 19
The God of the Liberals

Liberal Protestant theology emerged in the eighteenth century largely as an attempt to defend the credibility of the Christian faith in the increasingly sceptical intellectual climate of post-Enlightenment Europe. Its exponents believed that, if Christianity was to survive, traditional theology had to be stripped of the layers of outdated dogma and supernatural revelation that it had accumulated over the ages. Anything that clashed with scientific rationality had to be refashioned and clear distinctions had to be drawn between the historical core of the gospels and the later accretions of myth and fantasy. Arguments about the existence of God and the reality of miracles had to be squared with contemporary philosophical insights. The Bible had to be reassessed in the light of the newly minted tools of literary and historical criticism, and so on. It was a fearsome agenda that was tackled initially by eighteenth- and nineteenth-century German theologians; but their task was eased to some extent by an earlier German scholar who is remembered less for his theology than for his radical analyses of biblical texts.

Hermann Reimarus (1694-1768), a professor of Hebrew and oriental languages at Hamburg University, was one of the first European scholars to break with the tradition of academic piety and read the Bible in the same critical way as other types of literature. Drawing on his training and experience in Middle Eastern linguistics, Reimarus argued that the great variety of texts in the Old and New Testaments strongly suggested that they were not the absolute and literal words of God, dictated sentence by sentence to scribes who faithfully reproduced them as the books of the Bible. Rather, they were the products of their times, written by men who may well have thought themselves to be in touch with God but whose work was necessarily shaped by the cultural, religious and even political climate in which they were operating. It was a risky argument to advance at a time when caution was still needed by those who dared to question Christian orthodoxy. An indication of the peril in which Reimarus placed himself is suggested by the fact that his most controversial writings were not published until after his death, and then only in fragments under the editorship of the German dramatist Gotthold Lessing (1729-1781).

Reimarus began with a question about Jesus that has a surprisingly modern ring: which of the many words attributed to Jesus in the four gospels are likely to be authentically his own, and which were probably added later by the evangelists who wrote them? It must have seemed a baffling and unnecessary question in the early eighteenth century: why should anyone think that Jesus had *not* said all the words that Matthew, Mark, Luke and John placed into his mouth? Reimarus stuck to his guns, however, concluding that the most authentic words of Jesus were probably the eschatological passages in the synoptic gospels that spoke of the end of time, the second coming of the Son of Man, and the establishment of a new and godly kingdom on earth. They were words that must have seemed to those who heard them as a challenge to the secular powers of earthly rulers, but Reimarus believed that they explained a great deal that would otherwise be obscure. It was only by seeing Jesus as an imminent threat to the established political order, he argued, that sense could be made of his crucifixion by the Roman authorities. By the time he made his painful way to the place of the skull, however, Jesus had realised his mistake: God was *not* about to enter history and change it forever, so Jesus uttered the despairing words from the cross: 'My God, why have you forsaken me?' Then, not relishing the prospect of returning to their former mundane lives in Galilee after the excitement of the previous three years, the disappointed disciples stole the body of Jesus, deposited it elsewhere, and made up the story of his resurrection in order to claim him as a spiritual Messiah.

Reimarus' analysis was not very convincing and it did not last for long. Yet it was an important landmark in the history of biblical interpretation, less for its substance than for its pioneering attempt to read the gospels in a light other than that of piety and faith. Reimarus is rightly remembered as one of the first to apply the principles of literary criticism to scriptural texts, even if the application proved in this case to be of little enduring value. It was daring, original and dangerous. Albert Schweitzer (1875-1965), the Swiss theologian, missionary and musician whose own work on the life of Jesus (*The Quest of the Historical Jesus*) was to become a seminal text in the early years of the twentieth century, held Reimarus in high regard. Though rejecting the substance of his thesis, Schweitzer described Reimarus' writing as 'one of those supremely great works which pass and leave no trace because they are before their time'. Where Reimarus pioneered with caution, Friedrich Schleiermacher (1768-1834) followed with greater confidence.

Sometimes praised as the greatest theologian since Calvin and the father of liberal Protestant theology, Schleiermacher was one of the first theologians to take the intellectual challenge of the Enlightenment seriously. He set himself the task of reshaping Christian theology in a way that would avoid the somewhat vague religiosity of Kant and Hegel yet take proper account of modern developments in philosophy and science. Born in 1768, the year that Reimarus died, Schleiermacher was younger than Kant but an almost exact contemporary of Hegel. He was much influenced by the German Pietists, calling himself (somewhat to the chagrin of Count Zinzendorf's followers) a 'Pietist of a higher order'. He was particularly opposed to the Deist vision of God as a *deus ex machina* lurking in the wings of the universe with no particular part to play in the day-to-day lives of his creatures. Like the Pietists, Schleiermacher wanted a God who could spark in people 'a sense and taste for the infinite', not a God of formulae and propositions who distanced himself from the world of feelings and emotions.

Friedrich Schleiermacher's two most important publications were *On Religion: Speeches to its Cultured Despisers*, published in 1799 as an attempt to explain and defend Christianity to his sceptical friends, and *The Christian Faith*, published in 1821 as a systematic account of Christian doctrine for the modern world. Central to Schleiermacher's understanding of the nature of religious experience was the sensation that many people experience of something or someone that exists above and beyond themselves – a presence in their lives that they may not always recognise but upon which they may feel utterly dependent. Schleiermacher called it, in German, *Gefühl* – a word that does not translate easily into English but might in this context be rendered as awareness or discernment. So universal is this sense of a reality transcending the normal experiences of life that Schleiermacher regarded it as an innate part of human nature, an inborn intuition of God that everyone could experience. Indeed, he attached so much importance to *Gefühl* that he saw it as the essence of true religion; and anything that sat uncomfortably with it was liable to be devalued in his theological system. The doctrine of the Holy Trinity, for example, was a relatively minor consideration for him, not because it was unimportant in the historical sweep of the Christian faith but because it was not a natural way for people to experience a personal awareness of God. Even scripture and tradition were accorded less authority than people's intuitive awareness of a godly presence 'out there'.

Schleiermacher claimed that *Gefühl* reached his highest expression in Jesus of Nazareth. Jesus was fully human, just as we are, but unlike us he was overwhelmingly conscious of God in everything he did. He was more completely aware of the spirit of God and more dependent upon it than anyone before or since. If Jesus was able to do things that others regarded as miraculous, then that was simply the measure of his power to persuade people of the reality of God's spirit among them. Whether the reported miracles of Jesus 'really' occurred was not a matter of any great moment for Schleiermacher, though he did suggest that many of them could be explained in perfectly natural ways. The healings that Jesus performed, for example, could have been manifestations of mind over matter, and the resurrection might have been nothing more than the regaining of consciousness by one who had never really died but merely fainted. As for the ascension, Schleiermacher was content to say only that we shall never know what truly happened – the cautious position of an academic theologian in the first flush of the Enlightenment.

Schleiermacher's work was important in mapping out a way of experiencing God that did not depend for its authenticity on abstract and unverifiable statements about the nature of the godhead. In the notion of *Gefühl*, he seemed to have discovered a pathway up the mountain of divine encounter without the encumbrance of a knapsack full of paradoxical dogmas and doubtful superstitions. It was an appealing prospect in the age of Enlightenment, but also a dangerous one, for as Schleiermacher's critics pointed out, the God to whom the pathway of *Gefühl* might lead could all too easily become the created God of human yearnings and frailties. Self-righteousness and self-satisfaction might rise above a humble obedience to the God of scripture and revelation. If Schleiermacher was intent on jettisoning past orthodoxies, his detractors said, he had to recognise the price that he was paying for it. It was, nevertheless, upon this attempt to find God in the depths of human spirituality rather than the arcane formulations of traditional creeds or the convoluted arguments of academic philosophers and theologians that Schleiermacher's liberal successors (mainly German) built in varying ways.

Albrecht Ritschl (1822-1889), who was a young boy when Schleiermacher died, is among those most closely identified with the liberal strands of nineteenth-century Protestant theology. His teaching influenced an entire generation of theologians and his ideas were to mould the shape of liberal theology until well into the twentieth century. Ritschl was particularly anxious to shield the Christian faith from the potentially damaging repercussions of scientific discovery, and he tried to do it by drawing a clear distinction between the territories of science and religion. Science, he argued, dealt with objective facts about the world that could be tested and refuted; religion dealt with moral values that were authenticated not by experimentation but by their beneficial effects on people's lives. Ritschl was adamant that religion should never try to colonise the explanatory realms of science any more than science should claim jurisdiction over the moral concerns of religion. If this demarcation between science and religion was carefully observed, Ritschl thought, the two need never be in conflict. If, however, religion ignored the boundary with science and persisted with explanations of the natural world that relied on biblical or ecclesiastical authority, then it would be doomed to eventual extinction as science probed ever more deeply into the secrets of nature. In short, Ritschl was rejecting the God of the gaps.

Ritschl thought that the true essence of religion lay not in any adherence to revered doctrines or ancient rituals but in the claims it made about the conditions for righteous living. To be a Christian meant working to establish the kingdom of God on earth in reasonable and practical ways. It was about transforming societies through loving service, with Jesus Christ as the inspiration. It was not about assenting to a set of dogmatic beliefs, however hallowed they may be, nor was it about adopting an anti-intellectual stance towards the philosophical and scientific debates of the times. Religion was nothing if not an integral part of the fabric of contemporary society, and Christianity had no future if it set itself up as a counter-cultural force, decrying all that was rational and progressive. These views placed Ritschl much closer to the modernism of Kant and Hegel than to the medievalism of Augustine and Aquinas, but they did not set him entirely apart from the main stream of Christian tradition. He believed that, in a symbolic if not a supernatural sense, Jesus was the saviour of the world, and he believed in a personal and loving God who revealed himself to men and women in ways that complemented but did not compromise their natural human reason.

Another nineteenth-century beneficiary of Schleiermacher's pion-eering theology was Ludwig Feuerbach (1804-1872), a philosopher of Hegelian tendencies (he studied under Hegel in Berlin) who rejected the orthodox theistic idea of God as a being who 'really' existed somewhere in the ether, preferring instead to locate the creative spark of divinity within the very stuff of human nature. For Feuerbach, religion was not a matter of a God 'up there' revealing himself to humanity 'down here' in order to save them; rather, it was a matter of imperfect people on earth creating a perfect God in heaven. There was nothing particularly new in the notion of God being created in the image of man. The Greek philosopher Xenophanes (born *c.* 570 BC) had said as much in his famous observation that if horses and oxen

could think and draw, they would draw gods that looked like horses and
oxen. Feuerbach went farther than this, however, explaining *why* it had
been necessary for humans to create a God in their own image. God,
he thought, represented the instinctive aspirations of men and women
to be creatures of wisdom, love and mercy. In their hearts, people
sensed that love was better than hatred, justice better than treachery,
wisdom better than folly. Such values were deeply embedded in human
nature; but human nature being the fragile vessel it was, they could
never be fully or consistently achieved. They remained an aspiration,
not a continuing reality – an echo of how things could be if the word
of God was taken seriously.

For Feuerbach, then, religion functioned to give people a vision of
the ideal perfection of mankind, offering incentives for them to strive
towards it and raising them up when they fell by the wayside. Since
God was the embodiment of all that mankind would most dearly wish
to become, it was inevitable that he should be thought of in terms
of human virtues such as love, compassion and mercy, for there were
no other moral qualities that people knew about. It was categorically
impossible to imagine God in anything other than human terms; but
in him these qualities were elevated to perfection. God, therefore,
emerged as the projection of people's ambitions and aspirations,
an eternal statement of the deepest moral sentiments of humanity.
For Feuerbach, the true atheist was not the man who denied the
existence of a transcendent God but the one for whom the attributes
of love, wisdom, justice and compassion meant nothing, for to say
that they meant nothing was to reject the deepest moral aspirations of
humankind.

Other significant liberal thinkers of the late nineteenth and early
twentieth centuries included Rudolf Otto and Adolf von Harnack.
Otto (1869-1937) was among the best-known writers on religion in
the first half of the twentieth century, and his influential book *The
Idea of the Holy*, published in 1923, explored the implications of
liberal thinking for religion in general as much as for Christianity in
particular. Otto believed that if, as Feuerbach had argued, God was to
be understood as the divine dimension of every human personality,
then Christianity could not claim an exclusive route to communion
with him. Underlying all religion, Otto thought, was an innate human
capacity to experience things that lay beyond the ordinary range of
human perception. Schleiermacher had called it *Gefühl*: Otto called it
a sense of the 'numinous', and he identified the three states it could

invoke in those who responded to it. The first is *mysterium*: the sense of an encounter with something that is entirely different from anything experienced in ordinary life and that reduces people to silence. The second is *tremendum*: the feeling of awe in the presence of something that is overwhelmingly powerful. The third is *fascinans*: a deep spiritual awareness of mercy, grace and acceptance. Everyone, Otto thought, could recognise and experience the '*mysterium, tremendum et fascinans*' of the numinous, whether Christian or not. Jesus was a route into the mystery for those who had been nurtured in the Christian faith, but he could not be seen as the only route. Jews, Sikhs, Buddhists, Hindus and Muslims all had access to other, equally valid pathways to inner holiness. It was a radical argument to advance at a time when ordinary Christians still knew relatively little about other world faiths, not least because it cut across a central tenet of Christianity that (as Jesus is reported as saying in John's gospel) 'no man comes to the Father except by me'. As we shall see, the denial of Christianity's exclusive grasp on the truth was decisively rejected by twentieth-century theologians of a more conservative persuasion. The other major world religions were not to be sneezed at, of course, but they were not the repositories of the real truth about God. Only Christianity was that. According to the conservatives, Otto had got it wrong.

Adolf von Harnack (1851-1930), a leading German intellectual who taught church history at the University of Berlin, was another effective populariser of liberal Protestant theology who informally succeeded Schleiermacher and Ritschl as the intellectual leader of the liberal tendency in Europe. Harnack was very close to the German government in the build-up to the Great War, helping to draft the speech in which the Kaiser declared war on France and Britain in 1914. After the armistice in 1918, he was offered the post of ambassador to the United States but turned it down. Harnack believed that, in its formative period, Christianity had been moulded by Greek philosophy in ways that had never been intended by Jesus, and it had suffered ever since through its labyrinthine attempts to define God in ways that few ordinary Christians could really understand. In his view, Christian theology had to return to Jesus' simple and uncomplicated demands about righteous living that lay at the heart of the New Testament. If people wished to follow Jesus, they should be striving to create the kingdom of God in their hearts and in their communities by loving God and serving their neighbours. This, Harnack believed, was the kernel of authentic Christianity; and anything that blunted its appeal to ordinary men and women could be deleted from the catalogue of Christian doctrines with no great loss.

By seeking to shield Christianity from the potentially lethal assaults of scientific rationality, liberal theology cast a veil over at least one of the faces of the God of orthodoxy – the God without whose continuing involvement the universe could not exist. Liberal theologians foresaw the dangers that lay ahead if Christianity continued to press this claim, for it was clear even by the early nineteenth century that science was becoming skilled at explaining the regularities of the natural world without any reference to God at all. Pierre-Simon Laplace may not really have said that he had no need of the 'God hypothesis' in his work as a physicist, but it was an apt sentiment, indicative of the direction in which science was steadily moving. The more the Church tried to account for the natural world in terms of religious dogma or biblical authority, the greater would become its risk of being side-lined by an increasingly literate and sophisticated populace.

The liberal theologians were all too conscious of this. They understood that they had to work in tandem with science, not against it, accepting the things that the scientists were discovering about the cosmos without imposing their own doctrinal spin on them. It is probably true to say that, because of this, liberals were much better placed than their more conservative counterparts to withstand the impact of Charles Darwin's discoveries in the mid-nineteenth century about the evolution of species. Whereas liberals were able to accept evolution through random mutation and natural selection as the means that God had chosen to ensure the continuing development of life on earth, conservatives (of all stripes) felt threatened by the challenge that Darwinism posed to the Genesis accounts of creation. They responded by trying to discredit both Darwin and his theories. Matters came to a dramatic head at a meeting of the British Association at Oxford in 1860 when the Anglican bishop Samuel Wilberforce and the humanist scientist Dr Thomas Huxley clashed over the relative merits of Darwinism and creationism. Wilberforce, relying on a volatile combination of sarcasm and ecclesiastical authority, emerged from the encounter a humbled man. To his insulting question of whether Huxley was descended from an ape on his mother's or his father's side, Huxley famously replied that he would rather have an ape for a grandfather than a man who misused his intellectual gifts to obscure important scientific discussion. Liberal theologians, one feels, would have said 'Amen' to that.

It could be argued that liberal theology's abiding legacy to the Christian faith has been its success in allowing Christians to welcome each new scientific discovery about the world as a further step towards a deeper understanding of the religious impulses of humanity. It has done so by surrendering the claim to be better able than science to explain the natural world and emphasising instead the spiritual and moral qualities that the *idea* of God can inspire in those who seek to do his will. Liberal theology declares that God can be encountered most fully by looking inwards to the numinous qualities of the human spirit and then outwards to the moral obligations of Christians to build the kingdom of God on earth. Everything else, including God's traditional role in creation and a large swathe of traditional Christian dogma, takes second place.

Yet for all its appeal to modernity, liberal theology has not been without its risks. In reading the Genesis stories of creation as myths rather than facts, liberals have found themselves sitting on the thin end of an uncomfortably large wedge, for if Genesis is myth, so too might much of the rest of the Bible be. As their critics point out, liberals are obliged not only to say which parts of the Bible they believe to be myth and which to be fact but also to explain the reasons why they distinguish one from the other. This was to form a large part of the liberal agenda in the twentieth century. In the course of doing so, liberal theology provoked a backlash from two rather different quarters: evangelical fundamentalism and neo-orthodoxy.

Chapter 20
The God of the Fundamentalists

Though never an organised or coordinated movement, liberal Protestant theology was bound sooner or later to provoke a hostile reaction from more conservative quarters. The ideas of theologians of the stature of Schleiermacher, Ritschl and Harnack were indisputably Christian in their purposes, but to many traditionalists they seemed to be squeezing out ancient and hallowed Christian truths about a transcendent God and a sinful people – truths about judgement, atonement and salvation. In its deep desire to avoid anything that might be construed as scientific naivety, liberal theology was thought to be robbing religion of all that distinguished it from the fashionable ideas of the time, reducing faith to little more than an ethical humanism with a vaguely God-like figure in the background. Though undoubtedly liberating to some, others regarded this kind of theology as the modern face of unbelief, stripping God of his omnipotent and supernatural qualities. Reaction was predictable, and it came initially in the form of what has come to be known as evangelical fundamentalism.

One of the prime movers behind the evangelical response to the nineteenth-century liberal theologians was an extraordinary Dutch polymath, Abraham Kuyper (1837-1920). Kuyper began his career as a parish priest in the Reformed Church in Holland before turning to politics. In 1874 he was elected to the Dutch parliament where he remained for thirty years. Kuyper developed a distinctively theocratic approach to Christianity, not unlike that of Calvin and Zwingli before him, based on his unshakeable belief in the lordship of Jesus Christ: 'There is not a square inch in the whole domain of our human existence', he said in an inaugural address to the Free University in Amsterdam, 'over which Christ, who is Sovereign over all, does not cry: Mine!' Kuyper believed that, since earthly governments derived their legitimacy from the sovereignty of God, politicians could not ignore their ultimate accountability to him. Practising what he preached, he founded a Christian political party, the Anti-Revolutionary Party, which he led in thirteen national parliamentary campaigns. Between 1901 and 1905 he served as the Prime Minister of Holland, his parliamentary majority coming from an alliance between his own Anti-Revolutionary Party and the Catholic Political Party.

To advance his religious and political ideals, Kuyper founded and largely edited a Christian daily newspaper, *The Standard*, to which he contributed almost five thousand front-page editorials. Time and again in these editorials Kuyper stressed the absolute sovereignty of God over secular powers and governments. God's word, he thought, was more important than natural law or human reason and should always be at the heart of politics. Kuyper believed that any political movement that claimed to be Christian should base its policies on the Bible and should have no truck with liberalism or any other fashionable ideology. Indeed, he regarded 'modernism' as foremost among the threats to a Christian democratic society. On the eve of the twentieth century, he declared that 'there is no doubt that Christianity is imperilled by great and serious dangers'. Two entirely different ways of living were wrestling with each other in mortal combat: modernism, which was building an ungodly world of its own, and evangelical Christianity, where those who reverently bent the knee to Christ and worshipped him were the faithful heirs of the Reformed heritage. This, Kuyper declared, was the struggle both in Europe and America, and 'this also is the struggle for principles in which my own country is engaged, and for which I myself have been spending all my energy for nearly forty years'.

In 1898 Kuyper crossed the Atlantic to deliver what turned out to be a seminal series of lectures (the Stone Lectures) on Calvinist Christianity at the Princeton Theological Seminary in New Jersey. The lectures, which were widely disseminated among lay as well as theological audiences, had a huge impact on the growing strength of evangelical fundamentalism in the United States as Kuyper warned of the deep and corrosive conflict between Christian and secular views of the world order. The Christian view, he argued, looked upon the institutions of modern society and saw them as corrupt and ungodly, in urgent need of the redeeming and transforming power of Christ. The secular view, by contrast, saw the institutions of society as self-sufficient, able without any divine aid to meet the burgeoning needs of an increasingly wealthy and sophisticated electorate. The struggle between belief and unbelief was, for Kuyper, the defining struggle of the coming century, and it would end only when Jesus Christ was accepted as the Lord of nations as well as the head of the Church.

Kuyper's visit to Princeton in 1898 confirmed the theological seminary there as an important centre of Calvinist Christianity, rooted in a belief in the literal truth of the Bible. Princeton was already well known for its tradition of conservative theology that had been established by Charles Hodge (1797-1878) and carried forward by Benjamin Warfield (1851-1921)

and J Gresham Machen (1881-1936). Hodge was born into a conservative
Presbyterian New England family and ordained a Presbyterian minister
before embarking on an educational tour of Europe. He attended Friedrich
Schleiermacher's lectures in Berlin and was exposed to the ideas of Georg
Hegel in Tübingen before returning to Princeton where he remained
for much of his life. Hodge believed that theology and science both
proceeded on the basis of the collection and analysis of data; but whereas
science gathered its data from observations of the natural world, theology
gathered it from the Bible. 'The Bible is to the theologian what nature is
to the man of science', he wrote in his book *Systematic Theology*, published
in 1872, 'it is his store-house of facts.' Hodge regarded the Bible as the
verbally inspired and infallible word of God, full of timeless truths waiting
to be organised and interpreted under the guidance of the Holy Spirit. The
literal truth of the Bible extended not merely to its themes and passages
but to every word it contained; and if there were occasional inconsistencies
and discrepancies within its sacred pages, these were no more than minor
errors that the faithful reader could safely ignore. Since Hodge regarded
the creation stories in Genesis as factually true, he denounced Darwin's
ideas about evolution as atheism masquerading as science; and he was
opposed to Darwinism being taught in American schools and colleges.

   Hodge's high view of scripture marks him out not only as one of the
most strictly fundamentalist theologians of the modern era but also as the
harbinger of twentieth-century American evangelical fundamentalism. His
onslaught against the liberal ideas of Schleiermacher amounted almost to
character assassination. Schleiermacher, he thought, had had a pernicious
and debilitating influence on nineteenth-century Christianity, emptying it
of all its most important doctrinal content and turning it into a flabby
and subjective sentimentalism. What was *Gefühl* when confronted with the
ineffable mystery of Calvary or the glorious majesty of the Holy Trinity?
Hodge was merciless and uncompromising not only towards those who
peddled such abominably liberal ideas but also to those who were seduced
into believing them. He wrote: 'Christianity has always been regarded as a
system of doctrine. . . . Those who believe these doctrines are Christians;
those who reject them are infidels or heretics.' As for the content of
those historically enduring doctrines, Hodge identified them with a rigidly
Calvinist understanding of salvation. In particular, Arminianism, with its
rejection of the TULIP doctrines of unconditional election and irresistible
grace, and its willingness to acknowledge the human freedom to choose
or reject the gracious overtures of God, was for Hodge the treacherous
bridgehead to liberal heresy.

   The work of Hodge and his successors at Princeton laid the foundations
of twentieth-century American evangelical fundamentalism. The Princeton

theologians regarded the dogmatic traditions of the church as the gold standard of Christian orthodoxy. They held the scriptures to be the infallible revelation of the word of God; they inveighed against the vague, subjective emotionalism of Schleiermacher and like-minded theologians; and they bitterly resisted the invasion of modern modes of thought. Hodge and his successors, however, also stood in a tradition that later evangelicals of a more populist bent were wont to belittle – the tradition of orthodox catholic Christianity in which the dogmas and the rituals of the church were revered as the repositories of the eternal truths of the ages. Twentieth-century evangelicals were all too ready to bypass Christianity's rich heritage of sacrament and doctrine in their quest to recapture what they believed to be the immediacy and vibrancy of God's presence in the modern world. To them, the historical church was less a repository of everlasting truth than a hindrance to modern, flexible evangelism. Better to sing theologically shallow songs of praise to Jesus than to engage in the serious and demanding study of the foundational doctrines of the universal church. The Princeton theologians would, we feel, have been appalled.

An important catalyst for twentieth century American fundamentalism was the publication from 1910 onwards of a series of booklets called *The Fundamentals*. They were the brainchild of two wealthy Christian businessmen, Amzi C Dixon (1854-1925) and Reuben A Torrey (1856-1928), who were dismayed by the liberal betrayal of the Christian faith but heartened by the countervailing theological tradition of Princeton. It helped their cause that the booklets coincided with the revivalist meetings of the popular evangelist Dwight L Moody (1837-1899) and his musical collaborator Ira D Sankey (1840-1908). Twelve in number, *The Fundamentals* were written by leading conservative theologians and distributed free to pastors, church leaders, academics and teachers. Early volumes defended the literal truth of the virgin birth and the divinity of Jesus, and they attacked the contemporary penchant for reading the Bible as a collection of culturally nuanced documents rather than the literal word of God.

Spurred on by the success of *The Fundamentals*, groups of anti-liberal Christians in America began to compile lists of doctrines and beliefs that were, they claimed, obligatory for those who wished to call themselves Christians. They were, of course, precisely those that had been attacked by liberals for a hundred years and more: the literal truth of the Bible, the virgin birth, original sin, predestination, and the bodily resurrection and ascension of Jesus. Some of the items in some of the lists owed more to millennial fervour than to scriptural authority, as for example when the World Christian Fundamentals Association, founded by William B Riley

(1861-1947) in Minnesota in 1919 to prevent the spread of 'damnable heresies', declared it to be a central belief of true Christianity that Christ would return to rule on earth for a thousand years before the final judgement and resurrection of mankind.

As the 1920s and 1930s progressed, several American fundamentalist groups began to sink their differences and band together against a common enemy. It turned out to be a disjointed enemy, including not only nineteenth-century liberalism (now beginning to lose its appeal among European theologians) but also the emerging school of neo-orthodoxy, informally led by Karl Barth (1886-1968), that was just as much opposed to liberalism as the fundamentalists were. Matters came to something of a head in May 1922 when the liberal Baptist minister Harry E Fosdick (1878-1969) preached at the First Presbyterian Church in New York City on the text: 'Shall the fundamentalists win?' Fosdick pleaded for mutual tolerance between the two sides and urged each to respect the other's views; but the outcome was exactly the reverse. When Fosdick's sermon was printed and circulated throughout America, the smouldering fire of controversy between the traditionalists and the modernisers burst into flames. The ensuing conflict was reminiscent of the much earlier battles that had taken place between the theologians of Alexandria and Carthage in the days of the early Church fathers. The General Assembly of the Presbyterian Church in America passed a motion instructing the First Presbyterian Church of New York to ensure that, in future, every sermon preached there would explicitly uphold the five essential doctrines of the Christian faith: the infallibility of the Bible, the virgin birth, the substitutionary atonement of Jesus' death, the physical resurrection of his body, and the literal truth of the miracles. The battle between the liberals and the fundamentalists was now in the open.

A critical turning point came in 1925 with the so-called 'Monkey Trial' in Dayton, Tennessee, when John T Scopes (1900-1970), a high school teacher, was charged with teaching Charles Darwin's theory of evolution through natural selection. It was always likely to act as a focus of bitter confrontation between traditional and modern views about religion and creation. If Darwin was right, then the living world could not have been created by God in six days, and if that had not happened, then the creation accounts in Genesis could not be literally true. If the creation accounts in Genesis were not true, then other parts of the Bible might also not be true. The implications were unthinkable; and William Jennings Bryan (1860-1925), formerly President Woodrow Wilson's Secretary of State and himself a three-time Democratic candidate for the presidency, launched a fundamentalist crusade in the 1920s to banish the teaching of Darwinism from American classrooms. By the beginning of 1925 Bryan and his followers had succeeded in prohibiting the teaching of evolution from schools in fifteen American states, and Tennessee became the sixteenth when a bill was passed that year which made it unlawful to 'teach any theory that denies the story of divine creation as taught by the Bible and to teach instead that man was descended from a lower order of animals'.

The stage was set for a very high-profile confrontation. The American Civil Liberties Union (ACLU) promised its support for anyone willing to challenge the State of Tennessee, and Scopes was manoeuvred into becoming the fall guy. A young science teacher and part-time football coach, Scopes was not entirely sure that he really had been teaching Darwinism to his students; but he regarded the state law as unconstitutional and agreed to be prosecuted in a test case. William Jennings Bryan was recruited by local fundamentalists as the celebrity prosecutor, and Scopes was represented by Clarence Darrow (1857-1938), an agnostic attorney from Chicago hired by the ACLU. A carnival atmosphere pervaded Dayton in the summer of 1925 as the trial got under way. Banners decorated the streets, sidewalk vendors sold lemonade to perspiring tourists, and chimpanzees performed in street theatres. Nearly a thousand people were jammed into the Rhea County courthouse when the trial began on 10 July. In the event, Scopes was found guilty and fined a hundred dollars; but it hardly amounted to a victory for the fundamentalist movement. Bryan's handling of the case was widely thought to be embarrassing, and Darrow made the fundamentalists appear foolishly intent on turning back the clock of scientific progress. Bryan died six days after the trial ended. A year later the Tennessee Supreme Court reversed the decision of the Rhea County Court, albeit on a technicality.

It has been argued that, by allowing anti-evolutionism to become its rallying cry in the 1920s, the fundamentalist movement in America doomed itself to obscurity. There could be no long-term future for a God whose existence depended upon the falsification of Darwin's theory of evolution through natural selection. After 1925, the movement went into decline, its leaders quarrelling among themselves over relatively minor points of doctrine. Eventually, under the influence of new leaders like John Rice (1895-1980) and Carl McIntire (1906-2002), the new practice of 'biblical separation' came in as fundamentalists refused to cooperate or even have fellowship with other conservative Christians who were in contact with non-fundamentalists. Such was their sense of purity that Rice and McIntire refused to work with the rising young evangelical star Billy Graham (born 1918) because of his contacts with non-fundamentalist Protestant ministers and even with Roman Catholic priests.

By the end of the twentieth century such extreme separatism had all but disappeared as those in the mainstream Christian churches, even those of a markedly conservative disposition, began to mingle with other Protestants and Roman Catholics. Yet there is little doubt that the fundamentalist movement had been a powerful force in both America and Europe and was still exerting its influence over grass-roots religion as the century ended. Even though they now preferred to call themselves 'conservative evangelicals' or 'Bible Christians' rather than fundamentalists, thousands of local churches, especially in the southern states of America but also throughout much of Protestant Europe, still held fast to the acceptance of certain key doctrines as the authentic test of Christian faith: the literal truth of the Bible, the virgin birth, the physical resurrection of Jesus, the reality of the second coming and other such favoured dogmas. It might be said that the spirit of fundamentalism lives on whenever doctrinal rectitude is held to be of overriding importance in separating 'true' Christians from those who side instinctively with a more liberal approach to their faith. Even the storm over the teaching of Darwinism has yet to blow itself out in several American states, and it is not beyond the bounds of credibility that a reprise of the 'Scopes Monkey Trial' could yet occur.

One of the important legacies of twentieth century fundamentalism has been the elevation of a God of doctrinal purity above the traditional Protestant God of grace. From a fundamentalist standpoint, salvation depends as much upon the doctrinal position of the believer as upon any subjective response to the freewill grace of God. Those who deny the virgin birth or who see the resurrection of Jesus as a symbol rather than a hard historical fact have, in the eyes of the fundamentalists, placed themselves beyond any hope of salvation. They cannot be authentic Christians and they cannot expect a merciful reception into heaven when they die. In this respect, at least, fundamentalism has rejected the legacy of Pietism and Methodism with its emphasis on the subjective experiences of the heart rather than the objective exercises of the mind. Whereas a Pietist might have said: 'if your heart is warm give me your hand', a fundamentalist might say: 'if your beliefs are correct (that is, if they are the same as my beliefs) you may walk with me'. Those who value feelings above doctrines are, in fundamentalist eyes, to be distrusted as liberal sympathisers. By equivocating over dogmatic statements about Jesus, they have grievously misunderstood the nature of God. Yet in its insistence on the supremacy of the traditional dogmas of the Christian church, fundamentalism shares (perhaps surprisingly) a certain amount of common ground with a second but very different assault on liberal Protestant theology, that of neo-orthodoxy.

Chapter 21
The God of Neo-Orthodoxy

As the twentieth century opened, hopes were high among liberal Protestants in both Europe and North America that modernity would pervade and transform the Reformed faith, drawing in new converts who were seeking God but who had difficulty accepting the dogmas that came with the traditional package. In the event, liberal theology largely failed to provide a coherent context in which ordinary Christians could fashion their faith and express their beliefs, and it wilted under the twin assaults of evangelical fundamentalism and neo-orthodoxy. Fundamentalism, with its insistence on the infallibility of the Bible and the literal truth of such classical doctrines as the virgin birth and the physical resurrection of Jesus, fared quite well for much of the twentieth century as church communities throughout Europe and North America became explicitly evangelical in their theology and style. Some remained within the major denominations while others flourished outside them as free or independent churches. Neo-orthodoxy, which found fault with both liberalism and fundamentalism, also prospered, offering a comfortable home for Christians who wanted clearer doctrinal boundaries than the liberals could offer but who were edgy about toeing the uncompromising line of the fundamentalists. As a result, most mainstream Protestant churches that were not openly fundamentalist were, by the end of the twentieth century, treading a broadly neo-orthodox pathway, remaining faithful to traditional beliefs without necessarily insisting on doctrinal purity as a condition of membership.

The central figure in the neo-orthodox response to liberalism was the Swiss theologian Karl Barth. He is widely regarded as the most important Protestant theologian of the twentieth century and possibly the most significant since the Reformation. Almost single-handedly, he snatched Protestant theology from the grasp of the liberals and fundamentalists and reinstated it as the centrepiece of moderate Christianity in the West. The agenda of neo-orthodoxy had, however, been anticipated in the nineteenth century by an eccentric philosopher, cultural critic and amateur theologian who is widely seen as having laid down the foundations upon which Barth and other like-minded theologians were later to build. His name was Søren Kierkegaard (1813-1855).

Born in Denmark in 1813, Kierkegaard was known as the melancholy Dane – and not only because his name translated into English as 'churchyard'. Like his fellow Dane Prince Hamlet, he was tormented throughout his life by doubt and anguish. A stranger to happiness, Kierkegaard's view of the world was deeply tinted by thoughts of sin, suffering and grace. He was, it has been said, a pious neurotic who saw himself as an evangelical Lutheran. In 1830 he matriculated at the University of Copenhagen where he studied theology, philosophy and literature. Following the death of his mother in 1834 he sensed the need to discover himself before deciding what to do with his life. Much of his subsequent voyage of self-discovery is recorded in his *Journals*, which amounted eventually to over seven thousand pages in thirteen volumes. In 1837 he met a teenage girl, Regine Olsen (1822-1904), to whom he later became engaged; his inherent pessimism, however, persuaded him of the intrinsic incompatibility between marriage and his destiny as a philosopher, and he broke off the relationship. Kierkegaard was, throughout his life, a loner. A central theme of his writing is the issue of how to live as an individual person. It is said that when the Swedish writer and early feminist Fredrika Bremer (1801-1865) invited him to be the keynote speaker at a colloquium, he replied: 'Let no one invite me, for I do not dance'.

Such individualism was to become the distinctive mark not only of Kierkegaard's life but also his theology. Running through much of his writing is a rejection of the Hegelian view of God as the ground of social life and political progress. Georg Hegel, who still had another eighteen years to live when Kierkegaard was born, had seen God in the steady progression of human society towards a state of utopian perfection. For him, God was to be known not through individual experiences but through the onward march of human history towards ever higher states of rationality and freedom. Kierkegaard was dismayed by Hegel's rejection of the transcendent God of traditional Christianity in favour of a spiritual *Zeitgeist* whose actions were to be found only in the social and political processes of human societies. He wanted nothing to do with such a de-personalised view of God, believing instead that God had always worked through individuals. True Christianity, Kierkegaard argued, had never been woven into the fabric of respectable society: it had always been at its strongest and most authentic when it was a minority voice opposing the false fads and fashions of the times. In a society where everyone was Christian, true Christianity would not exist.

At the heart of Kierkegaard's understanding of religion was his belief in a personal God who could be known to individual believers and who could change not only their own lives but those of their communities as well. It was this, as much as anything else, that set him apart him from many of the liberal theologians of his day, with their doubts about a God as a being who 'really' existed beyond the human imagination or the witness of human history. For Kierkegaard, a belief in God was not merely a rational solution to a philosophical problem, it was a conscious leap of faith in which each individual believer risked disappointment in the pursuit of truth. God could be truly encountered only by responding in faith to a personal experience of the divine, and this (as Blaise Pascal had discovered two hundred years earlier) was always risky. Yet without both the subjective experience and the leap of faith, religion for Kierkegaard was little more than an ethical humanism.

Kierkegaard's traditionalist views and his gloomy personality made him a soft target for the satirists. In 1846 the Danish magazine *Corsaren* published a series of pictorial and written caricatures of him that reduced him almost to despair. A street urchin is said to have mocked him for his strident individualism: 'Wherever there is a crowd, there is untruth', he shouted after him. If the story is true, which seems unlikely, the intellectual calibre of street urchins in nineteenth century Denmark is truly remarkable. In his *Journals* Kierkegaard described himself as 'the martyr of laugh'. In 1848 he experienced a spiritual crisis that had many of the characteristics of what might now be called the 'male mid-life crisis', though in fact he was nearing the end of his short life. He became anxious about the future and intensely guilty about his earlier treatment of Regine Olsen. In the autumn of 1855 he was suddenly stricken with a disease of the spine and in November of that year he died at the age of forty-two. Kierkegaard never lost his faith in the justice of God or his sense of his own unworthiness. In his *Journals,* he wrote: 'If, after the Final Judgement, there remains only one sinner in Hell and I happen to be that sinner, I will celebrate from the abyss the Justice of God'. The hard-line Calvinists of the sixteenth century would have rejoiced to hear him say it.

Kierkegaard's legacy to both philosophy and theology was considerable, and it was his insistence that the heart of the Christian faith lay in a believer's relationship with, and commitment to, a transcendent God that was later to encourage Karl Barth (1886-1968) to stress the overwhelming reality of a personal, saving God. For Barth, Christianity was more than simply a system of doctrines, as the Princeton theologians had been teaching. It was a relationship between a holy God who spoke from beyond the world and a sinful people who bowed before mysteries that reason could not understand. For Barth, Christianity was not merely, as Hegel had argued, a symbolic story about the deep connections between human history and divine will: it was a celebration of the decisive intervention of a loving and creative God into human time and space, after which nothing was ever the same again.

Barth was the son of the New Testament scholar Fritz Barth. He was born in Basle but brought up in Berlin where he studied theology and was taught by (among others) the liberal theologian Adolf von Harnack. He held a number of pastorates in the Swiss Reformed Church before and during the Great War, emerging as a strident and at times intemperate critic of liberal theology. Yet like his near contemporary Dietrich Bonhoeffer (1906-1945), Barth did not limit himself to academic abstractions, for he always sought to test the strength of his theology in the contemporary world. He resisted the rise of National Socialism in Germany in the 1930s and he supported a number of church-sponsored movements against Hitler's government. He was one of the authors of the *Declaration of Barmen* in 1934, which set out the case for a Christian opposition to National Socialism and which articulated the struggle of the German Confessing Church against the encroachments of the Nazi state. In 1935 Barth was dismissed from his post at the University of Bonn (largely for political reasons), but he was immediately appointed to a chair in his home town of Basle, where he continued to teach until his retirement in 1962.

In his widely acclaimed commentary *The Epistle to the Romans*, first published shortly after the end of the Great War, Barth stressed the vast chasm of holiness and perfection that separated God from the human world. God was transcendent, majestic, ineffable and holy; he could be known, if at all, only through his revelation of himself in the gospel record of Jesus Christ. To claim, as those of a Hegelian disposition were wont to do, that God had his consciousness in the great sweep of human history was to compromise his holiness and his autonomy. It was panentheism at its worst. God, Barth insisted, was separate from the world and self-sufficient in his autonomous majesty.

One only had to read the Bible intelligently to realise that. Although the gospel of Jesus Christ was the only source of true knowledge about God, it was not, however, the kind of gospel that the world either wished to hear or was used to hearing. Properly interpreted, the gospel was prophetic and judgmental; but its impact had been grievously weakened by those who adapted it to suit the social and political fashions of the day. People needed to hear the eternal and authentic voice of God preached to them in clear and uncompromising terms, not to be led aimlessly up the foggy paths of liberal ambiguity.

It was a reasonable argument, though Barth was given to pursuing it with unreasonable vehemence. His denunciations of liberal theology in general and Friedrich Schleiermacher in particular sometimes bordered onto the paranoid. In *God Here and Now* he described liberal theologians as 'pagans' and made a point of distinguishing tartly between 'their God' and 'our God'. 'Their God', the God of the liberals, could not perform wonders, hear prayers, forgive sins or rescue people from the clutches of death. 'Our God', the sovereign God of scripture, could do all of these things and more. Barth wrote luridly and offensively in *The Sovereignty of God's Word* of the 'stench of godlessness' emanating from the liberal camp. 'We will only be rid of it', he observed, 'when we learn again to seek God in His Word, and to seek His sovereignty in the sovereignty of His Word, which is to say, in the sovereignty of His Son Jesus Christ.' Here, in a single sentence, is encapsulated the kernel of Barth's theology.

Much of Barth's theology harked back to the great historical themes of Christianity that had begun with St Paul, been elaborated by St Augustine, emerged anew from the birth pangs of Protestantism during the Reformation, and been all but abandoned by what Barth saw as the misplaced contemporary enthusiasm for rationality and modernity. He was particularly concerned about the mechanics of revelation. Where and how did God reveal himself? Liberal theologians had pointed to human experience and universal history as authentic vehicles of God's revelation; fundamentalists, by contrast, had stressed the infallibility of biblical revelations about him. Barth rejected both of these. God, he asserted, had revealed himself to mankind in Jesus Christ, not in history and not through the supposed infallibility of the Bible. Jesus alone was the Word of God and to know Jesus was to know God. Indeed, it was the *only* way to know God. Jesus was God's perfect and complete self-expression in human history; he was, as the author of John's gospel had put it, the timeless Word that became flesh and dwelt among men.

Where did that leave the Bible as a vehicle of revelation? Here Barth faced a dilemma. On the one hand, he obviously accepted that it was only through the Bible that anything at all was known about Jesus, and to that extent he had no option but to endorse the time-hallowed Protestant principle of scriptural authority. On the other hand, he parted company with those who argued that the Bible was the literal and infallible word of God, dictated sentence by sentence to men who had obediently recorded what they were told. Barth managed to steer a cautious third way between the two positions, seeing the Bible as a human creation, but one through which God challenged people to place their faith in Jesus Christ. Prophetic and evangelical the Bible may be, but it was still the product of many different authors and editors working over hundreds of years in constantly changing social and political landscapes. The words of the Bible could not therefore *themselves* be the Word of God – only Jesus was that. But the Bible could be used by God as a fallible and sometimes even sinful witness to Jesus, daring those who read it to commit themselves to him.

Barth also tried to steer a middle course in explaining the nature of God. He rejected the view of God as a remote and otherworldly figure, so far beyond the understanding of mortal men that he could be experienced only in the dreamy realms of mysticism and meditation. Barth certainly accepted that the fullness of God was beyond human comprehension, but he also understood that unless ordinary people could develop a personal relationship with God, there was little point in being a Christian. Somehow, God had to be earthed in the ordinariness of everyday life. In this, Barth was in agreement with the liberals. Yet he resisted the liberal penchant for seeing God almost everywhere – in nature, in the great sweep of world history and in the numinous depths of human spirituality. God, he believed, was far too holy and separate a being to become simply another part of the furniture of everyday life.

Barth found his middle way in his unswerving belief in Jesus Christ as the unique window into the character of God. If God had revealed himself in Jesus as loving, gracious and merciful, then he *was* loving, gracious and merciful. This did not mean that men and women could ever fully plumb the infinite depths and riches of God's love, but at least they had been given a sufficient glimpse of it in Jesus to confirm them in their faith. The story is told of a lecture that Barth gave towards the end of his career at a major American university. He was by now a figure of world stature on the theological stage, and as befitted an academic of such distinction, the lecture was attended by many dignitaries as well as staff and students. During the questions at the end of the lecture, a student asked Barth (somewhat to the embarrassment of the big-wigs seated alongside the great man on the platform) if he could summarise his life's work in one sentence. Without hesitation he replied: 'Yes. As my mother taught me: Jesus loves me, this I know, for the Bible tells me so'.

Barth's God was a brilliant and holy being, utterly different in nature from the flawed and imperfect grain of the human condition; but he was not a God who had turned his majestic back on the wretched and sinful faces of humankind. Quite the reverse: through his incarnation in Jesus, God had demonstrated not only his love for the world but also his willingness to be affected and changed by it. Barth well understood that the world could not actually add to the divinity of God or even deepen its quality, for to do so would be to rob God of precisely the perfection of holiness that set him apart from humanity. Since God, however, had freely chosen to involve himself in the life of the world, his relationship with it must somehow have left its mark on him. In saying this, Barth was rejecting centuries of classical Christian orthodoxy, stretching right back to the early church fathers, that saw God as so complete and so perfect that nothing could change his nature in any way, least of all his engagement in the sheer awfulness of so much of human history. To argue, as Barth did, that God could be changed through his dealings with his creatures, would have been seen as a grievous heresy by almost every major Christian theologian from Tertullian to the Reformation. Barth's rejoinder was simply that God chose to include the world in his perfection. He did not have to, but he did. Barth once remarked, with an obvious nod towards Hegel, that 'God could be God without the world, but he chooses not to be such a God.'

Barth's influence on twentieth century Protestant theology was immense; but he was not without his critics. Fundamentalists thought him weak on the authority of the Bible and liberals saw him as too firmly wedded to supernatural doctrines and propositions that had lost their credibility in the modern world. Even some of those who found themselves in sympathy with the general tenor of his views regretted his emphasis on Jesus as the sole channel of God's revelation. Others believed that he had exaggerated the vast and unbridgeable gulf between the worldly sinfulness of man and the transcendent glory of God. The critics had a point: if the holiness of God and the depravity of man are removed from Barth's theology, its arresting quality begins to fade. Moreover, if, as students of comparative religion were beginning to assert, God has revealed himself in different ways at different points in history, then the distinctiveness of the Christian faith comes into question. Jesus no longer stands as the *unique* revelation of God's love. It is perhaps no coincidence that the 'death of God' school (as it came to be known in the twentieth century) owed much to disillusioned followers of Barth.

Barth died in 1968, and although he had by then written some six million words of his lifetime masterpiece *Church Dogmatics*, the work remained unfinished. His ideas were brought to a wider audience largely through the endeavours of the American theologian and social ethicist Reinhold Niebuhr (1893-1971) who started his professional life as a left-wing minister steeped in the tradition of theological liberalism but whose conversion to Barth's theology of neo-orthodoxy in the late 1920s enabled it to reach across the Atlantic to North America. While Niebuhr rejected Barth's insistence on the absolute uniqueness of God's revelation in Jesus Christ, he certainly thought it possible for an historical figure like Jesus to point beyond himself to an eternity of grace. He even saw in Jesus the most complete and perfect personality the world has ever known. For Niebuhr, though, it bordered onto outright contradiction to regard Jesus as both human and divine. If the incarnation meant that God emptied himself of his divinity to come to earth in the human person of Jesus (the traditional doctrine of *kenosis*), then his life was a human life, not a divine life, and it was marked by all the weaknesses and temptations to which the frailty of human flesh is prey. It was an argument that harked conspicuously back to the ancient heresy of Gnosticism.

Niebuhr also had a more forgiving view of man than Barth. He thought that the classical Augustinian view of man as utterly corrupt and depraved was unduly pessimistic. Things had to be kept in perspective. Sin was an inevitable fact of human life, to be sure, but it was not original in the biblical sense of having stemmed from the lapse of Adam and Eve in the Garden of Eden. Rather, sin was rooted in people's lack of trust in the providence of God and in their failure to see the goodness of God at work in the world: and if that was the diagnosis, the cure was for people to accept their imperfections and strive for greater confidence in God. Niebuhr was rather more inclined than Barth to expect people to make some effort on their own behalf, though he had no illusions about the frailty of human morality. In this he parted company not only with Barth but also with one of the central planks of Reformed theology, for Niebuhr's vision of men and women working in partnership with God towards their own and their communities' salvation was deeply at odds with the classical Protestant view of the utter inability of people to help themselves in matters soteriological.

Niebuhr died in 1971, having perhaps done as much as any other twentieth-century theologian except Barth himself to transcend the increasingly sterile confrontations between the liberals and the fundamentalists. For two decades after the Second World War, he exerted a huge influence in American intellectual circles, and his work was taken seriously by sociologists, economists and psychologists as well as by theologians. Prominent American politicians, including President Jimmy Carter, have been among those who have acknowledged the impact of Niebuhr's thinking in their lives. Reinhold Niebuhr's views were taken up and elaborated by his younger brother Richard (1894-1962). Though not as wide-ranging as Reinhold in the themes he espoused or the fame he achieved, Richard Niebuhr spent much time pondering the nature of theology and the ways in which it could be used and communicated. He came to see theology, rather as Barth had done, as the other side of the coin of faith. Theology, he thought, must grow out of faith just as faith must grow out of a concern with the condition of people in their joys and sufferings. For Richard Niebuhr, theology and faith together made up the work of the Christian community as it reflected upon its moral actions, both past and present.

The legacy of neo-orthodoxy has been substantial, though it may still be too early to judge its long-term impact on European and North American Protestantism. Apart from the explicitly evangelical churches, most Protestant worship by the end of the twentieth century was probably as close to the spirit of neo-orthodoxy as to any other theological position. It held a theistic view of God, it preached the revelation of God in Jesus Christ, it held to the authority of scripture without necessarily believing every word to be a literal truth, it accepted most of the supernatural elements in the gospel stories, and it taught that salvation was largely but not exclusively a matter of God's grace. Roman Catholicism, too, has been touched by the neo-orthodoxy of Barth's theology and Reinhold Niebuhr's Christian realism. Among Barth's most enthusiastic disciples was the Roman Catholic theologian Hans Küng (born 1928), who argued in his book *Justification: the Doctrine of Karl Barth and a Catholic Reflection*, published in 1957, that Barth's doctrine of salvation was in line with the official teaching of the Catholic Church. Even contemporary liberal Protestant scholars occasionally acknowledge the important of Barth in emphasising the transcendence of God and the sinfulness of man. The God of neo-orthodoxy, it might be said, has so far stood the test of time rather well.

Chapter 22
The God of Silence and Suffering

The Second World War changed a great many things, including Christian (and also Jewish) theology. In the wake of the deaths and displacements of the countless millions caught up in the conflict, many found it impossible to believe any longer in a God who, as Arthur Ainger (1841-1919) had confidently asserted only a few years earlier, was 'working his purpose out as year succeeds to year'. As the spoils of war were being shared out by the victors at the Yalta and Potsdam conferences in 1945, it required a great leap of faith to believe that the time really was drawing near when 'the earth shall be filled with the glory of God as the waters cover the sea'. Trust in a benign and loving God seemed even harder when the nuclear age dawned in the skies above Hiroshima and Nagasaki and the diabolic evils of the Nazi Holocaust began to seep into the consciousness of post-war Europe. That six million innocent people should have been killed in the name of a monstrously perverted ideology was terrifying enough; that they should have been God's own chosen people, with whom he had entered into an everlasting covenant of salvation and protection, was destructive of almost everything that the Jewish and Christian scriptures had to say about him. Millions lost their religious innocence (and millions more their faith) in the 1940s and 1950s as they struggled to adjust to a world in which the signs of a beneficent God were few and far between.

For a while atheism, closely identified in the 1950s with the godless Marxism of the Soviet Union, was still not an entirely acceptable alternative to belief; but that was soon to change. From the 1960s onwards, institutional Christianity began to decline as non-belief became the norm for the vast majority of people in Western Europe. Suddenly, people seemed much less afraid of the fires of hell than of the furnaces of nuclear destruction; and theology had to take account of these vast and dramatic changes if Christianity and Judaism were to flourish in anything like their pre-war forms. New ways had to be found not only of understanding a covenant God of love who had seemingly abandoned his people to genocide, but also of explaining him to a world that was teetering on the edge of a nuclear doomsday.

Two very different men who each in his own way began the painful process of fashioning a theology for the post-war world from the legacy of devastation and genocide were the Jew, Elie Wiesel and the Christian, Dietrich Bonhoeffer.

Wiesel was born in 1928 into a Jewish family in the small town of Sighet in what is now Romania. His childhood world revolved around his family, the synagogue and the local Jewish community: he spoke Yiddish at home and from an early age he was able to read the Hebrew Scriptures. The young Wiesel had a natural affinity with Judaism, drinking in the mystical traditions of the Hassidic sect to which his mother's family belonged. His father, more prosaically, ensured that he acquired a sound basic education. The early years of the war left Sighet largely untouched, and its Jewish families believed themselves safe from the Nazi persecutions that were gaining momentum in Germany and Poland. It was, however, a false sense of security, and in 1944 Wiesel's adolescent world collapsed with the arrival of the *Schutzstaffel* (the SS) at Sighet. All the Jewish families in the village were deported to concentration camps in Poland, and the young Wiesel was separated from his mother and sister as soon as they arrived at Auschwitz. He never saw them again. He recorded his first impressions of Auschwitz in his book *Night*, first published in 1956. 'Never shall I forget that night, the first night in camp, which has turned my life into one long night. Never shall I forget that smoke. Never shall I forget the little faces of the children, whose bodies I saw turned into wreaths of smoke beneath a silent blue sky. Never shall I forget those flames which consumed my faith for ever. Never shall I forget that nocturnal silence which deprived me, for all eternity, of the desire to live. Never shall I forget those moments which murdered my God and my soul, and turned my dreams to dust. Never shall I forget these things, even if I am condemned to live as long as God himself. Never.'

Wiesel managed to remain with his father as they were starved, beaten and shuffled from camp to camp in open cattle trucks without food or proper clothing. In the last days of the war his father succumbed to dysentery, starvation and exhaustion. After the liberation of the camps in 1945, Wiesel spent time in a French orphanage before studying in Paris at the Sorbonne. Then followed a career as a journalist, writer and informal world ambassador before his appointment as Andrew Mellon Professor of Humanities at Boston University. In 1984 he was awarded the Congressional Gold Medal of Achievement and in 1986 the Nobel Peace Prize. In 2006 Wiesel received an honorary knighthood from the British government.

In his writings and interviews after the war, Elie Wiesel pondered deeply the question of why it had still remained possible for him to believe in God - for in spite of all the reasons he rehearsed for abandoning God, he did not do so. Ever since his experiences in the camps of Poland, he confessed to having 'tremendous problems with God'; but God had remained a continuing presence to be spoken to, argued with, berated, praised and called to account. In this respect, at least, Wiesel stood in the same tradition as the Jewish prophets of the Old Testament who had also had their 'problems with God'. Yet although God was always 'there', Wiesel wrote often of the silence of God, a silence that was, paradoxically, deafening in the dehumanising conditions of the concentration camps. The question, therefore, was: why had the voice of God not been heard in Auschwitz, Treblinka and Buchenwald when his own people, the Jews, were being slaughtered in their millions? Either God had spoken but had not been heard, or he had kept his silence. Which was it?

Wiesel found an answer to the question in the words of an old Jewish rabbi and poet: 'God is not silent, God *is* silence'. Yet somehow, the silence of God was not the silence of a passive onlooker, indifferent and uncaring. The silence of Auschwitz was deep and redolent with meaning. It was, for Wiesel, the genuine silence of God, but not a God who sat back and watched, unmoved, as the atrocities unfolded. For those who could grasp the paradox, the silence proclaimed the presence of a God who suffered with his people, who wept with them and who perhaps even died with them as they were herded into the gas chambers. It is a deeply moving vision of God that dare not be questioned by anyone who has suffered less than Wiesel and the countless other victims of the Holocaust. Yet it cannot pass without mention that Wiesel's eloquent account of a God who *could* have put a halt to the barbarism of the camps but who chose instead to suffer silently with his people in their degradation and despair is far removed from the historical God of both Judaism and Christianity. Judaism was founded upon the belief in a God who would deliver his people from all their suffering, however desperate their plight may be: as Wiesel put it, 'the Jewish people do not believe in a weak God'. Likewise, the early Christian church held fast to the image of a God who was above all passion and suffering, branding as the heresy of *patripassianism* the idea that the Father had shared the anguish of Jesus in his crucifixion and death. But heresy no more: it is now commonplace for Christian preachers to speak of a God who stands side by side with humanity in its pain and despair, sharing its misery and experiencing its hurt. From the almost unanswerable questions that the Holocaust posed about a God of everlasting love, a remarkable new face of God emerged that would have been unthinkable in earlier times: the face of a God who suffers.

If Wiesel articulated a meaning of God for Judaism in the suffering of the concentration camps, Dietrich Bonhoeffer (1906-1945) began a similar exercise for Christianity even though the experiences and the theological concerns of the two men were different. While Wiesel questioned God's presence in the Holocaust, Bonhoeffer questioned the moral responsibility of people when faced with great evil. Bonhoeffer was born in Breslau and studied in Germany and America. In 1931 he returned to Germany where he lectured on theology at the University of Berlin. He also served for a time as pastor to two German-speaking Protestant churches in London. In 1935 Bonhoeffer returned again to Germany where he collaborated with (among others) Karl Barth in establishing the German Confessing Church and helping to script the *Declaration of Barmen* that articulated a theologically grounded opposition to Hitler's democratically elected government. A strong opponent of Nazism, Bonhoeffer ran an illegal seminar for pastors of the German Confessing Church, castigating the anti-semitic policies of Hitler and calling for the Church to resist the Nazi's treatment of the Jews. For his efforts, he was banned by the Gestapo from preaching, teaching and, finally, speaking at all in public.

In 1939 Bonhoeffer joined a small, clandestine group of high-ranking officers in Hitler's military intelligence who were planning to assassinate the Führer. When his involvement in the plan was discovered, he was arrested and charged with conspiracy. He spent a year and a half in a Berlin prison; and when the assassination attempt in July 1944 failed and Bonhoeffer was found to have been associated with the conspirators who planted the bomb in the room where Hitler was standing, he was transferred to the concentration camps. Together with others of the conspirators, Bonhoeffer was hanged at Flossenbürg in April 1945, three weeks before the camp was liberated. To satisfy the sadistic whims of the camp commander, the men were forced to strip in their cells before their execution and walk naked to the gallows. Fifty years later Bonhoeffer was absolved by the German government of all crimes against the state.

Bonhoeffer has been widely regarded as a twentieth-century martyr for the Christian faith and is one of very few modern theologians to have been accepted equally by fundamentalists, liberals and those of a neo-orthodox disposition. His theology stretched beyond the dogmatic boundaries of sectarian Christianity towards a universal vision of God that demanded a morally committed response. Yet many of his beliefs and ideas are incomplete and provisional. Although his famous *Letters and*

Papers from Prison were gathered together and published in 1953, his ideas remain, like those of Blaise Pascal, in an unfinished form. Bonhoeffer wrote tantalisingly of 'a religion-less Christianity' and of 'a world come of age' in which a God of the gaps had been rendered obsolete, but there can be little certainty about his precise meaning. He does, though, seem to have grappled seriously with the idea that God's greatest gift to the world may have been the gift of human maturity, allowing people to grow out an infantile dependence upon him and to take the adult step of accepting responsibility for their own lives. To many, it seemed a daunting prospect – but then, as Bonhoeffer stressed, God's grace does not come cheaply.

In another posthumously published work in 1949, *Ethics*, Bonhoeffer tried to articulate an explicitly Christian basis for moral action in the face of great evil. It had obvious affinities with his broader themes of human maturity and responsibility. Bonhoeffer rejected the possibility of absolute moral certainty. Actions may be right or they may be wrong, but those who carry them out may not ever be entirely sure which side of the moral divide they are on. People may believe that their actions are morally justified if they lead to a morally valued outcome; but Bonhoeffer observed that the outcome of an action could stretch away into an infinite future where notions of 'right' and 'wrong' may be very different from those of the present. Think of biblical attitudes towards slavery. Or again, people may believe that an action is morally justified if it is done with a morally valid motive; but who is to adjudicate between a right and a wrong motive? Motives that are seen as morally wrong today may not always have been so. Think of the ethnic cleansing of Canaan, superintended by Yahweh and executed by Joshua. Bonhoeffer believed that, since morality is always at risk of turning out to be provisional, there can be no cast iron guarantee that any particular choice is the right one at the moment when it is made. Responsible action is, therefore, an adventure of uncertainty. We can never be sure we are doing the right thing. Bonhoeffer's own participation in the plot to assassinate Hitler is a poignant illustration: the Bible almost unequivocally condemns the taking of life, but might it not be morally justified if aimed at the removal of a murderous tyrant?

Nevertheless, Bonhoeffer was clear that people of goodwill must do *something* when they are confronted by the great evils and perversions of the world. To stand aside and do nothing would actually be the least moral course of action. So there is a dilemma: to fail to act in the face of evil is tantamount to condoning that evil, but there can be no certainty that actions that are taken to oppose evil are morally justified.

Each situation is different, and what is right in one context may be wrong in another. It is here, though, that Bonhoeffer's argument seems to turn back on itself, for he appears to conclude that there *is*, after all, an over-riding criterion by which the truth of a moral choice can be judged, namely, that it mirrors the selfless behaviour of Jesus. It cannot be a foolproof criterion, for many of the situations in which people are called upon to take a moral stand are very different from any that Jesus faced. Conspiring to murder an evil dictator would be one. Provided there is a clear and honest attempt to find the kind of choice that is consistent with Jesus' own selfless behaviour, then that for Bonhoeffer is the best that can be done. It has moral integrity and is a worthy offering to God.

In their different ways, both Elie Wiesel and Dietrich Bonheoffer found the presence of God in the atrocities of Nazi Germany. Wiesel saw the face of a God who stood silently with his people in their desperation and who shared their suffering. Bonhoeffer saw the face of a God who makes a moral challenge to people to resist the evils and atrocities in the world around them but who will not necessarily intervene to help them. Bonhoeffer's image was perhaps the more orthodox, but Wiesel's was perhaps the more compelling. The idea of a God who silently suffers with humanity has passed into both Jewish and Christian theology as perhaps the best that can be offered in response to the persistently troubling questions for post-war Judaism and Christianity: Where was God in Auschwitz, Treblinka and Buchenwald? Why did God not save his own people in their hour of greatest need?

Chapter 23
The God for the Twentieth Century

The second half of the twentieth century saw the emergence of new faces of the Christian God, some of which would have been unrecognisable to earlier generations. Among them were the faces of a God who was notably on the side of freedom-fighters, the poor, women, homosexuals, disabled people, black people and other oppressed communities. Christian theology acquired a range of qualifying epithets: liberation theology, feminist theology, Marxist theology, urban theology, post-modern theology, existentialist theology, historical theology and several others. God was metamorphosing into a deity whose diverse qualities (as if he needed reminding of them) became incorporated into the ways in which prayers were addressed to him: 'Sympathetic God', 'Understanding God', 'Suffering God', 'Gentle God', 'Challenging God', 'Kindly God' and so on. Feminists objected to calling God 'Lord' because it implied a male superiority that was offensive to women. When, to redress the balance, prayers and liturgies began to address God as 'mother', it upset those of a conservative nature who pointed out that God had always been recognised as a male figure and it was absurd to further complicate the already taxing doctrine of the incarnation by accepting that he had a feminine side as well. How could a 'mother' God have become incarnate in a human man who then called God his 'father'?

It was all part of the continuing search for images of God that could attract new converts in a post-modern world in which epic stories of faith and dogmatic assertions of truth had lost their power to engage the hearts and minds of an increasingly sophisticated populace. The time-hallowed face of the God of the Nicene Creed was still alive and well across great swathes of Christendom, especially in the developing world; to many observers in the West, however, it seemed to be showing its age. Thoughtful Christians found it increasingly difficult to believe in a God who had emerged in the distant past and whose identity had been set in theological aspic in alien cultures far removed from the complex and fast-moving world of the late twentieth century. God needed to be rediscovered, or at least reinterpreted, for modern times, and there was no shortage of those willing to try. Among the better known of them, at least in the short term, were Rudolf Bultmann, Paul Tillich and John Robinson.

Rudolf Bultmann (1884-1976) belonged to the last generation of outstanding theologians who grew up in the universities of the Kaiser's Germany and who began their scholarly careers in the aftermath of the Great War. He was born in 1884 at Wiefelstede, in what was then the Grand Duchy of Oldenburg, and he studied theology at Tübingen, Berlin and Marburg. After academic posts at Breslau and Giessen Universities, he returned to Marburg in 1922 where he remained until his retirement in 1951. It was during the Marburg years that Bultmann encountered his exact contemporary Karl Barth and found himself agreeing with much of what the arch-exponent of neo-orthodoxy had to say about the holiness of God and the sinfulness of man. Like Hermann Reimarus before him, however, Bultmann saw the Bible not as the absolute and unchanging word of God but as the cultural product of its times, needing constantly to be interpreted in a modern frame of reference if its messages were still to appeal. His project to modernise God by 'demythologising' the gospels reached a wide audience and came to be seen as one of the distinctive features of twentieth-century Protestant theology. Although the notion of 'demythologising' appears at first sight to involve dismissing the Bible as a work of fiction, Bultmann used it to signal the need to recast 'gospel truth' in ways that made sense in the modern world. It was a clumsy and unfriendly word and Bultmann himself did not much like it; but it has stuck.

Bultmann followed the lead of earlier biblical scholars of the stature of David Strauss (1808-1874) and Johannes Weiss (1863-1914) in arguing that the gospels had to be read and understood within the cultural framework of first-century Jewish Palestine. Like them, he believed that when Jesus spoke in eschatological tones about the coming kingdom of God, he was echoing the apocalyptic fervour of his age. His words were to be taken literally because that is how they were intended to be taken. Jesus meant what he said when he warned that wars and insurrections would break out, plagues and famines would engulf the world, stars would fall from the sky, and the sun would darken. In making these apocalyptic predictions, Bultmann argued, Jesus was speaking neither figuratively nor metaphorically. He was predicting real physical events that would herald the arrival of God's eternal reign on earth. They would, moreover, happen within the natural lifespan of many of those around him; and the New Testament narratives trace the growing voices of impatience and doubt among later generations when they failed to materialise. The author of the Second Letter of Peter wrote that: 'There will come scoffers who will say: What has happened to his promised coming? Our fathers have been laid to rest, but still everything goes exactly as it has always has done since the world began.' Why the delay?

For Bultmann, writing in the middle of the twentieth century, it was hardly a question worth considering. He could see nothing odd about the failure of the predicted apocalypse to arrive, for he knew that universal laws could not be suspended or overthrown by the idiosyncratic actions of God. Stars could not literally fall from the sky or the sun go out. Such things simply did not happen. The age had passed when God's capacity to change the processes of the natural world could be taken for granted. If Jesus' apocalyptic vision of the coming kingdom was to have any traction in the modern world, Bultmann argued, it had to be recast as a culture-bound story that, if read with modern insight and imagination, might still have something important to say to the contemporary world; and it should be the task of theology and preaching to dive below the surface and raise the treasures below. In short, Bultmann saw a pressing need to demythologise the gospel stories by lifting them out of their original settings and reinterpreting them in ways that harmonised with the mind-set of the twentieth century.

Bultmann suggested, for example, that although the words of Jesus about a cosmic cataclysm could no longer be taken in the literal sense in which they were intended, his vision of the kingdom of God was nevertheless a realistic blueprint for a just and righteous society for modern times. What Jesus proclaimed as an impending future event could be recast as a demanding but worthy aspiration for the present, and no intellectual compromise need be involved in doing so. To demythologise the gospels was not to reject the Christian message itself but only the ancient cultural beliefs in which they had become fossilised. If read with faith, a demythologised gospel could still provide meaning and purpose in people's lives. Although, for instance, misfortunes and tragedies could no longer be seen as personal warnings from God, a serious accident might lead the victim to review her lifestyle or rearrange her priorities in ways that reflected the gospel messages; and if so, then faith could trace the hand of God at work in the tragedy. It could no longer be said that God had *caused* the accident to happen, but it might be thought that he was somehow at work in it. As Bultmann put it in *Jesus Christ and Mythology*: 'Christian faith can only say, I trust that God is working here. Whatever it is that he is doing, I do not yet know, and perhaps I never shall know. But in faith I trust that it is important for my personal existence, and I must ask what it is that God says to me.'

Rudolf Bultmann's contemporary and sometime colleague Paul Tillich (1886-1965) also took seriously the reality of the situations in which people found themselves – situations of profound doubt, anxiety and loneliness as well as of assurance, certitude and acceptance. Like Bultmann, Tillich believed that unless theology dealt honestly with people's personal concerns and experiences, it had little to contribute to the welfare of humanity. Tillich was born in Starzedel, in Prussia, in 1886. After serving as a Protestant chaplain with the German army in the Great War he taught theology at Berlin before being appointed in 1924 as professor of theology at Marburg, where he overlapped for a year with Bultmann. Tillich soon moved on to Dresden and Leipzig before taking up a chair in philosophy at Frankfurt; but his outspoken criticism of Nazism forced him to leave Germany in 1933 and migrate to America, where he eventually took American citizenship. In 1954 he was appointed to a chair in theology at Harvard where he remained until his retirement.

A recurring theme in Tillich's attempt to reconcile people's questions about their existence with the insights of Christian theology was that of loneliness and estrangement. He noted that many people in the middle years of the twentieth century seemed to be drifting through life with little purpose or hope, alienated from their heritage and fearful for their future. In his book *Suicide*, published in 1897, the French sociologist Emile Durkheim (1858-1917) had earlier coined the term *anomie* to describe the mood in a society when the normal rules and expectations of civic behaviour have been eroded and nothing has taken their place. Cut off from their past, people could all too easily drift aimlessly in a cultural vacuum, failing to see any signs of hope in the present and surrendering the desire to build a better future. Tillich recognised the destructive power of *anomie* in the modern world, reflected strongly in the anxious writings of Nietzsche, Sartre and Camus, and he believed that it was the task of theology and preaching to restore a lost sense of meaning and purpose to human lives by reconnecting people to the ground and depth of their being.

There was, perhaps, nothing very new in the idea of people 'finding their true selves in the depths of their souls', for it had been a distinctive theme of liberal Protestant theology since the nineteenth century. Tillich, however, put a modern spin on it by defining the 'ground and depth of being' as God himself. He wrote most openly about 'ground' and 'depth' in his popular book *The Shaking of the Foundations*, published in 1949. In it, Tillich argued that God was not merely present in the ground and depth of being, he was the ground and the depth. 'The depth of being is what the word God actually means', he wrote in *The Shaking of the Foundations*, 'and if that word has not much meaning for you, translate it, and speak of the depths of your life, of the source of your being, of your ultimate concern, of what you take seriously without any reservation.' A part of God's life, he seemed to be saying, was lived in the deep experiences of the human spirit. The implications were radical. Tillich exhorted his readers to forget everything traditional that they had learnt about God, perhaps even the word itself, for if they knew that God meant depth, they knew a great deal about him. He wrote: 'You cannot then call yourself an atheist or unbeliever . . . for he who knows about depth knows about God.'

It was in some such way as this, Tillich believed, that Christian theology could address the *anomie* of modern men and women. By helping them to understand that God could be equated with the most important things in their lives, whether personal or social or political, the gospel of hope could reconnect their existence to their essence by introducing them to God himself. It offered the possibility of salvation this side of the grave rather than, as Christian doctrine had taught for almost two thousand years, the other side. The key to it all, as it had been throughout the history of Protestant theology, was grace. Grace, for Tillich, was more than forgiveness, more than benevolence, more than the showering of gifts. In grace, something was overcome, some blindfold removed, some obstacle unblocked. Grace occurred in spite of the separation and estrangement of modern man from God. Indeed, grace for Tillich was the very means by which the separation could be reversed. 'Grace is the *re*-union of life with life, the *re*-conciliation of the self with itself.'

The idea of God as 'ground' and 'depth' is sometimes named as 'panentheism'. A Greek compound word meaning broadly that 'everything exists in God', panentheism has always been viewed with suspicion by conservative theologians, for it narrows the gulf between the infinite perfection of God on the one hand and the finite imperfections of humanity on the other. It chips away at God's transcendence and holiness, making it difficult to know exactly where humanity ends and divinity begins. Conservatives also charge that panentheism risks diluting the perfection and glory of God by mingling it with the selfishness of human nature. If, as Tillich argued, God is defined as that which people take seriously in their moral and political lives, then God's nature must be shaped and influenced by the flawed morality of human actions. What does it say about God if people have nothing more serious in their lives than their own pleasure or self-interest? What if there is actually very little in the 'ground and depth of humanity' other than greed and self-satisfaction? These have proved to be telling questions for those of a panentheistic persuasion.

One of Tillich's most accomplished popularisers in Britain was John Robinson (1919-1983) whose book *Honest to God*, written while he was Bishop of Woolwich, was a publishing sensation in the 1960s. The book was described as 'a personal confession of convictions borne in upon him [Robinson] by the need to be utterly honest about the terms in which the Faith can truthfully be presented today'. Robinson observed that his book might seem radical, even heretical, but he was sure that, in the fullness of time, it would be seen to have erred in not being radical enough. The appeal of *Honest to God* owed a great deal to the fact that its author was a bishop in the Church of England, for if a senior Anglican cleric could openly and publicly question the transcendence of God and the divinity of Jesus, then a fundamental change must be taking place in the landscape of theological discourse. The result was to open the way for Christians to question things about God that had hitherto been beyond dispute in public places, including many ancient dogmas to which worshippers gave lip service in creeds, hymns and prayers while harbouring doubts in their hearts. To many readers, especially lay people, the book seemed to come as a great relief, for it authenticated beliefs that they had been harbouring in their hearts but had been too afraid or too inarticulate to express in public.

Robinson began *Honest to God* by tilting at a fairly soft target: the traditional God of Judaeo-Christian orthodoxy. For four millennia, this God had been described in anthropomorphic terms: that is, he had been known through the qualities and characteristics of a human person. He had a name (the LORD), a gender (male) and a dwelling place (heaven) and, at various points in the Bible, he was endowed with a wide range of human traits including love, anger, justice, mercy, faithfulness, creativity and jealousy. Like humans, he had the capacity to think, act, remember and anticipate. The quality and intensity of these traits and capacities were, of course, written on a cosmic scale in the biblical narrative of God, but always they were traits that were human in their essence if divine in their degree of perfection. In short, the God of traditional Christian theology was, in some supernatural sense, a person, and a belief in the existence of such a God was known as 'theism'. Indeed, theism was the *only* way in which most people could think about God at all, for they lacked the words and the ideas to conceive of him as anything other than a sentient being who 'really' existed somewhere in the ether.

All of this, Robinson argued, had made very good sense for almost two millennia but had become increasingly problematic for at least two centuries; for if God 'really' existed as a separate person, where was he to be found? Until at least the Reformation, it was not a question that posed any great difficulty; but by the middle of the twentieth century few believed any longer in the literal reality of a place called heaven. The simple and uncontested medieval understanding of heaven, earth and hell that had once defined the topography of Christendom had now given way to an unimaginably vast and complex universe; and in the process, the traditional dwelling place of God and his angels had disappeared. This had created a problem, for nothing had so far emerged to replace the age-old idea of God as a living person whose abode was 'up there' in heaven. No really new insights about God had been developed that could supplant the common – but, in Robinson's view, now inadequate – view of him as an old man living somewhere in the sky with his son Jesus sitting at his right hand and assorted other denizens of heaven in attendance.

From this beginning, Robinson dared to raise some fundamental questions. What if the whole idea of an all-powerful being who 'really' exists somewhere 'out there' is altogether too far-fetched for the twentieth century? Have we seriously faced the possibility, Robinson asked, that in order to make Christianity intelligible to the modern world we may have to abandon the idea of God as a real, transcendent being? He acknowledged that however disturbing and uncomfortable the thought might be, it had to be confronted. In the long term, he argued, the Christian faith would not survive if it continued to depend on assertions about God that no longer carried conviction. Indeed, Robinson believed that 'we shall eventually be no more able to convince men of the existence of a God out there than persuade them to take seriously the gods of Olympus. If Christianity is to survive, there is no time to lose in detaching it from this scheme of thought.'

It was at this point in his argument that Robinson found his ideas merging naturally into the stream of liberal theology running from Schleiermacher and Ritschl in the late eighteenth and early nineteenth centuries through to his near contemporaries Bonhoeffer, Bultmann and Tillich (who stalk the pages of *Honest to God* like the three wise men). Like Tillich, Robinson wondered whether, instead of seeing God as separated from the natural world, it might be more in tune with the twentieth-century mind to think of him as its deepest heart and centre. Perhaps God is neither 'up there in heaven' nor even 'out there somewhere else' but in the deepest places of the human personality. Belief in such a God, Robinson suggested, would still involve faith and commitment, for it would require people to open themselves unconditionally to the most serious events in their human experience as they encountered them in their daily relationships with each other. It would be to trust that the sacrificial giving of oneself in love was not in vain, for it would be in such a relationship that God could be most fully encountered. Whether people have known God, Robinson proposed, could be tested by the single question: how deeply have you loved? A true encounter with God had very little to do with religious rituals and observances and even less to do with religious doctrines and dogmas; but it had much to do with people's behaviour towards the poor and the dispossessed, the homeless and the imprisoned, the grieving and the despairing.

Rudolf Bultmann, Paul Tillich and John Robinson were among an innovative group of twentieth-century theologians who were trying to fashion new but serious images of God for their times. They saw their task as both important and urgent, for entire generations were growing up with little understanding of traditional Christianity and even less sympathy with many of its most cherished dogmas and rituals. Rightly or wrongly, the twentieth-century inheritors of the mantle of nineteenth-century liberalism perceived an imperative need to move people on from old-fashioned beliefs and assumptions that had become increasingly difficult to accept. Christianity could no longer credibly be discussed in terms of heaven 'up there' and hell 'down below' at a time when men were landing on the moon and probes were travelling to the distant reaches of the solar system. Popular jokes circulated in the 1960s and 1970s about astronauts returning to earth and reporting no sighting either of heaven or of God. People laughed – but the message stuck. There was no heaven 'up there' from which the Jesus of orthodox Christian doctrine descended ('he came down to earth from heaven') and to which he returned as a living man from the top of a mountain in Palestine.

Other staple ingredients of traditional Christianity were also in danger of being consumed in the melting pot of post-modern culture. Apocalyptic warnings about the second coming of Jesus fell largely on deaf ears – a response that seemed entirely appropriate whenever small groups of believers who had taken themselves to the tops of local mountains to escape the cataclysm traipsed sheepishly down again a week or two later, only to find the world unchanged. Miracles were dismissed as so much superstition. The relevance of ancient middle-eastern texts to the modern world came under question. The excessively elaborate rituals and pageantry of Christian worship were seen almost as pantomime, as far removed from the simple, self-denying life-style of

Jesus of Nazareth as it was possible to get. It is scarcely surprising that some theologians saw the need for new ways of expounding the moral core of the Christian faith to a Western world that had largely lost touch with its religious heritage.

How far these would-be twentieth-century reformers succeeded is hard to say. Christians who understood and endorsed their objectives were doubtless scattered throughout the mainstream churches as the century drew to a close, though they could hardly be said to have constituted a distinctive group or to have spoken with a concerted voice. The 'Sea of Faith' movement had its devotees, as did the Progressive Christian Alliance in America and the Progressive Christianity Network in Britain, and such names as Don Cupitt, David Jenkins, Richard Holloway, John Spong, Geza Vermes and Marcus Borg were familiar to many churchgoers on both sides of the Atlantic. The impact, however, of these movements and writers upon ordinary congregations up and down the land was probably quite small. Hazardous though it is to generalise, the majority of regular worshippers in Protestant Europe at the dawn of the new millennium were probably rather conservative in their religion, disliking change and resisting any challenge to their familiar beliefs. It is interesting, for example, that some of the most vehement opposition to Robinson came not from the secular press but from within the Church of England and, although *Honest to God* was a publishing sensation in the 1960s, it is probably now little read.

The hard truth seems to be that, by the end of the second millennium, there were few signs that the 'new theology' had taken hold in either pulpit or pew. When *Honest to God* was published, Robinson seemed to have positioned the established church in the forefront of theological openness and change, but it would be difficult to identify any great impact that the book may have had in the five decades following its publication. Robinson's fear that history may judge him not to have been radical enough now seems rather wide of the mark. Meanwhile, in spite of a decade of evangelism by the mainstream churches in Britain, organised Christianity continued its genteel but inexorable decline throughout the 1990s and into the new century. The religious issues dominating the opening years of the new millennium were not those about the nature and being of God but those of internal disharmony in an increasingly fractured society where traditional social mores were undergoing a radical transformation. As the Church of England, in particular, engaged in public civil war over the ordination of homosexual priests and the promotion of women to the episcopacy, it became increasingly difficult to discern the wellsprings of any major revival. The God of Christian tradition and orthodoxy may not actually have died, but only the most fervent believer could claim that he reigned supreme in all the earth.

Chapter 24
The God of the Past and the God of the Future

The Christian God has had an enduring and varied history. The recorded story of his life began in the Middle East some 4,000 years ago when a deity who called himself 'I AM THAT I AM' appeared to a man named Abraham and promised to make him the father of a great nation. It is very probable that Yahweh's origins stretch much farther back into the mists of human experience to a time when religion was beginning to replace magic as the fount of understanding about the world and when gods were taking over from sorcerers as supernatural help-mates in managing the vicissitudes of life. Whatever his origins, Yahweh has been a very versatile God. As well as being the God of the Jewish people for the four millennia that have passed since his appearance to Abraham, he has also been the God of the Christians for the last 2,000 years and the God of the Arab nations for the last 1,400 years. In his various revelations, this God has dominated the lives of countless millions of people, first in the Middle East, then around the Mediterranean world, then throughout the rest of Europe and finally across the entire globe. There is not a continent that has not been touched by the power, mystery and inspiration of the deity who entered into the covenant of circumcision with Abraham.

It goes without saying that this is a complicated history that cannot be fully understood. The questions, though, remain. In what sense can it be said that the God of the Jews is the *same* God who is also worshipped by Christians and Muslims? Is there only one true God who chooses to reveal himself in different ways to different people at different times, keeping them in the dark about his unique status and allowing them to beat culturally different paths to his door? Or are there different gods who may have had a common origin but who revealed themselves in history as separate deities for Jews, Christians and Muslims? These are, self-evidently, questions for faith rather than historical analysis, yet since each of these great world faiths believes in the living reality of the God whom it worships, they are entirely reasonable questions to ask.

There is the added problem, certainly for Christianity and probably for Judaism and Islam as well, that Christians have generally regarded their

God as the one fixed point in cosmic history, constant and unchanging across vast aeons of time. It is a belief that is clearly reflected in the traditional hymns and prayers of Christendom. He is the 'Rock of Ages' who was, and is, and is to be for aye the same. He existed before time began and he will continue to exist when time has ceased. Although Christianity has traditionally proclaimed the timelessness and the immutability of God, however, the historical record reveals a rather more complicated picture. As this book has tried to show, many different and often contradictory faces of the Christian God have emerged over the last four thousand years, challenging the notion of him as the everlasting and unchangeable 'Rock of Ages'. It is more faithful to the beliefs and experiences of generations of Christians to see God as a fluid and multifaceted deity whose image can alter from generation to generation. To believe in a God who has remained the same throughout the course of human history is to pose a great number of unanswerable questions.

Is the God who instituted the ritual of circumcision the same God who, according to St Paul, set no store by the procedure at all? Is the God who was once pleased by the sacrificial offerings of goats and cattle in the temple at Jerusalem the same God who was later offended by the odours of the altars? Is the God who led the ethnic cleansing of Canaan the same God whom Americans ask to bless their country and Britons beseech to save their gracious Queen? Is the God who forbade the Jewish people to eat kites, falcons, crows, pelicans and ospreys the same God whose existence St Anselm found to be philosophically necessary? Is the God who forbade the building of steps in front of altars the same God who is worshiped throughout Christendom at altars placed at the top of steps? Is the God of the Psalms, who led his people into quiet pastures and accompanied them in the valley of the shadow of death, the same God who delighted in the killing of thousands of Israelites during their wilderness years? Is the God who appeared to Moses amidst the terrifying sound of thunder on Mount Sinai the same God whom Elie Wiesel encountered in the searing silence of Auschwitz? Is the God of love and forgiveness who became incarnate in Jesus the same God who chooses some people for salvation and condemns others to perdition?

Is the God whose deeds and passions dominate the early books of the Old Testament the same God as the passionless, Hellenistic deity of the Christian creeds? Is St Augustine's God of awesome righteousness the same God who moved Nicholas von Zinzendorf to tears in an art gallery in Düsseldorf? Is the God whose existence was tested in the cosmological arguments of Thomas Aquinas the same God who warmed the heart of John Wesley? Is the God whom Martin Luther once despaired of ever pleasing the same God of abundant grace proclaimed by Jacob Arminius? Is the God who sternly commanded much of the civic life of sixteenth-century Switzerland the same God who inspired the liberation theology of twentieth-century Latin America?

Is the philosophically necessary God of René Descartes the same God who moved Blaise Pascal to a state of emotional fire? Is the supernatural God who was rejected by François-Marie Voltaire the same God who worked miracles of healing at the shrines of medieval saints? Is the God whose words can only be understood in the historical context of their time the same God whose Word is literally and eternally true? Is the God whose aid was fervently implored by the Christian armies fighting in the crusades the same God whose aid was equally fervently implored by the Islamic armies against whom they were fighting? Is the God who masterminded the military tactics of Jewish armies in Old Testament times the same God whose help is sought by Palestinians in their contemporary struggles against Israel?

Such questions are, of course, unanswerable in any modern sense of the word. They are, nevertheless, legitimate questions to ask about a God who is believed by his followers to 'really' exist, for we would expect such a deity to display a continuity of character and nature across the ages. We would expect the God who reveals himself to believers in one generation to be recognisably the same God who reveals himself to those in other generations, for otherwise there would be no coherent basis for a faith that proclaims the continuity of his actions in the world. At the very least, we would expect no blatant contradictions between God's revelations of himself at different times in history.

In fact, however, there are endless contradictions: the faces of the Christian God that have been revealed over four millennia have often been inconsistent and sometimes downright paradoxical. The God whose grace is freely available to all can hardly be the same God who predestines some to damnation. The God whose son died for the salvation of some can hardly be the same God whose son died for the salvation of all. The God who superintended the slaughter of soldiers and civilians alike can hardly be the same God who requires his followers to love their enemies. The God who created the world and its inhabitants, fully formed, in six days can hardly be the same God who works through the infinitesimally slow processes of evolution. The God who promised to protect his chosen people for ever can hardly be the same God who was powerless to prevent their systematic genocide at the hands of the Nazis. The God who was once above all passion can hardly be the same

God who weeps over the sufferings of his creation. It would be going too far to suggest that the God of Abraham has meant all things to all people in all ages, but he has unquestionably meant different things to different people in different ages. The God who has traditionally been seen as the immutable Rock of Ages turns out to be surprisingly flexible and adaptable.

The historically diverse and conflicting faces of God are likely to cause difficulties only to those who believe that he 'really' exists. It is only they, the traditional theists, who would expect to see continuity and consistency in the revelations of God's nature and character. For those who hold no such theistic belief in a transcendent God, the problem simply does not arise. If you do not believe that God is a real person, there is no particular reason for you to expect any consistency in the way he has been perceived by human beings across the ages. From this viewpoint, the historical portrait gallery of God has been stocked with nothing more eternal than the deepest expressions of people's hopes and fears, wishes and dreads, imaginings and yearnings. That is simply the nature of human creativity. Moreover, since any one revelation of God cannot be shown to be more genuine or more authentic than any other, there is little point in acclaiming one as true or condemning another as false.

Among those who would decline to call themselves theists (let us call them, collectively, non-theists), a distinction has commonly been drawn between 'a-theists' and 'panen-theists'. It could be said that a-theists are in the more comfortable position, for since they have no belief in any kind of God, they can afford to view the recurrent battles over truth and falsehood with bored indifference. For the a-theist, God is a human invention; and since human inventiveness has proved to be infinitely variable, it is hardly surprising that claims and counter-claims about God have been equally varied. The 'real' God cannot stand up and be counted simply because he is not there.

Panen-theists are less well defined in terms of their beliefs about God, and it is harder to generalise about them. Yet as this book has tried to show, there have been those throughout the history of Christian thought and experience who have challenged theistic orthodoxies about God without rejecting the possibility of a divine dimension to human experience. They have held fast to the *idea* of God while rejecting the theistic view of him as a transcendent being outside time and space. They have, in their different ways, raised some challenging questions for a post-modern world. What if God exists not as a transcendent being but in the shared beliefs and common rituals of a community of faith? What if he is the name that people give to the human impulses that move them to awe, inspire them to love, sustain them in their tribulations, and enable them to forgive? What if 'getting to know God' is getting to know the deepest, noblest and most generous aspects of the human spirit? What if 'trust in God' is the trust that love is better than hatred, honesty better than deceit, hope better than despair, compassion better than selfishness? What if 'belief in God' is the belief that a life lived in the service of others is a life well spent? Such questions involve a faith and trust in God, but it is not the transcendent God of the theists. Rather, it is a God who is to be found in the lives of people who have consciously committed themselves to the values of the Christian gospel, and who express that commitment by loving God with all their heart and soul and mind and their neighbours as themselves.

A number of the writers discussed in this book may perhaps be seen as panen-theists, though that is most emphatically my categorisation, and they may well object to it from their graves. There have always been, however, those who have understood God as the faithfully articulated expression of humanity's highest aspirations for itself and the world. This kind of interstitial point between theism and a-theism can perhaps be glimpsed in Peter Abelard's vision of the cross as a moral inspiration to righteous living; in François-Marie Voltaire's plea for a religion that 'taught much morality and very little dogma'; in Desiderius Erasmus' humanistic philosophy of Christ; in Ludwig Feuerbach's definition of an atheist as one for whom the attributes of divinity such as love, wisdom and justice mean nothing; in Friedrich Schleiermacher's emphasis on the importance of the way people respond to their feelings about God; in Rudolf Bultmann's assertion that the gospels can be inspirational without being literally true; in Elie Wiesel's experience of God within the profundity of silence; in Paul Tillich's equation of God with depth and love.

These writers can hardly be called a-theists, yet in their writings they do not obviously seem to be traditional theists. They occupy a place between the two, dispensing to a greater or lesser extent with the creedal God of Nicaea and Chalcedon while still preserving the divine idea as a template for righteous living. Such views were able to be fully explored for the first time, without fear of ecclesiastical retribution or the threat of eternal punishment, during the golden years of liberal Protestant theology in the nineteenth century. In the twentieth century they formed a small but moderately influential repository of liberal thinking at a time when a-theism was becoming the norm in the Western world. There is nothing surprising about the emergence, from the eighteenth century onwards, of symbolic rather than literal ways of thinking about God. Human progress in all aspects of life has depended upon people's capacity to change their mental gears when to do so opens up the possibility of new insights and advancements. The switch from religious literalism to religious symbolism has been, for many Christians, one such powerful change.

What, then, of the future? In *The Golden Bough*, published in instalments at the turn of the twentieth century, Sir James Frazer argued that the evolution of human understanding about the world could be likened to the gradual weaving, over aeons of time, of a colourful tapestry made up of black, red and white threads. In the early stages of its making, the tapestry was coloured largely by the black threads of magic; but with the steady development of human knowledge and understanding about the natural world, the black became overlaid first with the dark crimson streams of religion and then with the wide white rivers of science. Frazer was more inclined than many other social anthropologists to see these phases as broadly sequential, albeit with substantial overlaps: first there was magic, then religion, and finally science. He argued that, as a methodology for understanding and controlling the natural world, magic had been no more able to survive the arrival of religion than religion would, in the long run, be able to survive the arrival of science. Religion would continue to be practised in certain forms and places, but it would eventually cease to command the allegiance of the masses unless it relinquished its unique claims to know the truth about the universe.

Frazer's analysis caused a stir in late Victorian and early Edwardian society. If he was right, science would eventually take over from religion as the arbiter of knowledge, and technology would replace prayer as the most effective way of harnessing its processes. It seemed that, for the first time in human history, the need for God would fade away as science and technology eased themselves into the driving seat. Frazer asserted, moreover, that the process was irreversible: there would never be a retreat from science to the older religious and magical modes of thinking. Short of the total collapse of modern civilisation and a cataclysmic reversion to ancient and less sophisticated cultures, religion would eventually cease to be of any value as the arbiter and regulator of knowledge. *The Golden Bough*, therefore, was seen by many as a deliberate and even offensive challenge to the religious certainties of late nineteenth-century Britain.

Frazer has, self-evidently, been largely vindicated in his views. For the most part, science *has* superseded religion as the arbiter of knowledge about the natural world and religion is no longer the dominant force that it once was in most people's lives. Biblical truth and ecclesiastical authority no longer command the unquestioning allegiance that they once did. Although Frazer was writing at the dawn of the modern era in science and technology, it was nevertheless a bold prediction for him to make, for God was still an indispensable element in people's understanding of how and why things happened. Prayers were still offered up to God in the confident expectation that he would answer them, and 'acts of God' that seemed to have no known or rational explanation were daily events. The dispute between scientists and churchmen in the middle of the nineteenth century over Charles Darwin's theory of evolution was a turning-point in the competition between science and religion for ownership of knowledge. While leading scientists such as Thomas Huxley were using observation and experimentation as a way of understanding the history of life on earth, leading clerics like Bishop Samuel Wilberforce were still placing their faith in the authority of the Bible and the teachings of the Church.

Events, however, have moved on rapidly since Frazer began to publish *The Golden Bough* in the late Victorian period. For the most part, the Bible is no longer seen, even by most of those who would count themselves believers, as a source of scientific truth, and God no longer intervenes in the processes of the natural world to cure illnesses, send rain, eliminate famine, or banish wars. He no longer appears in the syllabi for university courses in physics, astronomy, mathematics or medicine, and it is to science and technology rather than to God that people look for improvements in the quality of their daily lives. Most people, especially in the most highly industrialised countries of the world, seem to get along perfectly well without God, and the mythical Martian visiting the earth might have difficulty grasping the traditional Christian assertion that nothing happens without God's knowledge and concern. Where, the Martian might ask as he surveyed the vast diversity of human activity, is the evidence for such a breath-taking claim? If it were true, surely God would appear as the centrepiece of every news item in the papers and on the television.

There is another sense, too, in which the orthodox God of Christian faith may be said to have had his day: no longer is he accepted unquestioningly as judge, jury and executioner in the trial and sentencing of human souls. Only a hundred and fifty or so years ago, most Christians still believed that after death their souls would be judged by God and dispatched by him to either the paradisiacal gardens of heaven or the fiery cauldrons of hell. Judgement was real, and salvation was devoutly to be hoped for. But that kind of imagery has undergone a radical change. The spectre of divine retribution may continue to be celebrated in the dwindling number of evangelical Victorian hymns that are still sung; but it is rare to find the kind of hell-fire preaching that made eighteenth- and nineteenth-century congregations squirm with alarm. Rarely now do Christian preachers berate their hearers for playing fast and loose with their souls. Rarely do sermons dwell upon the redemption that is available to abject sinners who are washed in the blood of the lamb. Such images no longer carry much conviction in the post-modern world. People's beliefs and expectations have changed, and so too have these staple ingredients of historical Christianity.

To say that God has lost some of his traditional functions is not to say that he has disappeared without trace down the soakaways of history. People have always needed beacons of solace and light in a dark and threatening world, and the twenty-first century may be no different in this respect from any other. Indeed, it could reasonably be argued that beacons of light are needed more urgently now than ever before as the world threatens to tear itself apart in sectarian strife, burn itself up through its profligate use of carbon fuels, or suffocate itself in a materialistic stampede for wealth and possessions. The omens are far from bad: if opinion polls are to be heeded, most people in Europe and North America, including many who would never dream of setting foot inside a church, believe in the existence of something beyond the realms of human perception that offers them comfort and hope and that gives meaning to the triumphs and tragedies of their lives. For much of human history, these symbols or icons of religion have been called gods, and people have been adept at discovering or inventing the gods best suited to the needs of their times. The Christian God, no less than any other deity, has been shaped by the evolution of human needs and the creativity of human inventiveness. That is why he is a God who is continually changing and moving on.

All of this suggests that God might have as enduring a future as he has had a successful past. Religion, it seems, is hard-wired into the human psyche. Yet although people seem to need *some* kind of god, most will not settle for *any* kind of god: to survive, God must be credible within the cultural milieu of the times. This has always been the case, and (as this book has repeatedly shown) divine images that were believable in one generation have often had to be refashioned for later ones. Momentarily, however, the process appears to have stuttered. The God who heard prayers and intervened in the world to disrupt the natural laws of cause and effect began to lose his near-universal credibility several decades ago; but nothing of any great appeal seems to have taken his place.

The failure of Western nations to find a widely acceptable face of God among the *fin-de-siècle* confusions of post-modernism has arguably been a factor in the continuing decline of institutional religion, to the point where entire generations are now growing up with no understanding of *any* kind of God, theistic or otherwise. New images of God may be needed if religion is to become much more than the private solace of a small minority of traditionalists and enthusiasts.

Hazardous though it is to forecast the religious tastes and inclinations of future generations, some broad predictions may be ventured. In many parts of the developing world, the theistic God of traditional Christian belief is likely to thrive, at least for a while; but not everywhere. The first decade of the twenty-first century was witness to a growing gulf of religious belief and practice between poorer and richer countries in the Christian world (exemplified in the profound splits that occurred between African and European Churches over issues about human sexuality and the authority of the Bible) and the gulf is likely to widen in the short term. Wherever the Bible continues to be seen as the infallible word of God, and wherever such traditional doctrines as the virgin birth, the reality of miracles and the bodily resurrection of Jesus continue to be accepted without demur, the traditional God of almost two thousand years of Western Christianity will still hold sway in the hearts and minds of faithful believers.

In other parts of the Christian world, however, the future is likely to be markedly more heterodox. There will be a continuing place for the orthodox God of Christian belief, and he will continue to be worshipped in places that still acknowledge the weight of Christian tradition and the authority of ecclesiastical teaching; but this God is never likely to regain the dominance that he enjoyed throughout Christendom for the better part of two thousand years. A God who created the world in six days, who brought dead people back to life, and who became incarnate in the human person of Jesus whilst still remaining wholly and completely God will find the going increasingly tough in a world of quantum mechanics, genetic engineering and molecular biology – to say nothing of people's exposure to new religious beliefs and practices in an age of mass travel. As each new generation becomes increasingly detached from the stories of the Bible, there will be ever fewer guardians of the traditional message. Indeed, the trend is already well underway as churches close in their hundreds through the lack of both ministers and congregations. A decade of intensive evangelisation at the end of the twentieth century did little to stay the decline.

Will any other faces of God emerge with sufficient conviction to supplement the traditional faces of the Christian God? History suggests a positive answer. Who could possibly have predicted, on the eve of the Great War in 1914, that images of God would be commonplace before the century was out that allied him to the cause of political freedom fighters, black people, women seeking ordination in the church, gay liberation movements, supporters of nuclear disarmament, friends of the earth and many others? Although the contours of the future faces of God may be obscure (for who can predict the moral issues that will engage the hearts and minds of generations yet unborn?), the processes through which they might emerge are perhaps more predictable. Religion in the future will probably set less store by the weight of tradition and the pronouncements of the formal guardians of religion than by the experiences of ordinary men and women. For two millennia the Christian Church has been highly effective at imposing its own ideas of truth upon a largely passive and uncritical flock; but the temper of post-modernism (and probably of whatever will succeed it as well) is unimpressed by either tradition or authority. Theology has become demotic as theological discourse has been democratised. Anyone can now do it, openly and honestly, without fear of ecclesiastical reprisals. The new watchword might be: think for yourself! In the future it may no longer be a matter of the Church telling the faithful what they must believe; rather, the faithful will increasingly be telling the Church what they are reasoning out for themselves. Heterodoxy will become the acceptable order of the day, and institutions that claim to be the guardians of an absolute truth are likely to find the going increasingly tough. Half-hearted attempts by the Church of England in the early twenty-first century to reinstitute heresy trials for doctrinally aberrant clergy collapsed, almost inevitably, because they were out of tune with the spirit of the times. They are not likely to return.

If God does ever return as a major force in modern life, he is likely to be a God whom people have rediscovered for themselves – a God to whom they can relate in an honest and useful way, freed of the pretence to believe things about him that sometimes strain their credibility beyond acceptance. The century-old words of Albert Schweitzer have a prophetic ring about them. 'He comes to us', wrote Schweitzer at the end of *The Quest of the Historical Jesus*, 'as one unknown, without a name, as of old, by the lakeside, he came to those who knew him not. He says the same word, follow me, and sets us to those tasks which he must fulfil in our time. He commands. And to those who hearken to him, whether wise or unwise, he will reveal himself in the peace, the labours, the conflicts and the suffering that they may experience in his fellowship, and as an ineffable mystery they will learn who he is.'

Bibliography

List of related literature and materials
on which the book is based

P Ackroyd, *Albion: The Origins of the English Imagination*, London: Vintage, 2004

K Armstrong, *A History of God*, London: Vintage, 1999

W Barclay, *The Apostles' Creed*, Berkhamstead, Hertfordshire: Arthur James Ltd, 1998

T Barfield ed, *The Dictionary of Anthropology*, Oxford: Blackwell Publishers Ltd, 1997

G Barraclough ed, *The Times History of the World*, London: Times Books, 1999

K Barth, *God Here and Now*, London and New York: Routledge Classics, 2003

D Bonhoeffer, *Letters and Papers from Prison*, London: SCM Press Ltd, 1971

D Bonhoeffer, *Ethics*, London: SCM Press Ltd, 1955

M J Borg and J D Crossan, *The First Paul*, London: Society for Promoting Christian Knowledge, 2009

J Bowker, *God: A Brief History*, London: Dorling Kindersley Publishing Inc, 2002

R Bultmann, *Jesus Christ and Mythology*, London: SCM Press Ltd, 1960

J Burge, *Heloise and Abelard: A New Biography*, New York: HarperSanFrancisco, 2003

M Bragg, *The Book of Books*, London: Hodder and Stoughton, 2011

G Bray, *Biblical Interpretation Past and Present*, Leicester: Apollos (Inter-Varsity Press), 1996

W R F Browning ed, *Oxford Dictionary of the Bible*, Oxford: Oxford University Press, 1996

J M Byrne, *Religion and the Enlightenment: from Descartes to Kant*, Louisville, Kentucky: Westminster John Knox, 1996

J Cannon ed, *The Oxford Companion to British History*, Oxford: Oxford University Press, 1997

The Catholic Encyclopaedia, www.newadvent.org 2004, 2005

P Collinson, *The Reformation*, London: Weidenfeld & Nicolson, 2003

J M Court, *Dictionary of the Bible*, London: Penguin Books Ltd, 2007

D Cupitt, *The Sea of Faith*, London: British Broadcasting Corporation, 1984

D Cupitt, *After God. The Future of Religion*, London: Weidenfeld & Nicolson, 1997

C Darwin, *The Origin of Species by Means of Natural Selection*, London: Penguin Classics, 1985

R Dawkins, *Unweaving the Rainbow*, London: Penguin Books Ltd, 1998

R Dawkins, *The God Delusion*, London: Bantam Press, 2006

J Drane, *Introducing the New Testament*, Tring, Hertfordshire: Lion Publishing, 1986

J Drane, *Who is Jesus?*, Carlisle: Hunt and Thorpe, 1997

E Duffy, *The Stripping of the Altars*, London and New Haven: Yale University Press, 1992

Durkheim E, *Suicide: A Study in Sociology*, New York: Free Press, 1971

Encyclopaedia Britannica, Online Library Edition, www.library.eb.co.uk

J Frazer, *The Golden Bough*, Ware, Hertfordshire: Wordsworth Editions Limited, 1993

O Gingerich, *The Book Nobody Read*, London: William Heinemann, 2004

A Graham-Dixon, *Renaissance*, London: BBC Worldwide Ltd, 1999

S J Grenz, *A Primer on Postmodernism*, Grand Rapids, Michigan: Wm B Eerdmans Publishing Co, 1996

R Hattersley, *John Wesley: A Brand From the Burning*, London: Little, Brown - Time Warner Books, 2002.

R Holloway, *Dancing on the Edge*, London: Fount Paperbacks, 1997

Internet Encyclopaedia of Philosophy, www.iep.utm 2005

W James, *The Varieties of Religious Experience*, New York: Collier Books, 1961

D Jenkins, *The Calling of a Cuckoo*, London and New York: Continuum, 2002

G S Kirk and J E Raven, *The Presocratic Philosophers*, Cambridge: Cambridge University Press, 1960

H M Kuitert, *Jesus: the Legacy of Christianity*, London: SCM Press, 1999

R Le Poidevin, *Arguing for Atheism*, London and New York: Routledge, 1996

D MacCulloch, *A History of Christianity: The First Three Thousand Years*, London: Allen Lane, 2009

H McKeating, Studying the Old Testament, London: Epworth Press, 1979

B C Metzger and M D Coogan, *The Oxford Companion to the Bible*, Oxford: Oxford University Press, 1993

M Meyer, *The Secret Gospels of Jesus*, London: Darton, Longman and Todd, 2005

J Moltman, *The Crucified God*, London: SCM Press, 1999

P C Moore ed, *Can a Bishop be Wrong?*, Harrisburg, Pennsylvania: Morehouse Publishing, 1998

C Morris and P Roberts eds, *Pilgrimage: The English Experience from Becket to Bunyan*, Cambridge: Cambridge University Press, 2002

M A Mullett, *Martin Luther*, London: Routledge, 2004

M A Murray, *The Genesis of Religion*, London: Routledge and Kegan Paul, 1963

R E Olson, *The Story of Christian Theology*, Leicester: Apollos (Inter-Varsity Press), 1999

W E Paden, *Interpreting the Sacred*, Boston: Beacon Press, 1992

M Palmer, *The Question of God*, London: Routledge, 2001

J Polkinghorne, *Science and the Trinity*, London: SPCK, 2004

M A Powell ed, *The Jesus Debate*, Oxford: Lion Publishing plc, 1999

A Richardson, ed, *A Dictionary of Christian Theology*, London: SCM Press, 1982

J Riches, *The Bible. A Very Short Introduction*, Oxford: Oxford University Press, 2000

J A T Robinson, *Honest to God*, London: SCM Press Ltd, 1963

D Rosman, *The Evolution of the English Churches 1500-2000*, Cambridge: Cambridge University Press, 2003

B Russell, *History of Western Philosophy*, New Edition, London: George Allen and Unwin Ltd, 1961

E P Saunders, *The Historical Figure of Jesus*, London: Penguin Books Ltd, 1995

E P Saunders, *Paul A Very Short Introduction*, Oxford: Oxford University Press, 2001

E Schuster and R Boschert-Kimmig, *Hope against Hope*, Mahwah, New Jersey: Paulist Press, 1999

A Schweitzer, *The Quest of the Historical Jesus*, London: SCM Press, 2000

A G R Smith, *Science and Society in the Sixteenth and Seventeenth Centuries*, London: Thames and Hudson, 1972

J Stacey, *Groundwork of Theology*, London: Epworth Press, 1984

D F Strauss, *The Life of Jesus Critically Examined*, London: SCM Press, 1973

The Revised English Bible, Oxford: Oxford University Press, Cambridge: Cambridge University Press, 1989

T L Thompson, *The Bible in History*, London: Jonathan Cape, 1999

P Tillich, *The Shaking of the Foundations*, London: Pelican Books, 1962

M Tully, *Lives of Jesus*, London: BBC Books, 1996

P Vardy, *The Puzzle of God*, London: Fount Paperbacks, 1999

G Vermes, *The Changing Faces of Jesus*, London: Penguin Books Ltd, 2000

Wikipedia: The Free Encyclopaedia, www.wikipedia.org, 2004 onwards

E Wiesel, *Night*, London: Penguin Books Ltd, 2008

A N Wilson, *God's Funeral*, London: Abacus, 2000

A N Wilson, *Paul. The Mind of the Apostle*, London: Sinclair-Stevenson, 1997

I Wilson, *Jesus: the Evidence*, London: Weidenfeld & Nicolson, 1996

R Winston, *The Story of God*, London: Bantam Press, 2005

N T Wright, *Evil and the Justice of God*, London: SPCK, 2005

Index

Is God the eternal and immutable presence that Christianity has commonly proclaimed him to be – the Rock of Ages? John Butler offers a different perspective through a personal exploration of the changing images of God within the main streams of the Christian faith over a period of some four thousand years.

Butler takes the reader on a kaleidoscopic odyssey that begins with the pantheon of deities in Bronze Age Canaan from which the God of the early Old Testament emerged and ends with the radical images of God that were surfacing in the late twentieth century. The story is told largely through the record of the Bible and the ideas of key writers and thinkers whose authority or persuasiveness have allowed their visions of God to become embedded in the major Christian traditions. The book concludes with a discussion of the central question raised by the analysis: why is it that people across the ages have claimed to have experienced so many different and sometimes contradictory faces of the Christian God?

Written in an elegant and engaging style, this informative book will appeal to Christians, atheists, students, and those who are simply interested in the cultural and intellectual history of God.

> This beautifully written book tells the fascinating story of the evolving portrait of the Christian God from Abraham to the present day. It is an illuminating read for those who feel the need to cross their fingers whenever they say the Nicene Creed – and for many who don't! **Richard Llewellin,** former Bishop at Lambeth

John Butler is Emeritus Professor at the University of Kent and a guide at Canterbury Cathedral. He is the author of the acclaimed *Quest for Becket's Bones* (1995) and the prize-winning *Red Dean of Canterbury* (2011).

The Lutterworth Press
P.O. Box 60
Cambridge
CB1 2NT

www.lutterworth.com
publishing@lutterworth.com

ISBN 978-0-7188-9296-8

9 780718 892968

P8-BYF-190

Cover image: *The Creation of the Sun and the Moon*, Michelangelo (1508-1512)